ISLAND IN CHAINS

ISLAND IN CHAINS

INDRES NAIDOO
Prisoner 885/63

PENGUIN BOOKS

PENGUIN BOOKS

Published by the Penguin Group
80 Strand, London WC2R 0RL, England
Penguin Putnam Inc, 375 Hudson Street, New York, New York 10014, USA
Penguin Books Australia Ltd, 250 Camberwell Road, Camberwell,
Victoria 3124, Australia
Penguin Books Canada Ltd, 10 Alcorn Avenue, Toronto, Ontario,
Canada M4V 3B2
Penguin Books (NZ) Ltd, Cnr Rosedale and Airborne Roads, Albany,
Auckland, New Zealand
Penguin Books India Pvt Ltd, 11 Community Centre, Panchsheel Park,
New Delhi – 110 017, India
Penguin Books (South Africa) (Pty) Ltd, 24 Sturdee Avenue, Rosebank,
Johannesburg 2196, South Africa

Penguin Books (South Africa) (Pty) Ltd, Registered Offices:
Second Floor, 90 Rivonia Road, Sandton 2196, South Africa

First edition published by Penguin (UK), 1982
First published in South Africa by Penguin Books (South Africa)
(Pty) Ltd, 2000
New edition published 2003
Reprinted 2005

ISBN 0 140 29535 6

Typeset by CJH Design in 10.5/13 point Life
Cover design: Mouse Design
Cover photograph: Jürgen Schadeberg
Printed and bound by CTP Book Printers, Cape Town

*To Nelson Mandela and all other political prisoners,
and in memory of all those who gave their lives for the
liberation of our country, South Africa*

Contents

Foreword

I had been reflecting on the contents of this Foreword. Then, a few days ago, an incident occurred that changed what I was planning to say.

I was in a one-way street in central Pretoria, almost double-parked, as I waited for traffic to ease so that I could swing across the road to enter a basement parking facility. I heard a loud, gruff voice calling in Afrikaans: '*Meneer Maharaj, is dit Meneer Maharaj*?' (Mr Maharaj, are you Mr Maharaj?). I looked around. It was the driver of a car parked alongside me. He was big and heavily built. Broad shoulders bearing the signs of overweight; thick, short neck, sagging jowls almost falling off his face. White-haired. A heavy, almost handlebar type moustache capped his thick lips. I could not place the expression in his eyes. Uncertain, aggressive, fear, hatred?

'Don't you recognise me?' 'Not really,' I replied as I scanned the recesses of my mind. He offered me a clue: 'I was your worst enemy,' he said. The 'your' was couched in the Afrikaans '*julle*' – the plural. My mind was in rapid scan search. The categories were now narrowed: security branch, police and prison warder. I have been through two rounds of torture – in 1964 and 1990 – at the hands of the security branch; in the periods of detention, awaiting trial and imprisonment I had been through twenty-two police stations and prisons. Just as he began to offer his surname 'Van . . .' I blurted out 'Suitcase!' That was it: Van Rensburg, better known among us prisoners on Robben Island as 'Suitcase'.

The conversation was fleeting – I was late for my appointment and finding a gap in the early morning traffic was not easy. I asked where I could contact him. He would not give me that information. He kept repeating: 'I am afraid of you people; I live in fear of you people'. I offered my phone number. He said he did not have a pen to write it down. He queried why I would want to see him. He was incredulous when I replied that I would like to have a chat with him. 'Why? Would you really be prepared to talk to me?' he asked.

I was holding up traffic. If I had stayed I am sure I could have persuaded him to meet me. Whether he would have kept the appointment is another matter. The thing that stands out: he kept saying, 'I am afraid of you people; I live in fear of you people'.

What has this fleeting episode got to do with a Foreword to an updated reprint of Indres Naidoo's book *Island in Chains*?

Van Rensburg gained his nickname and notoriety from his conduct in the single cells section of Robben Island. He does not feature in this book. The story about him appears in Nelson Mandela's autobiography *Long Walk to Freedom*. He was specially brought to Robben Island to give those of us in the single cells section hell. He wore a swastika sign tattooed on his arm. He was open – no, boastful – about his racism, his belief in the white master race. Life under his regime on Robben Island was a running battle. We fought back and bested him over and over again. But he would not relent. He kept up his campaign of harassment and humiliation as if it was a mission assigned to him personally by his Führer. He was no great intellect – he was cannon fodder of the race supremacists ruling South Africa.

Van Rensburg interacted with us thirty-odd prisoners on a daily basis. Did he not get to know us? I went back to skim through

Indres' book. I could only find three sentences in the entire book where the word 'hate' appears.

In one case Indres recounts the brutal treatment meted out to political prisoners by a head warder. In this context he makes these observations: 'Delport made no bones about his hatred of political prisoners . . . The warders hated him as much as we did – even his family, we were told, stood in fear of him.'

In another case Indres describes the role played by Brigadier Aucamp, the person who was in charge of security on the Island and in all the prisons in South Africa. He describes Aucamp as 'our most dangerous opponent. He was shrewd and cunning; the most powerful man on the Island, and he loathed political prisoners.' And he concludes: '[H]e could have come out straight from the Gestapo. We hated his guts, he was the source of all our misery, and when rumour strengthened that he was very sick, we could not wait for him to die.'

The only other instance where the word 'hate' appears, is when Indres describes how prisoners were made to run all the way to work with Alsatian dogs barking and snapping at their heels. 'We felt,' says Indres, 'the constant pressure to humiliate us, perpetually to reduce us to nothing in the warder's presence. They hated us and we hated them, it was quite simple.'

Today it is cliché to talk about the lack of bitterness on the part of former political prisoners and freedom fighters. Within South Africa and abroad there is unanimity that there is no single action that the ANC has undertaken since its unbanning that is regarded as having been motivated by revenge or hatred. If I were to single out one special hallmark of *Island in Chains* it is that Indres Naidoo and Albie Sachs found a way with a quiet and unassuming dignity to tell the story like it was.

On the other hand, the Van Rensburgs of our country were brought up by their leaders in their political, social, cultural and even religious activities never to forgive or to forget. Their leaders brought them up, for example, to behave and think as if the Anglo-

Boer War of 1899-1902 had never ended.

Van Rensburg lived through the period when political prisoners were released, the ANC and other organisations unbanned. He heard and experienced the conduct of the ANC in the negotiations and in government. No one can be ignorant of the consistency with which Madiba has held out the hand of friendship and with which the ANC pursues the goal of nation building, reconciliation and reconstruction.

But the fear expressed by Van Rensburg, however much it is out of sync with reality, is real. It gave me a jolt when I saw it.

Since its publication in 1982 *Island in Chains* has been read by hundreds upon hundreds of young activists in the anti-apartheid struggle. It inspired and gave courage. It demystified fear of prison, steeled us and reinforced our humanity. I know of no activist who, by reading this book, was deterred from engaging even more fully in the Struggle.

But South Africa in the year 2000 is virtually another country. The changes that have already taken place have moved us light years away from 1982. And change continues unabated. Everything around us is changing – even ourselves. And so it should be.

When I was approached to write this Foreword, I agreed to do so with some diffidence and misgiving. I knew I would have to re-read the book. I was not sure I wanted to. But I did and am deeply grateful. Confronting the past is a constant act of renewal.

And then I bumped into Van Rensburg. There he was trapped in his fear, unable to confront his past and therefore unable to drink at the well of renewal. How many Van Rensburgs are there in this beautiful country of ours?

There are those who say: forget the past; let's just get on with the future. Our apartheid past ensured that communities grew up, lived, even interacted and died without knowing each other. At best we were indifferent towards each other. More often we were taught to be suspicious and to fear each other. And fear is cradled in the bosom of hostility.

Out of this terrible past – terrible for all of us in all the communities in South Africa and across the divides of colour, class, ethnicity, gender, language and religion because in different ways we were dehumanised and precluded from living in an environment in which our humanity could flower and flourish – a nation is evolving and emerging. Do not judge the wondrous colours and pattern of the butterfly's wings from the appearance of the larva.

The quality of what we bequeath to posterity will in part be determined by our willingness to understand others who are destined to be part of the South African nation.

There will be no better time than now for the story-tellers from every walk of life in our country and continent to tell their stories so that we may better understand the experiences which have shaped them, so that we may know them and thereby know ourselves.

Seventeen years later I happenstanced to re-read *Island in Chains*. This time round I am awed by the humanity that found a way to flourish in the midst of inhumanity. The real issue, Mr van Rensburg, is not that you were, in your words, our 'worst enemy' on Robben Island. It is that in the South Africa of today you are your own worst enemy.

Thank you Indres. Thank you Albie. A nation without a past has no future. *Gracias a la Vida!*

Mac Maharaj
August 1999

Foreword to the first edition

Robben Island, an exposed piece of prison land surrounded by freezing sea only miles away from the sunny beaches and luxury hotels of the Cape Peninsula, has long been a centre of suffering and struggle. In its dry soil lie the bones of dozens of princes of the East banished and interned there centuries ago for leading popular revolt against the vast plunder of the Dutch trading empire. Later the mangled bodies of mutinous slaves, many still alive, were cast into the icy waters that batter the Island's shores. In the last century the great leader of people's resistance to British colonial rule, Makanda, died heroically trying to swim to freedom from exile on the Island. Later still it became a place to which lepers were banished. And, finally, in our times, when South Africa has grown, through the sweat and suffering of the working people, to be a rich, beautiful and technically advanced country, the racist rulers have converted the Island into a harsh prison camp – a grey, soulless, cruel spot, designed to crush the spirit of the bravest and truest leaders of our revolt against the apartheid system, to douse once and for all the flames of rebellion in our hearts, to deter and subdue us for ever.

That was the intention but, as this narrative by one of its victims proves, the racists failed. The struggle continued, on the Island and off, the fires of resistance continued to burn, and Robben

Island became nationally and internationally synonymous not with defeat but with courage and indestructibility.

Prisoner 885/63 arrived on the Island in chains in 1963, three years after the massacre of Sharpeville, the banning of our organisation and the use of the South African Defence Force to crush a peaceful national three-day stay-at-home had proved to us that purely peaceful struggle was no longer enough. He was one of the first volunteers for Umkhonto we Sizwe, 'Spear of the Nation', the armed wing of the African National Congress set up under the leadership of Nelson Mandela to express in fullest form the claims of our people to self-determination. In a calm and precise manner this book recalls the tortures to which he and others were subjected, the cruel work regime in the quarry, and the courageous fight back of the prisoners: their fight for food, for health, for warmth, for news, for song, for beauty, for dignity.

This book could not have been written inside the country where its contents most need to be known. Comrade Indres Naidoo, as prisoner 885/63 is better known to us, was banned in South Africa immediately after his release from prison, one result being that no word of his may be published there. Once outside the country, he told his experiences to Albie Sachs, a lawyer who was himself imprisoned and banned in South Africa. Together, and working nights and weekends, they grouped the themes into chapters, and so produced this book. It is a narrative of one of the central episodes of recent South African history, the story of an island in chains, the story of resistance, as seen through the eyes of one who lived through it all for ten years. Thousands of others went through the same experience, and possibly each one would have a different way of recalling it, one with more attention to political analysis, another with greater introspection and reflection, a third with more passion and lyricism, another with a different literary style altogether. Yet this is a completely true story, told by a participant in his own voice, authentic to his personality, true to the character of our struggle, true in feeling, true in spirit, true in its very South African detail.

Who, after reading this story, will quickly forget the picture of the prisoners heaving and pulling the giant roller round and round while the warder rides on top cracking his whip . . . or the earthquake . . . or the joy of the prisoners on seeing a school of whales . . . or the extraordinary journeys of the prisoners, first to the island at the beginning of their sentence and then back across a changed country a decade later? And who can remain unmoved by the calmness and strength of Nelson Mandela and other leading prisoners kept in a prison within the prison, yet somehow managing to make their presence felt all the time, to remain in touch with their fellow prisoners?

The story, like our struggle, is filled with courage, amazement, humour and compassion. One of its most moving aspects is the way to reveals the process whereby even some of the sternest and most cruel of the guards, people conditioned by the ethics of a dog-eat-dog society to regard their fellow human beings as inferiors, as enemies to be despised, who constantly spied on and betrayed each other, came to learn gradually under the impact of the intense solidarity and humanity of the prisoners that mankind can live by another code, a code of mutual support and comradeship, that even under the grimmest conditions people imbued with the spirit of liberation can sing and retain their curiosity and live with the conviction that a new world is in creation.

When we in the ANC talk of liberation, we not only think of the brave patriots attacking the installations of apartheid, of the youths boycotting schools, of the workers demanding humane conditions of life – we think of the processes taking place in the very depths of South Africa's prisons. Liberation to us means in the first place the total destruction of all the structures of oppression and exploitation associated with apartheid, the complete elimination of racism and exploitation of man by man from our society; we do not wish to reform apartheid or make it more beautiful, we wish to abolish it in every shape and form. But to us liberation is not simply the wiping out of a scourge, it is the building of a new society based on new principles, and imbued with a new consciousness. And these new relationships of equality and brotherhood will not come about merely because we will have a new Constitution based on the principles of our Freedom Charter – they are being born right now in the daily struggle against apartheid, for we are already creating the new South African nation in embryo in the very battle to destroy the old. In that sense liberation is now, even before victory, even in the very bowels of captivity.

The prisoners on Robben Island came from every part of our country – because revolt was in every part of our country – they were factory workers, teachers, peasants, clerks, doctors, traders and lawyers, some were in their teens, others in their sixties, they spoke all the many different languages of our land, and yet in the course of a common struggle with common aims they established a firm comradeship, a new genuinely South African personality, drawing heavily on all the rich traditions of culture and struggle of our people, creating a new patriotism of liberation. The new is created in opposition to the old, a nucleus of freedom and transformation that grows and extends itself, which one day will overwhelm the racists themselves, destroying the structures that protect their greed and cruelty, enabling them to discover their own suppressed humanity, leading them out of the *laager* into the human race, freeing their children to grow up as children and not as the offspring of a master race.

The child whom Prisoner 885/63 describes as mounting a little platform each day to fire a toy gun at the procession of barefoot prisoners filing past his garden is now an adult carrying a real gun, possibly shooting hard-working peasants who are building a new life in Angola or Zambia, or fighting our brothers in Namibia, or shooting down workers or schoolchildren in the streets of Johannesburg or Cape Town. This is what we are fighting against, this is why we feel we have not only a right but a duty to fight, to destroy the cycle that perpetuates cruelty from one generation to the next, to wipe out the colonisation of the minds of oppressor and oppressed alike, to eliminate the myths of superiority and inferiority that flow from and reinforce exploitation. Perhaps that child grown adult is now dead, shot by one of his intended victims, because we too have arms now, we too have the capacity to fight, we too are expressing our power.

We want peace in South Africa. We want the country's wealth to be shared amongst all who produce it, we want the doors of learning and culture to be opened wide so that all may enter. But we know that as long as the system of apartheid survives, whatever its form and whatever its name, we can have neither peace nor security, nor can we hope to see a true extension of knowledge and culture.

At the time of writing there is great excitement in South Africa, a massive campaign to secure the release of Nelson Mandela and all other political prisoners. There is talk by the regime of closing down Robben Island prison, and moving its inmates to Leeuwkop prison (also described in these pages) on the mainland near Pretoria.

To those who have battled so hard in the world outside to focus attention on Robben Island, whether from humanitarian motives such as the International Red Cross or, in its different way, the International Defence and Aid Fund, or from political solidarity, such as our friends in the socialist countries, in the Scandinavian bloc, anti-apartheid workers in other Western countries; to our allies in brother African countries, many themselves recently freed from colonialism and racism; to our valued supporters in Asia, the Middle East and Latin America; to all the men and women of principle in the United Nations Organisation who believe in the Charter and Declaration of Human Rights, to you all we say: read this book and you will see how important your efforts have been to the prisoners on the island. And we call upon you to draw the necessary conclusion: redouble your efforts, give even more impetus to your valuable work.

And to those who make money out of trading with apartheid, who send the regime arms and oil and provide it with finance and diplomatic protection, who talk about building bridges and 'peaceful solutions' while our people are being shot down in the streets and murdered in the torture-rooms, while the population of neighbouring countries are bombed and massacred by the racist regime, to you we say: study this book and remember that just as those associated historically with the slave trade are today abominated, so those who make money out of apartheid will equally be condemned by future generations and even by their own children.

Above all, we commend this book to our fellow countrymen and countrywomen, to all South Africans, of all ages, all backgrounds, all colours. This book is the voice of struggle, the voice of the oppressed, the voice of the future. It expresses what is embodied and crystallised in our slogans: *Amandla Ngawethu, Maatla Kea Rona*, Power to the People; a slogan that emerged in the early 1960s and became a call that was heard in Soweto during the uprising, it spread and was echoed across our country. It simply means *Mayibuye iAfrika* – we are determined to seize power. It is a declaration of confidence in our just cause and emphasises what James Mange and his comrades said: Never on our knees.

Francis Meli
Director of External Publicity
African National Congress of South Africa

Introduction

My family has been active in politics for several generations.

My grandfather, C K Thambi Naidoo, was a founding member and the first president of the Transvaal Indian Congress, and a close associate and comrade of Mahatma Gandhi. He went to prison fourteen times during the course of the Struggle.

My grandmother, Veeramal Naidoo, gave birth to her youngest son Mithlin while in prison in the early part of the twentieth century. Her mother, Mrs N Pillay, was amongst the first female passive resisters to be imprisoned in 1906.

My father, Narainswamy 'Roy' Naidoo, was adopted by Mahatma Gandhi and spent fourteen years in Gandhi's ashram in Gurukula, India. He studied under Gandhiji and the great Indian philosopher Rabindranath Tagore. When he returned to South Africa, he immediately became involved in the political struggle. He was chief welfare officer during the Defiance Campaign of 1952 and he worked closely with J B Marks, Moses Kotane, Nelson Mandela, Walter Sisulu, Dr Y Dadoo and Bram Fischer, amongst others. He was imprisoned six times for defying the unjust laws of the country and he was awarded the World Peace Council Award posthumously in 1959.

My mother, Manonmoney 'Amah' Naidoo, was vice-president of the Transvaal Indian Congress (1986). She was also the vice-president of the South African Women's Federation (1960). She was imprisoned twice for defying the apartheid laws of South Africa. In October 1988 my mother was invited to India by Prime Minister Rajiv Gandhi to mark the Centenary of Jawaharlal Nehru, honouring her and her family's contribution to the Struggle.

All my brothers and sisters were imprisoned at some time or other for ANC activities in South Africa.

My sister Shantie was detained and sentenced from 1969 to 1970. My brother Murthie was detained in 1964 and again in 1985. My sister Ramnie was detained at the age of nine. My brother Prema was first detained at the age of sixteen and again in 1982 and then sentenced. My nephew (Prema's son) was detained and wrote his matriculation examinations in detention.

As far as I know, more than twenty members of my family have been in prisons all over the country.

In 1991 the Naidoo family was awarded the Indicator Human Rights Award for their contribution to freedom and democracy in our country, South Africa.

My prison experiences are recounted in *Island in Chains*. The book was first published in 1982 and was translated into Dutch, Portuguese, French and German. The American edition was called 'Robben Island'. In the USSR it was serialised in the national youth magazine. Radio Maputo also serialised the book on its Southern African Service. In 1983 the book won the Martin Luther King Memorial Award. This award is presented annually on the anniversary of King's assassination to a literary work which reflects the ideals for which the civil rights leader fought and died. In 1993 a London theatre group put on a play based on the book.

Island in Chains was immediately banned in South Africa. However, ANC underground units managed to smuggle hundreds of copies of the book into the country. It was much sought after. In the Western Cape activists used the book in their underground political study groups. In the Johannesburg and Pretoria area comrades made photocopies of the book which went from hand to hand all over the country. At least one person was arrested for being in possession of a copy of the banned book.

In 1985 the Canadian High Commissioner in Harare and his wife were in Maputo on their way to Johannesburg to attend comrade Helen Joseph's 80th birthday party. The wife offered to take a copy of *Island in Chains* signed by me to Comrade Helen, which she successfully did.

The 1994 election saw many of my comrades from Robben Island elected to Parliament. But I will always remember the hundreds of comrades, ex-Robben Islanders who were killed by the apartheid regime's assassins or who died in prisons in our country – people like Comrades Joe Gqabi, Zola Nqini, Sipho Hashe, Bram Fischer, Caleb Mayekiso, William Khanyila and many others. I think too of those who died before Freedom Day, 27 April 1994, like Martin Ramogadi, Zola Brain Mjo, Kistin Doorasamy, Joe Mati, Tshalimani, Rex Lupondwane, Peter Ntshabaleng, Judson Kuzwayo (who, incidentally, shared my birthday and we always hugged and kissed each other on that day on the Island), and many, many more. I think of those hundreds who went to prison strong, healthy and determined young men and women. Leaders of the people, they suffered physical and emotional abuse and became physically and/or mentally disabled for the rest of their lives, like Comrades Ernest 'Jambo' Malgas, Philip Sello, Twebe, Hlekani. The list goes on and on.

I would like to take this opportunity to thank all my comrades who served time on Robben Island with me for their courage, their determination, their will to continue the Struggle and to survive the brutalities of the Island. Special mention must be made of my two comrades-in-arms, Shirish Nanabhai and Reggie Vandeyar, whose comradeship and friendship has never waned. I thank my family who have always stood by me through thick and thin. They were a tower of strength, not only to me but also to many of my comrades, especially my mom, who was a source of endless encouragement and instilled a fighting spirit in all of us. Thanks to Justice Albie Sachs, then a professor of law in Maputo, who spent weeks and months in his oven-hot apartment taking notes of my story, putting them together in book form and finding a publisher. Finally, I thank my partner Gabi Blankenburg, who nagged me to get down to writing the epilogue for this edition and to get it published in South Africa.

In writing *Island in Chains*, which was a small link in our struggle in prison and, for that matter, an even smaller link in the chain of our struggle for the liberation of our country from centuries of oppression and humiliation, I have documented the horrors of the apartheid regime in the hope that it will help to heal the wounds of those of our people who sacrificed and suffered so much for freedom. We will march together to realise the African Renaissance.

<blockquote>
In your chain of Friendship and Comradeship
consider me as a small link.
</blockquote>

<blockquote>
From Robben Island to Exile to Parliament.
</blockquote>

Indres Naidoo

Island in Chains was published by Penguin Books India in 2000.

PART ONE

TO THE ISLAND

ONE

Trapped

As soon as I struck the match to light the fuse I knew that something was wrong. It was just after midnight on 17 April 1963 and an hour after the last train had passed, and we were planning to blow up a signal box in open country about nineteen kilometres from Johannesburg. The flame of the match was to be the signal for my comrades, Gammat and Shirish, to light their fuses. Reggie was keeping watch some distance away, but a small fire was burning where Gammat was supposed to be.

'What the hell are you doing?' I shouted.

Reggie yelled, 'Light the bloody fuse!'

Then there was the loud blast of a police whistle.

'Run,' Reggie yelled. 'It's the cops.'

We jumped a nearby fence and ran about twenty metres to the car. Suddenly the whole place lit up. We were surrounded by twenty to thirty heavily armed policemen carrying sten guns and rifles and wearing railway workers' clothes. As they closed in Lieutenant Swanepoel shouted: 'Put up your hands. Stand still.'

Reggie had a crowbar – our only weapon – but as Swanepoel shouted we all threw up our hands. I heard a shot but it was only

3

when I looked down and saw blood that I realised that my right arm had been struck by the bullet. This was the first time I had come across Swanepoel, 'Rooi Rose': heavy, with a thick red face, short crew-cut hair and always angry.

'What are you doing here?' he yelled in Afrikaans.

All three of us replied simultaneously. 'We came with Gammat Jardien.' We realised we'd been led into a trap: Jardien had supplied the dynamite, trained us, and suggested the target. The regional command of our organisation, Umkhonto we Sizwe, the armed section of the African National Congress, had previously investigated him. They had chosen the day, but otherwise all the initiative had come from him.

I thought nervously of the fuse still burning only metres away. We should have been in our car and far away by now. 'Who is Gammat Jardien?'

'Gammat has a sister round here and we've been to see her.'

A policeman was sent to look for Gammat. He returned after five minutes, saying there was no one else around.

Then the explosions went off, one after the other. We'd stuck the dynamite with insulation tape to the signal box and a tool shed. The explosions were very loud, and we were shocked by the noise. We'd never heard an explosion before. The first comment by Swanepoel was, 'Ah, soldiers of Mandela' – referring to Nelson Mandela, our commander-in-chief, who was transferred to Robben Island prison in May 1963. Swanepoel hit me across the chest with the butt of a rifle and as I fell down he and another policeman dug their rifles into me.

Reggie protested. 'What are you doing? Can't you see the man has been shot?'

Swanepoel said, 'Oh, coolie, you're a loudmouth,' and that was the end of Reggie. They got him down. He was a big guy, nearly ninety kilograms, and well built but, for the next fifteen minutes or so, every policeman had a go, pushing their rifle butts into him. They assaulted him so badly that when they had finished he couldn't even stand up.

We were lifted into a car and driven away under heavy guard to Protea police station in Soweto. By the time we got there my right shoulder was collapsing. I was full of pain. My whole body was aching. But the shoulder, I had no idea why, was really collapsing. I begged the police to call a doctor but they refused, saying, 'Coolie, you're going to die [*jy sal vrek*].'

While Swanepoel was making a phone call I felt I was going to bring up, so I made a dash for the window and vomited. Two policemen ran and grabbed me, obviously suspecting that I was attempting to escape which, with all the police around, would have been quite impossible.

'Take the coolie to hospital,' Swanepoel said when he returned.

I was dragged out of the charge office by two black policemen, and when we got to a panel van in the yard they picked me up physically and threw me into the back of the van and jumped in after me. With three armed whites in front we went off to the Coronation Hospital, where the doctor ripped my shirt open at the back and found the bullet sticking out between the shoulder blades. The hole was in my arm, and that was where the blood had flowed out, but the bullet had travelled up to my shoulder and across the shoulder blade. All the doctor did was to take a pair of tweezers, close them around the bullet and pull. The bullet came out – it was that easy. He suggested that I should be hospitalised for two weeks, but the police refused, so he insisted that they sign a document accepting responsibility for me, which they did. Later he gave me a dose of painkillers and handed more over to the police for me to take later. In fact I never saw the painkillers again.

Back in Protea police station I couldn't see my two comrades anywhere, but as I sat in the reception area I heard screaming coming from the back rooms and began to make out their voices. What was happening to them I didn't know, but I could hear shouts: 'Please leave me alone. I don't know, I don't know . . .'

I was sitting and listening and thinking, 'God, I'll be the next going in there.' I don't know how long it was, but after some time Reggie and Shirish appeared. They were so disfigured they were not recognisable; their faces were swollen, their eyes were closed and they could hardly walk. Shirish's face was so messed up, he couldn't even put on his specs.

The police then took me to my home and started banging loudly on the door, so I gave them my key so as not to let them frighten my family. As we entered, the whole family was there, my two brothers, two sisters and my mother, stunned. The police turned my room inside out, cut pillows open, dug into the fireplace, broke some tiles there, opened up floorboards, looked everywhere.

I was so full of pain I could hardly talk, but when I lay down I could rest for only two minutes before the pain started again and I would have to get up; I would lie down, get up, lie down, get up, lie down, to keep the pain away. My family was agitated, demanding an explanation, and when one of the policemen pulled out a chair to sit down one of my sisters kicked it away and said that this was her house and he needed her permission to sit. I felt this was wrong but was too weak to say anything.

Unfortunately, when the police lifted up my radio they found the programme of the Communist Party, 'South Africa's Road to Freedom', and also an American counter insurgency book with the writings of Che and Mao on guerrilla warfare. They also took a box of letters written by sports people from all over the world to Dennis Brutus who had been one of the prime organisers of the campaign to get South Africa kicked out of international sport. My comrade, Mac Maharaj, who ran a sports magazine and had been staying at our place, had left the letters there and the police took them all away. They also took a box file of letters and telegrams of sympathy on the occasion of the death of my dad. He had been well known for his political activities, having grown up as a child with Gandhi and then having been to prison many times, like my grandfather and grandmother before him. We did not know whether to ask the police for a receipt – if we didn't we might lose the sympathy letters, but if we did it would be admitting possession of the banned literature – so we decided not to ask for one. As we left, my whole family crowded round and assured me they would do everything possible and get the best lawyer for me.

At Marshall Square police headquarters, the next stop, I was stripped of my belt and put into a large bare cell, bigger than any of the cells I had been in previously when arrested for such relatively minor offences as distributing leaflets, entering locations* without permission, and trespassing, but it was totally dark, with only a small high window. The pain was dreadful: I couldn't stand it. I kept walking up and down until the pain was so bad I started kicking the door and screaming, 'Help, help.'

The door opened and a white hand came through the grille.

'What's wrong, friend?' The voice was sympathetic.

'Man, I'm in pain, terrible pain. Get me some tablets please.'

'I can't help you there, man, but do you smoke and have you got blankets?'

The white prisoner went away and returned with a blanket and a lit cigarette. What a relief it was. My first cigarette in hours. I tried to pick up the blanket, but I was too weak – I couldn't even lift it. All I could do was to sit on it for a few minutes and then, when the pain started, get up and walk round the cell. It was the longest night in my life.

At about ten o'clock in the morning they opened the cell and took me down to the charge office where I met my two companions. Then we heard a cop shout, 'Abdulhay Jassat! Laloo Chiba!' The three of us just looked at one another as we heard the names of two other comrades. My reaction was 'God, what's happened? Have they rounded up everybody else as well? Did somebody break down?'

---

*The term used in those days for black townships.

7

Then we saw Jassat and Chiba, looking quite fit. I don't know what they thought of us. We didn't talk, and all five of us were taken in two cars to Johannesburg Railway Police headquarters. It was a new building without any lifts working, and we had to walk up six flights of stairs, being pushed and pulled the whole way, until eventually we ended up in a small room where we saw about six heavily armed policemen waiting for us.

The first person to be taken away was Jassat. I don't know how long he was away, it could have been anything up to an hour, maybe more. All we heard was him screaming 'I didn't do it. I know nothing about it. Ma, please help me, help me.' And loud cries. There we were, just sitting and looking at each other. Up to now, from the arrest onwards, we hadn't said a word to one another, and we all sat very gloomily, full of pain, saying nothing.

Eventually Jassat appeared. He was of medium height, like me, but thin, less broad than I am, and when I looked at him I didn't know whether to laugh or cry. He looked like Frankenstein, with heavy feet dragging, arms hanging down at his sides, tongue dangling out of his mouth, a sort of bluish colour, with marks all over his slender face. He collapsed into a chair.

The second person to go was Laloo. Some time later he, too, dragged himself back into the room in the same way.

The third was Reggie . . . identical thing. What worried me was that he was in a bad condition when he left the room, but we could still hear his screams as they went for him. It is always terrible to hear someone screaming, but when it is someone close to you, whose voice you know, whom normally you hear talking or laughing, it is unbearable.

＊

Then it was my turn. Up to this time I really didn't know what was happening in this room of theirs, and when I got there I

8

found between twelve and fifteen Special Branch men standing around, all in plain clothes, moving this way and that. They included Lieutenant Swanepoel, Major Brits, head of the Railway Squad I think, and also Colonel van den Bergh, later to become head of the Bureau of State Security (BOSS).

At the time we didn't recognise any of them – before, we had known all the SBs (Security Branch) in Johannesburg – but this was a new group, this gang, and only later did we realise that they were the ones who (according to the reports we had read in the press) had been sent to France for special training some years earlier, when the Algerian War was still in progress, and had come back and formed the new Security Branch. They were now getting stuck into us.

They asked me my name, address, age, work and such routine things. Then: 'Who instructed you to go on these acts of sabotage? Who is the leader of the group?'

'I want to see my lawyer, please.'

I felt a punch, and before I realised what was happening they had surrounded me and were kicking and pushing me, saying 'Now we're playing rugby' – one policeman would dive full length on to me, hitting me on the side, then another would come up and kick me as though I was the ball. If ever I felt like crying, it was then. I had never realised I could cry that way, and I begged them to stop, pleaded with them, and all they kept on saying was 'Will you talk, coolie? You're going to talk.'

'Ask Gammat Jardien, ask Gammat Jardien. He was the one who took us down. He was the one responsible.'

'You lie, coolie, you lie.' They grabbed my beard and pulled it again and again. 'Why do you communists all have beards?'

Major Brits stopped them. I don't even remember what he looks like any more: I don't even know if he's alive or dead. Van den Bergh was very quiet, a nonentity, and with people coming and going I'm not sure if he stayed, but he certainly knew what was going on.

'Are you going to make a statement?'

Like a fool I mumbled over and over, 'Ask Gammat Jardien. Gammat Jardien knows everything.'

The next thing, I felt a wet cold canvas bag being put over my head. Who put it there I don't know, but they started squeezing a knot and choking me. I gasped for air, and every time I breathed in, the canvas hit me in the face. I was choking, my nostrils and mouth were blocked by the wet canvas; the harder I tried to get air into my lungs, the tighter the bag clamped over me, cutting off the air, preventing my lungs from working.

'Coolie, today you're going to die.' Laughter. 'We've got the bastards.'

I was struggling, thrashing around, almost unconscious. Laughter and talking amongst themselves. The bag was released and I swallowed air desperately, but then the canvas slapped back into my mouth and once more I started to choke, my body in a total panic.

'Coolie, you're going to talk.' More laughter.

I kicked my legs and arms as hard as I could, feeling my head go dizzy. The bag opened. I was finished. I could hardly stand. I begged them to leave me alone, and repeated, 'Gammat Jardien is the person. Ask Gammat Jardien.'

They pushed me into a chair, and I found my shoes being taken off and two policemen holding my hands behind the back of the chair. One of the group started hitting me on the soles of my feet with a rubber baton and a terrible pain shot up my leg. I don't know how long they kept it up, but still I kept pleading with them and cried that they should ask Gammat Jardien.

They told me that I was going to hang, our whole group would be hanged, and they jeered at our lawyers. 'We know your Bram Fischers,' they said. 'We know your Joe Slovos. They can't do anything for you now', referring to two famous lawyers who were part of our movement.

Next I felt all sorts of wires being attached to me, like a patient

10

during an operation, some on my hands, some on my feet, each attached by four little leads, taped with Elastoplast between my fingers and toes. My arms were stretched out at my sides and I was held down from behind, and then I saw the main lead running to a dry cell battery, a very crude-looking instrument, just a battery and wires, and as they attached the lead to the battery I felt a dreadful shock pass into my body. My whole being seemed to be in shock – I learned afterwards that it was only for a few seconds, but at the time it seemed like five or ten minutes.

The current stopped.

'It's Gammat Jardien,' I screamed. 'Ask Gammat Jardien. Gammat Jardien knows everything.'

Again the shock travelled through my whole body, convulsing every particle of me, going on and on for ever, absolute pain from top to toe. It was the worst pain I had ever experienced and I kept on screaming to them, begging, pleading with them to stop, but the more I cried the more they went on applying the shocks. Swanepoel was the man in command, conducting the whole operation, giving the instruction when to attach the leads and when to stop. I was growing worn out with pain, exhausted by how much my body hurt, feeling myself on the edge of life, near to death.

Eventually Major Brits intervened: 'Let the *koelie* go, we'll see him again.'

I assume that I reappeared in the room in the very same state as the other three had done. How I managed to get there I don't know. Shirish was led away and we heard the same screaming, all of us sitting quietly, not saying a word. The thought that ran through my mind was 'What are the other comrades saying?' While torturing me the police had kept on saying, 'We know everything. Reggie has given us a full statement. Jassat and Laloo have given us full statements, you are the only bloody fool; you'll see, your comrades have sold you out'. And now I wondered.

11

Long after dark, we were taken back to Marshall Square and I spent the night alone again in my big cell. The next morning we were driven in cars to Railway Police headquarters and, full of pain and full of doubt, placed in the same room, ready for the same performance. Jassat was the first to be taken away again but this time there were no screams. Nothing.

While we waited they took photographs of us, and later a doctor appeared and examined each of us, bringing a mattress and telling us to lie down, with the assurance that we would survive, we wouldn't die. He also gave us AP cods for the pain. Jassat reappeared after half an hour looking as he had done when he had gone in.

I was the fourth one to be taken away, and as I entered the interrogation room Lieutenant Steenkamp, head of the Natal Security Branch, introduced himself to me, shaking my hand and offering me a seat. He asked if I smoked and gave me a cigarette, which was most welcome, and then he introduced me to Sergeant Nayager who was sitting at another table close by.

'We're both from Durban and we're not brutes like those fellows from the Transvaal. We don't believe in treating people like they do.' He spoke in a friendly, sympathetic way.

'Naidoo,' he said. 'That's your name, isn't it. Naidoo ... Nayager, any relation?'

Sergeant Nayager was cleaning his revolver. We hated him, he had a terrible reputation.

'If Nayager was my relative I would have committed suicide long ago.'

Nayager jumped up and started threatening me with his gun, but Steenkamp told him to sit down.

'Tell me something. It's not important, but why do all communists have beards?'

I didn't want to explain that whenever one of our leaders was arrested I swore not to shave until he was released, and that as soon as one was released my mother would plead with me to shave it off, so I looked at Nayager, who had a Lenin-type goatee, and pointed.

'You mean like that?'

Steenkamp burst out laughing, and then started questioning me about explosions in Natal, telling me that he knew my comrades from Durban: Billy Nair, George Naicker and the others, and that he was sure they wouldn't get involved in stupid things like us people from the Transvaal. After asking where I had been on certain days he suddenly changed his attitude.

'Listen, man,' he said confidentially, 'we can get you off if you co-operate; you know the maximum penalty for sabotage is death, and the prosecution will ask for the death sentence in this case – you were caught red-handed. I'm a personal friend of Balthazar, I play golf with him every Wednesday' – he was referring to Vorster* – 'We can send you anywhere in the country, give you money, buy you a car, buy you a house – you're a young man, only twenty-six, you've still got a long way to go; we can send you out of the country, we have many friends overseas. What do you say?'

I just kept quiet, did not say a word, and he told me I did not have to reply straightaway and could ask for him any time and he would come along.

Then he let me return to the room where the others were. Up to this time we still had not talked to each other. It never dawned on me that we had not eaten for the last two days, until the police went to a restaurant and bought us some take-aways; I must have had about two or three spoonfuls of food, but I just could not eat.

That evening we were taken back to Marshall Square, and this time we were allowed to stand together while an ordinary prisoner cleaned out a cell for us.

We were all put into the same cell, with lots of new blankets;

---

*B J Vorster, Minister of Justice from 1962. Elected prime minister after the assassination of H F Verwoerd in 1966.

this was the first time that we actually smiled at each other after being locked up. We had not talked once, but now for the first time we asked one another how we were feeling; however, we were restrained in our talking and, even when one of our group said we would be appearing in court the next day and that was why our treatment had improved, the conversation never flowed. While we each had sympathy for the others, we still had doubts in our mind and did not know who to trust and who not.

TWO

Trial

While we were preparing our beds we were all called downstairs, and we got the shock of our lives when we saw our comrade 'Babla' Suliman Saloojee there, with five paper carrier bags around him. There was joy on our faces. We could all have grabbed him and kissed him on the spot. There was only one policeman there, a young guy in uniform and Babla introduced himself as advocate Saloojee – he was in fact just a clerk like me – and then in his gravelly working-class voice said, 'Hello comrades, how are you?' He told us not to worry, that we were appearing in court the next day and that they'd got the best lawyers for us, we mustn't worry about our families, about anything, we had the support of everyone.

This gave us a tremendous feeling that we were not isolated, and removed the worry that we had caused political embarrassment to the Transvaal Indian Youth Congress and the South African Indian Congress, our organisations. Although allied to the African National Congress, these organisations had not been banned like the ANC and had not come out with any public statement in favour of armed struggle.

Babla asked the policeman if he could give us the parcels but the young cop took all the cigarettes out, saying that we could not smoke. He also objected to our having Cokes, because we weren't allowed liquor, so Babla told him to taste the Cokes and, while he was drinking, smuggled the smokes across to us. Each bag had fruit, chocolates, toilet things, and the exact brand of cigarettes each of us liked: Texan for Laloo and me, and Viceroy for Shirish and Jassat – one plain, one filter.

We took our new possessions into our cells, and now there was more life in us, even our conversation changed and we became more friendly to each other.

The next day, on the way to court, with armed police all around us, we heard people in the streets saying, 'There they go, there they go. *Amandla!*' ('Power to the People!' – the ANC salute.)

Our lawyers were shocked by our appearance and made strenuous protests to the magistrate, while our supporters in the back of the courtroom buzzed and cried out 'Shame!' as the details of our torture were mentioned.

The prosecutor replied that we had been injured first in the explosion and then while trying to resist capture, and the magistrate ordered that we receive a full medical check. We constantly heard shouts of *'Amandla!'* from the spectators' section, and even one of the press men, Gerard Ludi, a member of the Congress of Democrats which mobilised whites in support of the ANC, gave us a clenched-fist salute as we passed by him; only years later did we learn he was a spy. Women in the gallery wore the green, gold and black uniform of the South African Women's Federation; we felt elated by all the support.

The lawyers were tired out, having made one application for bail after another in a whole series of political cases, all without success, and they were not keen to make one on our behalf that had no hope at all, but we insisted, and they agreed. At the very moment they were arguing on our behalf, a policeman whispered to the prosecutor who stood up and told the court that yet another leading comrade had jumped bail. Naturally, our application was refused.

*

We had no defence – we had been caught red-handed; and a few weeks later we were before the judge, having been found guilty, waiting to hear his sentence.

'Tell the accused to rise.' The judge looked severely down at us, his dark gown and formal white collar making him a grim figure in his big carved chair.

We stood up in our neatly pressed suits, clean-shaven on the insistence of our lawyers – I had lost the battle on this one – and wondered what he was going to say.

Our lawyers had proved that the last train had passed by the spot a good hour before the explosion, and also that the car which Gammat Jardien had used had been insured by none other than Lieutenant T J Swanepoel. Further, in my case, there had been character evidence that my father and three uncles had been like adopted sons to Mahatma Gandhi, that three generations of the family had struggled for the rights of the community (we had thought it better not to stress the number of times they had been to jail), and that I had left school early to support my family. I had told the judge how I had grown up in a political atmosphere, selling newspapers door to door from the age of ten, and how, when legal protest had been outlawed after the shooting at Sharpeville in 1960, we had felt there was no alternative but to resort to organised and disciplined violence as a means of securing our rights.

The court was packed tight, with people overflowing into the corridors, and we could hear the faint buzz of a vast crowd outside.

'I have heard what the accused have said in mitigation,' the judge's voice was quiet and modulated, 'and I accept that they were instigated to commit their crime by one Gammat Jardien and also, for the purposes of sentence, that they were assaulted

17

after their arrest.'

Faint flickers of hope began to rise in my breast.

'However, they willingly participated in these serious acts and have to be dealt with seriously as a warning to anyone who in future might be contemplating setting off explosives or engaging in other forms of sabotage.'

I felt numb inside.

'The accused all come from good families . . .'

Hope started to rise again.

'. . . And none of them has any convictions for crimes of violence . . . Taking all circumstances into account, the sentence of the court is as follows: each of the accused will serve ten years' imprisonment.'

Where we got the courage from at that moment I don't know, but, like one person, we raised our fists in the air in the *Amandla* salute. The response from the gallery was one big roar of '*Ngawethu!*' ('To the people!')

Although I had already geared myself to at least fifteen years and we had agreed that, whatever the sentences, we would put up our fists and show no signs of dismay or shock, a cold shiver went down my spine. I could see my mother in the gallery with tears rolling down her cheeks, my brothers and sisters as well. But to encourage them I gave a special gesture in their direction. *Amandla!*

Immediately we heard calls from the gallery: 'Don't worry, comrades, you'll never serve your sentence, you'll be free long before that.' We also heard cries that they would get Gammat Jardien. Hundreds of people queued to say goodbye in the cells below the court, and the crowd outside was so thick that when we were placed in the van it could not move. In fact the van began to rock backwards and forwards, and the black policemen in it with us panicked and begged us to appeal to the crowd to let us through. The face of one of my closest friends (Essop Pahad) pressed up against the mesh. 'Don't worry, comrades,' he shouted, 'you'll never serve ten years, you'll be out long before then.'

THREE

The Fort

'Strip!'

We took off our clothes and stood stark naked in the yard of the Fort, an old prison built into a hill in Johannesburg, a dreadful, crumbling place of incarceration for thousands of prisoners awaiting trial or newly convicted.

The warders mocked us for the nakedness they had ordered, prodding with their batons into my dark skin and flicking their straps into the pale face of comrade Shirish, getting as close as possible to his glasses.

'Tausa!' We remained still. *'Tausa! Hangpaal koelies, tausa!'* ('Dance! Gallows coolies, dance!')

We refused, we had seen other prisoners doing the *tausa,* and we were not going to do it: the naked person leapt into the air, spinning round and opening his legs wide while clapping his hands overhead and then, in the same movement, coming down, making clicking sounds with the mouth, and bending the body right forward so as to expose an open rectum to the warder's inspection.

The white warders moved away, leaving us to the mercy of the black warders, saying that we were the ones who had tried to blow up a train of black workers. *Kieriekops* (sticks with heavy round knots at the top) flashed around us as the black warders chased us from one part of the yard to the other, threatening to beat the life out of us. We just ran and ran, exhausted and humiliated, knowing that our sentence had just begun.

I had often been to the Fort before but only to take food to our leaders, such as when the Treason Trial had started in 1956 or during the state of emergency after the Sharpeville massacre. Now, exactly three years later, I was there as a prisoner.

During our trial we had looked forward intensely to the food brought in by our families and the chance to have a few words with them. Laloo had suffered because the warders had insisted that he speak only English or Afrikaans and his wife knew only Gujarati so that the two of them had simply had to stare at each other for the whole visiting period with tears in their eyes and saying nothing; but Reggie and I had used every second to keep in touch with our folks.

Our first cell had been bare of anything except three mattresses and a bucket of water. But then, to comply with a court order that we receive medical attention, the warders had marched with batons to the hospital section, chased the sick prisoners out and given us their beds. Finally, in the last part of our trial we had been placed in a large cell with about a hundred and fifty other prisoners, all members of the Pan-Africanist Congress (PAC), a breakaway group of the ANC, who had set up a communal sort of existence with food collected and shared, cultural activities in the evening and lots of books. The PAC was then at its peak and most of these prisoners had been arrogant and hostile to us in every way, making life miserable for us on every occasion, some even calling us communist agents and threatening to kill us. Fortunately, a group of about fifteen of these chaps had been friendly and had given us a great send-off when we went to court in the mornings and a great welcome when we came back in the afternoons, crowding around to find out what had happened at the trial.

'*Trek julle klere aan* – get dressed.' It was winter and cold and we put on the old pairs of short pants issued to us and red and white skippers – short-sleeved shirts with droopy necks – no shoes or socks.

'*Hardloop, koelies* – run.' We ran barefoot to a cell, not very large, which we found to be filled with a number of common-law (non-political) prisoners all scrambling frantically for something in the centre.

We stood looking at the commotion, not comprehending, and then suddenly realised what had been happening: the prisoners had been rushing to grab blankets and mats from a pile in the middle of the cell. We ran forward.

All that was left was one blanket and one mat for the three of us.

'Take everything back!' We heard a huge, tall, common-law prisoner speaking, and miraculously a big pile of blankets and mats grew once more in the centre. Only the big prisoner did not move, keeping a stern eye on the other prisoners rushing to do his bidding. A small pile of blankets and a mat – they happened to be of the best quality – remained undisturbed by his side. 'Now give them six blankets each,' he said firmly. 'The best.'

We protested, saying we only wanted our share and nothing more, but he told us to shut up, it had nothing to do with us.

The cell was like a dungeon, with little windows high up letting in some pale light through iron bars and wire grilles. We looked at the blankets and mat we had received. They weren't exactly good, but they were a little less dirty than the others, with fewer lice and a stink that was just a bit milder.

'Now make up their beds.'

We were quite naïve and did not know how to make up the beds, so we watched the prisoners folding them neatly so as to make a sort of cocoon. We then got inside the beds to get some warmth and heard the big prisoner asking us if we wanted to smoke.

Shirish and I said 'yes', and he made us two long brown paper *zolls*, lit them and gave them to us. We were nervous because we knew that convicted prisoners were not allowed to smoke, and we were not sure whether this was a plot against us or not, nor did we know how to smoke without being caught. So we took a few puffs and passed the *zolls* back to the prisoner whose name we learned was Choekoe. That day he had been sentenced to five years in prison, and we realised that he was one of the top gang leaders in prison, having already served ten years or more. We took a few more puffs, still feeling uncertain.

Later that evening, when we heard a black warder calling our names softly through a window, Choekoe was the first to jump up to see what was happening. He returned with cigarettes and chocolates sent to us by our comrades still in the remand section, and he told us firmly not to worry, he would look after the goods. We insisted that he take some smokes for himself but he refused, saying he had his own tobacco and that whenever we felt like a smoke we must just ask and he would light up one of our stock and give it to us. Even the chocolate we had practically to force on him before he agreed to have some for himself.

The following morning we were all moved to another, much larger cell with about a hundred and fifty convicted prisoners in it, and once more Choekoe saw to it that we had the best place in the cell and got our blankets. Also in the cell were two other political prisoners, both from the PAC, who had been convicted of attempting to leave the country illegally, given three years each, and one had another three years added on for breaking his banning order. The rest of the prisoners were in for murder, rape, house-breaking and other similar offences – we were quite a mixed crowd.

That night Choekoe called the three of us and asked us what our policies were, what was the policy of the ANC, what did we think of the South African situation? We told him that we were embarking on a period of armed struggle, that we felt it was going to be a long and hard struggle in which many lives would be lost, but that we were certain of victory sooner or later.

He then asked us: 'Is it not possible to get victory this year, in 1963? Don't you think you'll be able to overthrow the regime this year?'

We explained that it was not possible, but that we hoped that before our sentences expired our country would be liberated.

He then called one of the PAC leaders, Selby Ngendane, and told him he was stupid, he had been talking through his hat all this time, saying they'd be liberated by the end of the year, that we three young men understood the situation far better than he did, and that he was more inclined to believe us.

Selby, a national executive member of the PAC, replied that they were members of the PAC and that the PAC would liberate South Africa before the end of 1963 . . . Choekoe would see.

Food and cigarettes continued to come in to us from the remand section and Choekoe continued to guard them for us. We also got information that pleased us very much. On the day we were sentenced we were told a PAC member had stood up and made a moving speech in our praise and called upon the house to stand up and sing the National Anthem in our honour. One of the PAC leaders had strongly objected, saying that when, only three days previously, one of the PAC national leaders had been sentenced no one had made speeches or sung the National Anthem, and now, when three foreigners were being sentenced, they wanted to sing the Anthem. He had gone on to accuse us of being communists and of not being sincere in the Struggle. 'Yes,' was the reply of the man who had spoken in our favour, 'our national leader had been sentenced a few days earlier for trying to run away from the country, while these three brave young men had done something constructive and positive in the struggle against the oppressor; the house must stand and sing the National

Anthem.' The majority of the hundred or so had stood up and sung in our honour, while only a few, including the PAC leader, had remained seated and silent.

We left on a Saturday morning for Leeuwkop Prison, our hair cropped short on a cold, wet, rainy, early winter's day.

FOUR

Leeuwkop

There was tremendous tension in the air as we drove past the two large stone lions that guarded the front gate of Leeuwkop Prison and into the heart of the maximum security section. White warders armed with Belgian FN rifles, and black warders carrying *kieriekops* or old .303 rifles, stared down at us from high catwalks that criss-crossed the walls of the prison.

In the yard itself about fifteen warders closed in on us as we left the van and ordered us to strip. We took off our things and threw them on the wet cement.

'*Teen die muur, teen die muur* – against the wall.'

We did not know what to do, and the warders began to push our naked bodies against the wall and force us to lift our arms. We were facing the wall and I half noticed a bucket right in the centre of the yard. We called it the *bakkie,* or shit bucket. We heard shouting and screaming coming from the common-law prisoners who had travelled with us, and I tried to turn round to see what was happening, but a warder smacked me and said, '*Dit is donker agter, koelie, kyk voerentoe* – it's dark behind you, coolie, keep your eyes to the front.'

I could hear a prisoner crying and heard warders shouting, '*Kak hom uit, kak hom uit* – shit him out.' The prisoner was answering, '*Daar's niks, baas, daar's niks, baas* – there's nothing, boss, there's nothing.'

During all this commotion I noticed a number of warders walking towards us, laughing and giggling, and heard them talking amongst themselves.

'Yes, we've got the coolies, the dynamite coolies.'

Next thing, I felt something going right into my rectum. I immediately pulled back and heard a warder chuckling and saying, '*Hy's nog 'n maiden* – he's still a virgin.'

'*Draai om* – turn around.'

In the middle of the group of warders a prisoner with a completely shaven head, wearing heavy black pants and jacket, was standing with a tin in his hand. He walked over to me and before we could do anything he had slammed thick grease on to our heads and bodies: liquid soap. Then he was ordered to take us to the hospital and we moved off, the three of us, some black warders and a prisoner dressed in black who beat us and shouted at us all the way that we were coolies, murderers of innocent people, this was jail and we would be fixed up, here the white man was boss and we would do what he said. He was very violent, very aggressive.

In the hospital he picked up a blade and tried to shave our heads with it but we refused and, after some argument, he brought out a big electric sheep-shearer and set about us. As he worked he hummed the Italian song 'Funiculi, funicula'. He had a good voice, a real deep bass, and after three or four passes all our hair lay on the ground. He worked away busily, singing and abusing us all the time and then suddenly we noticed that he was whispering to us: his name was Lucas, he was from Johannesburg, and when he had the chance he would help us; in the mean time, we must forgive him for what he was doing. When the warders came near, he shouted rudely as before.

26

My pants were ripped at the back and had old bloodstains inside, and when I showed them to a warder named Kumalo he said, 'Coolie, you're lucky to get pants,' so I put them on. Next, he took us to the showers but changed his mind and said it was too cold and led us to the isolation cells.

The small cell was bare except for a gallon tin near the door: no bed, no seat, nothing. I put my plate of food down and looked around. A light covered with mesh shone in the ceiling, and outside the high windows I could see a cage into which warders could come from the catwalk whenever they wanted to peer down on us. I wondered who it was who had designed and built the place, this prison constructed between two hills near the Pretoria highway, dominated by catwalks, this strange piece of cruel, custom-built architecture.

Every half hour or so, a warder would enter the cage and stare down at me, barefoot, freezing cold in my torn shirt and pants, my head shorn, with nothing to do, nowhere to sit. From time to time I would walk around to try to keep warm, but the cement floor was icy. Then I would sit in a corner, trying to work out what time of day it was, wondering if my two comrades were in the same condition. When I felt thirsty I looked around for water, but could find none.

'Exercise time. Run!'

At one end of the courtyard was Kumalo with a *kieriekop*, at the other the head warder, Liebenberg, commonly known as Magalies, with a cane. As we passed Magalies he would lash out at our legs, shouting 'Faster, coolie, faster,' and at the other end Kumalo would hit at us with his *kierie*. My strapped arm hampered me, but we had to run at full speed. Suddenly I became aware that we were being accompanied by three or four common-law prisoners running between us, and at first I thought the one behind me had accidentally kicked my leg. I almost fell but managed to keep my balance. But then he tripped me a second time and this time I went sprawling on the ground. Magalies and Kumalo burst out laughing and the common-law prisoners joined in. When I got up my knees were bruised, my elbows were sore, but they kept shouting, '*Hardloop, hardloop* – run, run.'

During the half-hour, we must each have been tripped at least half a dozen times, and when Reg went to Magalies to complain he was simply beaten with the cane and ordered to carry on running.

By the end of the exercise period we were all exhausted. We could hardly stand. We were told to take a small sisal mat and three dirty blankets into our cells, as well as a plastic litre bottle of water and about ten sheets of toilet paper.

Supper consisted of a small piece of prison-baked bread, a mug of thick green synthetic soup, another mug of black coffee and a piece of meat.

I looked at the meat. Since the age of four I had not eaten meat, but there was no vegetable on the plate. Hungry, starving, I made up my bed and tried to have my first meal of the day. The bread was so hard I could hardly break it. The soup was inedible and the coffee dreadful. But somehow I managed to get them down into my stomach and crawled into bed leaving the meat on the plate. I tried to sleep, but no sleep would come, not even after the light went out after the eight o'clock bell.

The next morning at 5.30 the bell rang. I got up and sat on my bedding and about two minutes later a warder came and put the lights on. 'Oh, coolie, you're still sleeping, no food for you today.'

He was out on the catwalk, talking down to me. I jumped up, protesting that I had been up and was just trying to make my bed, but he did not listen.

'Run, you dynamite coolies, run. You'll never complete your ten-year sentences, you're too soft, you're too lazy.' Magalies was enjoying himself as he beat us while we ran round the yard. My arm was better now with the strapping removed, and Reggie could move more freely now that his plaster had been removed, but we hated our daily exercise-time when Magalies and Kumalo would get together to make our lives an absolute misery. We had both lost a lot of weight – Reggie maybe twenty kilograms, I about ten kilograms.

One evening, while I was singing freedom songs, I heard someone in the cell next to me joining in. I stopped to try and identify the voice, but could not make it out. So I changed to another song. This time, people on both sides of me took it up, and every time I changed they followed, but who they were was a total mystery until at about three o'clock my cell was opened, and I got the surprise of my life to see Comrade Joe Gqabi coming out of the cell next to mine, and further on Comrade Henry Makgothi and two other comrades. We felt great joy at seeing them, realising we were not alone, and although we could only greet each other in a very discreet way Joe managed to tell us not to worry, we were together now. For the half-hour we were made to run what struck me about these four comrades was how fit they were, you could see their muscles bulging.

Lieutenant Mann – 'Irish, and proud of it' – interrogated me in the boardroom. 'Tell me about your organisation. Show us that you have really changed, that you've repented of your actions, and we can move you up from "D" classification to "A" group with all its privileges. Right? Have you really turned over a new leaf?'

'I'm not prepared to answer questions about any organisations.'

'What's the matter with you Indians? You've got a long history of civilisation, you wore silk long before the white man, and here you are jumping from tree to tree with these barbarians, what's wrong with you, man?'

I said nothing, wondering what group I would be classified in.

'Right. You're wasting your time, the government will never be overthrown. Normally prisoners get a third off their sentences if they behave, but you aren't normal prisoners and you'll serve the full ten years. If you want to survive you'd better behave yourself – you fucking coolies, you think you're clever, we'll sort you out.'

He was very cold, and sent me out of the room.

A young warder on a bicycle, with one hand on the handlebar and the other waving a pistol, steered Shirish and me along a hard, stony path that cut our bare feet. Sweat started to seep into our torn shirts and our few toilet things bumped up and down against our hips where we had tucked them into our dirty pants.

We arrived at a vast dam site where about a thousand prisoners were working: some digging, others carrying huge loads of sand on their backs, moving in all directions, constantly harassed and beaten by about thirty white and black warders who moved amongst them, lashing out with canes and pieces of rubber hose.

'Where's the other coolie?'

The young warder explained that Reggie was in hospital.

'OK, load them up.'

Two common-law prisoners were ordered to bring us each a hundred-pound sisal bag and see to it that it was fully loaded up. We lifted them on to our backs and nearly collapsed.

'OK, over there. Quick. Hurry. Move. Get along you lazy fucking coolie.'

We staggered towards a small hill of sand being built about two hundred yards away. The huge weight threatened to topple us at every step. My shoulder ached, I felt the muscles in my neck stretching to bursting point and my feet struggled to find a hold on the ground.

Nearby there was a van with a machine gun, and on fixed posts we could see a number of white warders staring down at us with FN rifles. Four people were walking with me and I suddenly noticed that the load seemed lighter and more secure. 'Don't worry, comrade, we'll help you.' They told us they were from the

ANC and that comrade Joe had asked them to keep an eye on us. 'First thing, watch out for your toilet things.'

I looked down at my pants. My toothbrush and soap were already gone.

'We'll ask the other prisoners not to overload your bag, just stick with us and try to keep out of the way of the guards.'

Some of the common-law prisoners co-operated, others did not; however, wherever we went we found the four comrades surrounding us and shielding us. But the guards sought us out.

'Waar's die koelies? Waar's die koelies? – where are the coolies?' And when they found us they struck us continually with their canes, all over our bodies, our legs, our backs, even our heads. Because of my dark skin I could hide more easily, but Shirish, with his fair skin and glasses, was an easy target, and he really suffered that day.

The ground was littered with stones, and most of the time we had to move at running pace, so even when a stone pierced our feet we could not stop to remove it. What helped me was that when the warders could not find me, the prisoners would fill my bag with a little bit of sand and then put in lots of other bags to make it look bulky.

Where he got it from I don't know, but at lunchtime, as we sat resting with a group of thirty-five ANC comrades, we were able in a clandestine manner to smoke some tobacco smuggled in by Joe.

After introducing us to the other comrades, Joe told us that he had something important to discuss with us . . . for our ears alone. 'There's a gang leader who's planning a mass escape and he would like you to join in. What do you think?'

We were electrified. Like all prisoners, we were always dreaming of escape, imagining how we would miraculously get away and go into the underground and lead the revolution to success. But we were always nervous. Who was this gang leader? What chance of success did he have? Could we trust him?

31

We were introduced to the man – Joe had emphasised his own caution – and promised to think the matter over and give our decision the next day.

Counting: we were always being counted. In the morning, at mealtimes, in the evening, on the way to work, on the way from work, hundreds and hundreds of us being counted, slowly, over and over again by impatient warders who could never get the numbers right . . . especially in the late afternoon when they wanted to knock off work. The warders got furious, one count was never enough; we would stand in lines waiting to be counted, and after the thousand or so of us had been counted we would form up in rows again, sure that there would be a recount, maybe two or even three. Some of the bolder ones among us, better known to the warder, would suggest politely that if four prisoners were missing from the jail why did they not simply subtract four from the previous total?

I ran as fast as I could, my leg chained to the leg of Henry Makgothi, my wrist to his wrist. Each movement of mine threatened to pull him down, we tugged against each other, with the warders on horseback getting closer all the time. We stumbled and fell and got up and ran again, soon at the back of the vast mass of prisoners all running desperately back to the prison, their chains rattling in the dust.

Now I knew why our comrades had insisted that Shirish and I line up right at the front of the queue that had been getting ready to head back to the prison.

Black warders on foot lashed at us with sticks, our feet tore on the sharp stones and the horses, skilfully guided by their riders, kicked at our ankles. Henry tried to run smoothly, but I kept stumbling and pulling him over and I felt especially bad that he was suffering so many blows for trying to help me along. I lost sight of Shirish and his partner, frantically trying to keep going as the horses rode into me and the blows rained down. It was a nightmare. I just could not get used to running in chains, I never believed that we would reach the jail alive.

Eventually we arrived, bleeding and exhausted at the courtyard and stood, drained and panting, as the warders counted us, interminably counted, counted, counted, until they got the figures right; our legs ached and little pools of blood formed around our toes and ankles, mixing with the sand and dust and the chains.

We were running naked, our clothes bundled in our arms: a thousand of us streaming across a yard to place the clothes in a pigeon-hole, then racing, the cold air beating against our skins, to a door containing a metal detector, leaping through the doorway, one after the other, and then grabbing the first set of clothing we saw in a pigeon-hole on the other side, irrespective of who had worn it the previous day, dressing as we ran, ducking blows and hearing insults as we sped towards the kitchen, grabbing a plate of food from prisoners handing out the evening meal – worried that if we missed we would go without food – picking up a mug and dipping it on the run into a large container of coffee and rushing into a big courtyard where we were given five minutes to squat and finish eating.

That evening we lined up and were counted with our comrades, jubilant at being locked up with them, and were beginning to tell them about our experiences of the day when the cell door was flung open and a warder shouted: '*Julle koelies kom uit! Julle dink julle is slim, nè?* – You coolies, come out, you think you're clever, hey?'

We were marched back to the isolation cells.

✳

We waited for hours on end on the bitterly cold midwinter cement for the weekly inspection by the commanding officer, a colonel,

33

our identity cards open in our outstretched hands, our blankets and mats neatly folded on the ground nearby.

As the CO walked past I decided to call for his attention. His immediate reply was: '*Ja, koelie, wat soek jy?* – Yes, coolie, what do you want?'

I said that I had a complaint to raise and he said that in that jail no prisoner had the right to complain. But I insisted. I said I would like to see a doctor, so he asked why and I showed my feet, cut to ribbons. He said, 'That's nothing. I don't see anything wrong with your leg,' and went off.

Two days later, the warder in charge of the hospital came looking for the 'dynamite coolies'. As he escorted us to the hospital he told us that we had some nerve complaining to the colonel, that he would see to it that we would be well and truly fixed up, and that when the doctor found us fit for work we would really be in the shit.

At the hospital, prisoner Lucas came up to us and told us not to worry, he would look after us and ask the doctor to detain us in hospital. He then brought us tobacco to smoke and also copies of the *Rand Daily Mail* which had a story of huge demonstrations taking place in London in solidarity with us. It also had a photograph of a placard demonstration in Johannesburg where little kids were carrying banners reading I WANT MY DADDY! I WANT MY MOMMY! I WANT MY BROTHER! I WANT MY SISTER! These referred to comrades detained under the newly passed ninety-day detention law, and to those of us who were in prison.

One paper also carried the story of our comrades Abdulhay Jassat and Laloo Chiba, who had appeared in the Supreme Court and on the first day had had the charges against them dropped, only to be detained again immediately under the ninety-day law.

We stripped naked for the doctor, and the warders shouted that we were all lazy and work-shy and this business of seeing the doctor had to stop. One by one we were taken to be examined and when my turn came I recognised one of the district surgeons who had examined us after our torture. I did not have to explain anything to him, he could see the bruises and cuts on my feet and the marks on my body and he enquired how my right arm was; I told him that the bullet wound had healed completely. His instructions were that both I and Comrade Shirish should be detained in hospital for two weeks, and when the warder in charge of the hospital protested bitterly, saying we were lazy and did not want to work, he stuck firmly to his decision. The warder was furious, but there was nothing he could do.

Prisoner Lucas helped us a great deal, smuggled in newspapers regularly – at great risk to himself – as well as tobacco, and also gave us a bed each with two clean white bedsheets. Our meals were brought to us by him, pre-prepared and warmed up, and he saw to it that we had a hot bath every evening. In the presence of the warders, however, he would always be hostile, pretending to hit us and to be making our life as miserable as possible.

White warders on horseback and black warders on foot chased us to and from another dam being built by hundreds of medium-security prisoners, but this time we were not chained, though the beatings still continued, and when we complained about being barefoot we were given shoes and stockings.

One day, a black warder came up to me and whispered, 'Your leaders have been arrested not far from the prison.' When I asked him to name the leaders arrested, the only name he could recall was that of Nelson Mandela. I pointed out that Comrade Mandela was already serving a sentence and he promised to re-read the article and bring us the full news the following day. When I got back to prison I told Reggie and Shirish, and the following day we got the full terrible story.

The police had swooped on a farm at Rivonia near Johannesburg and arrested Walter Sisulu, Govan Mbeki, Ahmed Kathrada, Dennis Goldberg and others whom we knew to be leaders of the high command of MK.* Our movement had suffered a terrible blow.

The gang leader who had approached us about escaping came once again to Shirish and me. 'We'll attack the warders, grab their rifles and pistols and make a run for it. Alexandra Township is only about five kilometres from here. We can hide there or, if necessary, fight it out. What do you think? Will you join us?'

Shirish and I looked at each other, not committing ourselves.

'Do you know how to use the machine pistol on the truck?'

'I've never handled one before but I've got the theoretical knowledge,' I answered.

'Good. You two can take over the machine pistol and a number of us can get away in the truck. Good, good. We'll do it next week, so you've still got lots of time to think it over. Let me know.'

'Reggie, what do you think?'

We were shouting across the isolation section, wanting him to hear us clearly but anxious lest a warder come by.

'You guys should go, take your chance.'

'But we can't leave you behind.'

'Don't worry about me; this is your chance, take it, go. I can look after myself.'

'But we're in this together. Three of us came in, three of us go out.'

'Go, man, this is your chance.'

I was rapidly losing weight and my comrades insisted that I should eat meat, since our rations were so meagre and so terribly

---

*On 11 July 1963 police raided Liliesleaf Farm in Rivonia and arrested Walter Sisulu, Govan Mbeki, Ahmed Kathrada, Raymond Mhlaba, Bob Hepple, Rusty Bernstein and Dennis Goldberg. All were charged with sabotage, along with Nelson Mandela, James Kantor, Andrew Mlangeni and Elias Motsoaledi in what came to be known as the Rivonia Trial.

36

prepared that we could not afford to do without whatever scraps of protein we were offered. Reluctantly I made the decision to start eating flesh; ten years would be a long time and I felt I had no alternative.

Suppertime came and as usual we ran in the queue to collect our food. I stretched out my arm and took hold of the plate. It had thick green soup with a piece of bread on top, and there, sticking out at the side, was a piece of meat – a big pig's ear covered in hair. I ran with the plate and my cup of coffee to the cell and, after we were locked up, I put the plate down and lifted out the ear. It was full of dirt and bristles and I shouted to my comrades, 'Is this what you call meat?' Sympathetically they told me to leave it and to hope for better luck the next time, so all I ate that day was the bread and coffee – the soup was too ghastly, the pig's ear was just too much.

Two days later, I received two small pieces of meat and put them in my mouth – my first meat in twenty-four years. It did not go down well. I felt nauseous but I forced myself to swallow it. That whole afternoon I felt like vomiting.

We were ordered to line up just before lunch. There were more guards than I had ever seen, rifles and pistols everywhere, and dogs panting on the leash, occasionally barking. Rapidly we were marched off under heavy guard to the prison, all one thousand of us, and locked up – even though it was only lunchtime.

We never went back to the dam; in fact we were simply kept locked up all day, day after day. We were moved to a large communal cell where we were together with the thirty-five ANC comrades, allowed out only three times a day in the mad rush for our food, knowing that if we were found talking we lost our meals, if we ran too slowly we lost our meals, and if we missed the outstretched plate we lost our meals. Sometimes the whole cell would be locked up for the day without meals, as a punishment. Regularly, the group of thirty-five, now thirty-eight, would be arbitrarily moved from cell to cell to prevent us from returning to where we might have hidden contraband. The cells were always crowded – hundreds to a cell – and we were always being shifted around and counted.

Although chained and heavily interrogated, the leaders of the escape bid never mentioned once to their interrogators that they had included us in their plans to get away.

'Mr Commanding Officer.'
   'Yes, what is it now?'
   'I have a request to make.'
   'Well, what is it?'
   'We need more toilet paper.'
   'What?'
   'There are dozens of us in our cell and we only get forty small single sheets a day for the lot of us. We need at least three sheets each time we use the toilet, so we have to ration the paper and most of us go without it most of the time.' (I did not tell him that we also used to tear blankets in strips to make up for the shortage.)
   'You're talking rubbish. You're lucky to have a lavatory at all; most of you don't even know what a lavatory is – it all comes out of our taxes. You break the law and we have to pay even more for you to waste paper just as you like . . .
   'Let me tell you something. The train from Johannesburg to Durban travels eight hundred kilometres and may have a thousand passengers; they don't all shit at the same time; some today, some tomorrow, some the day after. Well, the same applies to you. Request dismissed.'

Nearly forty of us scrambled into six showers for our weekly wash, and after five minutes of bumping into each other under the jets we ran out into the freezing yard to slap ourselves dry. We did not mind our lack of combs because we had no hair, but we could have done with some soap and towels.

I was thirsty, but was I thirsty enough, that was the question. There was someone sitting on the toilet, making a terrible noise and stench. 'Silence, silence there,' someone shouted each time the man's bowels erupted. To get at the water tap meant kneeling down next to him, pushing my hands round his legs, and trying to catch a few drops from behind him. Better to stay thirsty a little while, and yet, when he finished, somebody else would probably take his place and I would never be able to get to the tap.

'Hey, comrade,' I shouted, 'are you going to be long?'

I could see the strain on his face as he forced his bowels to work; his pants lay curled round his ankles, his bare knees jutted out in front of him.

'Sorry, comrade,' he shouted back. 'I've got terrible cramp, I'll be as quick as I can, give me a chance.'

The stink was powerful. He was bending forward as he strained to finish. I told him not to worry, I only wanted to get to the tap, but I wasn't really all that thirsty.

'Yes, what is it now?'

The commanding officer was angry and long-suffering as usual.

'Blades. We need more blades, and a proper razor.'

'But you get five blades a week.'

'Yes, for forty of us, and we have to hold them between our finger and thumb and scrape our beards off without any soap. Before the week is over we are tearing our faces and fingers with them.' (The blades were brand-named Solingen, made in the Federal Republic of Germany, and we were convinced that they had been used and were resharpened before they got to us.)

'OK, you can have a safety razor at weekends. That's all. No more blades. Five is plenty. The white man can't throw all his money away on these trivialities.'

One evening two packets of tobacco came flying into our cell. As we swooped to pick them up we knew that the black warder we had managed to speak to – normally they were banned from our area – had followed our suggestion and had gone to the office of *Spark,* as the still legal pro-ANC newspaper was then called. (It had been called *Guardian, New Age, Advance, Clarion* and *People's World* in previous years; each one banned in turn.) We had in fact suggested he get five rand from them to buy us some tobacco, and keep the change. So now we had tobacco but nothing to light it with.

The next night a flint came flying in. Now we had tobacco and a flint. But we did not know how to use the flint.

'Easy,' said one of the common-law prisoners. 'You take the prison toothbrush, scrape a little off it, strike the flint, and the scraping catches alight.'

We tried it out, and he was right. The prison toothbrush was dated 1942 and, for some reason, the flint only worked with this war issue. Now we had tobacco, a flint to make a spark, toothbrush scrapings to make a light, but no paper to roll the tobacco in.

We looked around and saw one of the prisoners reading the Gideon Bible – the only reading matter allowed us.

'Would you mind handing over your Bible, please.'

'I'm sorry, but it's the Bible.'

'But there's nothing else. What else can we do with the tobacco? We can't eat it.'

'That's not my problem. I'm not parting with my Bible.'

'OK. Let's put it to the vote.'

The debate was heated. We went on for a long time, but that guy never stood a chance. There were just too many smokers in the cell and – maybe we were wrong – we won the day by a large majority. I must say that the thin leaves made excellent smoking paper.

One comrade was put in charge of the tobacco and he made six long *zolls* and we divided ourselves into six groups, each group going to the wall and smoking very carefully, trying to keep down the smoke while the other comrades maintained watch.

Those two packets were the only two we ever had. They lasted only three or four glorious days during which, bit by bit, the Bible became slimmer, but we rationed the paper carefully and there was always something left for the comrade to read.

The Hindu priest was saying prayers for five of us in a room in the reception section and, although we were happy to have him there, I must say our attention was not really on his words – it was on the beautiful plates of food piled up behind him.

'Right,' the young warder told us formally, 'your families have sent in food for your Diwali Festival, two kilograms in weight for each of you, and you have exactly three minutes to eat it.'

Our mouths were watering. We could hardly believe our luck, and we rushed forward to plunge our hands into the delicious sweetmeats and cakes laid out in front of us.

'Time up!'

We protested. We had hardly started. But the warder ordered us back to our cells and, very disheartened, we marched out, leaving the beautiful food behind us virtually untouched.

'Yes? Oh, it's you again. Now what is it?'

'Our families sent us in food for Diwali and we weren't given enough time to eat it.'

'It's your own bloody fault. Every prisoner has his chance, we are very fair. For some it's Christmas, you had your religious holiday, you must learn to eat more quickly.'

The warder marched us down a corridor, opened a door and ordered us to enter; there we saw all the food the priest had brought laid out on a table. The warder told us that his instructions were to lock us in the room and keep us there until we had finished eating.

We asked if we could take the food to our cell, hoping to share it with our comrades but he refused, and we were locked up with enough food for ten people – with orders to eat it all. We cut the cake into pieces and dug into it. We tasted every single sweetmeat. We devoured the chocolate. We ate and ate and ate and by the time we had finished, half an hour later, we could hardly move.

When the warder opened up he found us sitting around with practically no food left over. The chief warder who was with him said, 'God, look what they've done to the food,' complaining that we had even eaten the portions intended for them. They searched us to see that we had no food hidden away then marched us back to our cells, past the kitchen where the other prisoners were taking their lunch. The warder insisted we take our lunch as well and we tried to refuse, but he insisted. So we took it and, when we got back to our cell, we handed it over to our comrades.

About October, the three of us were called to the office where we met members of the Special Branch who took each one separately into a room and asked us to make a statement about the whereabouts of the dynamite that Gammat Jardien had sold to us. We were told that from a total of one hundred sticks of dynamite originally in the box we had only used eight, so they were investigating further charges against us, based on possession of the other ninety-two sticks.

None of us made a statement, we denied all knowledge of the dynamite. Reggie was taken away to Security Branch headquarters and once again interrogated, but he stuck to his story, and on his return gave us a full account of the interrogation. He also mentioned that, for the first time, the Special Branch had been very civil to him, though they had said that we had been lucky to get only ten years, and they would see to it that it was doubled on some charge or other in the future.

We had no reading matter or writing materials to help us get through the long day in our cells. All we managed to do was to smuggle in pieces of tar from which we made dice for the game of ludo, improvising a board by drawing on a blanket. But we organised lots of classes: English language, general knowledge and history, followed by geography, general science and Zulu language with half an hour's break for exercise.

The language classes were especially important since the people in our cell came from all over South Africa and spoke many different tongues; not all of them knew English which was the main medium of communication, so these classes helped bring us together.

After supper, which was always served early in the afternoon to enable the warders to get home early, we sang freedom songs and held political discussions. In fact, we sang freedom songs throughout the day.

One of our comrades imagined the scene and described it to us: 'Thousands of people are gathered round the courtroom where the Rivonia accused are to be charged, singing ANC songs and shouting *"Amandla!"* Many of them are dressed in the uniform of the ANC, and amongst them we can see Winnie Mandela wearing traditional clothing, while next to her is Albertina Sisulu, with hundreds of police standing around with stenguns and dogs . . . walking through the crowd, carrying his gown over his arm, is advocate Bram Fischer, leader of the defence team.'

The oration went on for about two hours as the speaker described the arrival of the *kwela-kwela** van and the roar of *'Amandla!'* from the crowd when our leaders climbed out of the back to enter the court. He told us about the journalists from the international press and the letters of solidarity sent in from all over the world. We were spellbound.

Henry Makgothi, otherwise known as Squire, a leading light

---

*The closed police pick-up vans were known as *kwela-kwelas*.

43

in the organisation, the comrade who sustained me on that terrible day when we had been chained together, had a vivid sense of dramatic detail, and he made us feel that we were present at the Rivonia trial, even though we had absolutely no information at all about it, not the faintest scrap of news.

'Don't worry, you'll never serve out the full ten years.' That was the constant refrain of the group of thirty-five ANC prisoners who had all been sentenced to two years for leaving the country illegally, after having been captured and handed over to South African Security by the Northern Rhodesian colonial police.

We came from Natal, the Cape, the Transvaal. One of the prisoners was even from Namibia (then called South West Africa). We represented a wide variety of backgrounds, but we stuck firmly to each other, and when a warder barked out, 'Who's making all that noise?', ready to punish some individual, we would all move forward together.

'Oh, all right. Be more quiet next time.'

Most of us had never set eyes on one another before, and our backgrounds were totally different, but while we were together our comradeship was of the highest calibre. We were literally from far and wide, some spoke Zulu, some Xhosa, some English, some Sotho, some Afrikaans, some were illiterate, others had university degrees. But we were all together for the same reason; all in the same fight for the same goals, suffering the same hardships.

It was a bitter time for all of us, a time of hardship and suffering, yet we were all sustained by the feeling that something very special was happening; that through our comradeship and our day-to-day struggles in support of each other, something very fine and deep was growing – we could feel the new South African nation in birth, right there in the dark depths of prison, and this gave us strength to fight on, and great hope for the future.

FIVE

Journey

We sat crowded together on the floor of the speeding van, a dozen pairs of people, legs linked by chains, wrists by handcuffs, bumping along in an increasingly hot atmosphere.

Four truckfuls of chained prisoners were heading in convoy through the darkness. We could hardly see each other's faces, just feel our bodies pressed together in an uncomfortable mass, and as light began to filter into the van all we could make out was a tangle of arms and legs and chains, and faces with drawn expressions. We wanted to stretch but there was no way of doing so – we were on top of each other and had to endure, for hour upon hour, a discomfort and an agony that were getting worse all the time.

Eventually we stopped at Bloemfontein Prison, right in the centre of the country, where security people from the Cape took over from those of the Transvaal, and they gave us just a short chance to stretch. But one of the trucks would not restart, and its load was distributed among the three remaining vans, so that now we were even more squashed up against each other than before, even more tortured by our own bodies, by ourselves.

It was blazing hot. Sweat poured down our bodies. As the van carried us on endlessly comrades found that they needed to have a piss, and we appealed to the warders to stop somewhere, but they would not listen to us. Eventually, some prisoners made their way to the back and tried to piss through a gap under the van's door; that turned out to be all right when the van was travelling uphill, but the minute it started moving downhill all the piss would pour in and we would find ourselves sitting in it.

I tried to hold out as long as possible, but my desire to pee became overwhelming. So I tugged at Squire and we manoeuvred our way over the hunched-up bodies of the other prisoners all huddled together. There was no room, and some of the prisoners literally carried us as we lurched and fell in the speeding van, making apologies all the way. Our progress was slow: we tripped over knees and chains; pulled against each other; toppled over together, hurting the people we crashed into – more apologies. When we finally got to the back, sweating, bruised and panting, I knelt down thankfully, with Squire at my side, and held my penis for at least ten minutes before anything would come out. Then it poured out, hot and burning and very protracted.

The worst moment was when one of the comrades said he had to have a shit. We appealed to him to hold on until the next stop, but he said that he had already held out for too long and could not keep it in any more. He, too, had to make his way with his partner to the back of the van and, after having his shit right near the door, he suddenly realised that he had no paper or anything to wipe himself with. After a long discussion he tore the bottom part of his shirt and used it to clean himself, but unfortunately, there was no way he could push the shit out, and this made the van even more uncomfortable: the stench, the exhaustion and frustration, the urine and the shit, and bodies piled upon bodies.

Frequently a comrade would scream out that he had cramp in his legs, but there was nothing we could do to help, the van bumped up and down and the cramps became worse all the time.

After sunset we could not even see one another. By this time the van was a real inferno, stinking of sweat mixed with the shit and with wet piss all over the floor and seeping into our clothing. We talked quietly to one another, telling each other to have courage, to have patience.

The van made about two stops, but even then we were not allowed to get out, but stayed trapped in our travelling hell while the warders stretched their legs outside. Eventually we reached Richmond jail, a small prison in the heart of the Karoo semi-desert, where we emerged into the freezing night air, breathing frantically, straightening our aching arms and legs, and feeling the sweat turn cold on our bodies.

The head of the jail, a lieutenant, was very polite to us, apologising for giving us only porridge and saying that we had arrived too late for him to prepare anything else. He asked that our handcuffs and chains be removed, but Magalies, who had accompanied us from Leeuwkop, refused to allow it. Then, after the meal, the lieutenant came along and asked politely who wanted tea – we thought he was pulling our legs, so we kept quiet, but he insisted and wanted to know if we had lost our tongues. At last one prisoner timidly said 'Yes', and the lieutenant instructed the local prisoners to bring us all some tea and apologised for the fact that it was in tins and not in proper cups.

We were locked up in two cells, still chained, and all we had was one blanket per pair: no mats, nothing. And we froze.

At about 5.30 we were woken, and again the lieutenant brought us hot tea and a quarter-loaf of white bread each. The bread was really delicious, in fact many of us went up to the lieutenant and thanked him, and as we were leaving he gave us each a further half-loaf and commented that he was sorry he could not do more for us, adding that he wanted us to remember our short stay in Richmond. It was obvious that he knew who we were, and we long remembered our short stop there, even though the conditions were so primitive. In fact, when Magalies noticed him giving us

47

the extra bread, he came running over to try to stop this, calling out, 'Why are you giving these pigs bread? They don't deserve it', but the lieutenant calmly insisted and since he outranked Magalies who was only a sergeant, we were able to keep the precious half-loaves.

Our next stop was at a modern jail in a little town in the Hex River mountains, and our eyes popped when we saw a roll of toilet paper – more than one roll – and also a washbasin where many of us had our first good wash in days; we took as much toilet paper as we could fold into our pockets – it was like gold and we felt like kings having it there.

We tried hard to see the Cape mountain scenery we were passing through and, eventually, Cape Town itself, but the peep-holes were too small and we could have been anywhere rather than in the beautiful Cape. When we arrived at Cape Town harbour the truck pulled in right next to a little passenger boat called *Diaz* and, still handcuffed and chained – many of the prisoners had never seen the sea before, let alone been on a boat – we were taken on board and placed in a hold below deck. We were counted three or four times; the hatch was then closed upon us and the boat started to move.

We could see the sea splashing outside, a little bit rough, and the boat rolled from one side to the other. It was frightening for many of the prisoners, especially as the waves hit the portholes and as we felt the chains heavy on us, trapped in the hold. Some of the prisoners trembled, others became seasick and made a dash to the toilet, dragging their partners with them, their chains rattling loudly.

Going through our minds over and over again was the question: 'What is Robben Island like, that dreaded prison we have heard so much about? What is the Island really like?'

PART TWO

ROBBEN ISLAND

SIX

'This is the Island'

All we could see was the harbour itself, and bushes, and warders; scores and scores of warders armed with stenguns, some holding Alsatians. A colonel and a major stood in the group, and there were no other human beings around; just prison personnel, keeping us under close guard as we clambered ashore in our chains, lurching and pulling against our partners.

We were placed in large prison trucks and driven about five hundred metres into the court of a half-completed set of prison buildings, where again all was quiet, without another prisoner in sight; just our group with chains clattering and warders issuing commands to each other and the occasional bark of a dog.

As we staggered out of the trucks the warders surrounded us and suddenly the shouting started. '*Dis die Eiland* – this is the Island. *Hier gaan julle vrek* – here you will die.' Words like '*kaffir*', '*koelie*' and '*boesman*' went flying left, right and centre. Batons rained down on us and we ran wildly around, trying to protect ourselves, our chains rattling loudly, one pulling in this direction, the other in that, all of us colliding and falling over as we ducked the blows. We looked up to see the senior officer enjoying the spectacle. Even when Head Warder Verster, the person in charge of security on the Island, eventually instructed the warders to take off the chains and the handcuffs, they continued to beat us, and our protests were simply ignored.

One young warder came up to me and said, *'God, hier's 'n koelie hier. Wat maak die koelie hier?* – God, here's a coolie. What's the coolie doing here?'

'Sir,' I replied in English, 'we are not coolies.'

That really set him off.

'God, watter taal praat jy jong – God, what language are you using, man – *die plek is Robben Eiland* – this is Robben Island – *en in die plek ons praat nie daardie kaffirboetie se taal nie* – and here we don't use that kaffir-lover's language – *nog, hier ek is jou baas* – what's more, here I am your *baas.'*

I insisted on speaking English, saying that I did not understand Afrikaans, so he called out to Verster, *'Hier's 'n koelie wat my Meneer roep, en hy sê hy kan nie Afrikaans praat nie* – Here's a coolie who calls me "Sir" and says he can't speak Afrikaans.'

Verster then walked up to me. 'Yes, coolie, so you don't know you must address me as *Baas*? If you know what's fucking good for you, you will learn to speak Afrikaans bloody fast. Most of my warders don't speak English and what's more you must remember to address every single warder as *Baas*. There's no "Sir" on the Island, only *Baas.'*

He then asked me if I knew what he was called by the prisoners, and when I said that I didn't he said that he was called Spy Thirteen and was a famous warder, well known to every prisoner on the Island, as well as to hundreds of prisoners in other jails all over the country.

After the chains were off we were made to strip and, leaving our clothing in one big bundle, stark naked to the wind, we moved to another pile of clothes, harassed, kicked and beaten all the way. This second pile was a heap of mixed-up stinking, dirty short pants, and khaki shirts with short sleeves and no collar. We had not seen a pair of shoes since our struggle at Leeuwkop, and we did not get any now; in the shortest possible time we had to put on our pants and shirts and then run about a hundred metres to the kitchen – the ground was covered with gravel and at every step our feet were pierced, but we could not stop for a moment.

At the kitchen we were given a metal plate with steaming hot porridge and we had to carry it while being chased towards our cells in 'B' section. Our hands were burning, our feet were being torn, and blows fell on our heads, shoulders and backs as we rushed along. The warders lashed out at us with batons and pieces of rubber hosepipe, leaving us alone for only five minutes while we tried to gulp down the scalding porridge. We did not even have spoons and when we asked for some we were told to use our bloody fingers – I personally could not manage more than a few scoops with my fingers, and soon we were rushed into our cells: fifty into B1 and fifty into B2, the first occupants of a new, freshly painted prison block.

From the windows which ran round the cell, we could see that the walls were immense, at least thirty centimetres thick; the iron bars in each of the windows were at least three centimetres in diameter. There was a row of sisal mats on the floor, one for each prisoner, and smelly blankets so thin you could look right through them. There was nothing else in the cell, except for a section at the side with a tiled bathroom, three cold-water showers, three handbasins, four washing tubs and, in a corner where one would expect a toilet, two buckets behind a low wall.

Ours was a cell of political prisoners, six convicted as ANC and forty-four as members of the PAC. We were all very tense, unsure what to do after the warders had disappeared, so most of us simply stripped and got into our beds, and when the bell rang for sleeping time at 8 p.m. with the midsummer sun still in the sky, and the lights never switched off, exhausted after the journey and all the tension, we soon fell asleep.

SEVEN

Reception

A loud bell at 5 a.m. startled us and we staggered out of bed in a general rush to the bathroom. By the time I got to the buckets, both of them were overflowing with shit and piss, right on to the floor. It was a chaotic scene, chaps running to the taps, others not knowing where to relieve themselves, and no toilet paper around – absolutely no toilet paper. I decided to hold out.

At 5.30 our cells were opened and in walked some warders, who chose two prisoners to carry out the buckets – the contents spilling all over the floor – and then chased us with batons out of the cells.

In the yard we found ourselves in the centre of a semicircle of warders and each of us had to run to a warder who frisked us with his hands while we stretched our arms in the air, swearing at us, calling us pigs and saying that we would die on the Island. While their hands searched our bodies in the most humiliating way possible, they told us that here the white man was boss, and they hurled as many insults at us as they could, crude insults, repeated over and over again, as though they could not be in our presence or touch our bodies without saying something vile, reminding them and us of their power to do with us exactly what they liked.

From there we were once more made to run to the kitchen through a barrage of blows from batons and rubber pipes, and this time we got a plate of ice-cold porridge with a thick congealed skin over it, a mug of what they called black coffee and another mug of what they described as soup.

We sat in long rows in the open, for the first time seeing hundreds of other prisoners, mostly political but some common law. As we squatted over our food, warders moved constantly in between us, and if we turned our heads even a fraction we got a crack with a fist or a baton. We were not allowed to talk at all. We simply had to eat as quickly as possible and listen to the abuse. By 6 a.m. the eating was over and we were already assembled into different work groups, all the new arrivals being ordered to step aside.

While the other groups were going out in *spans* (teams) to work, we were marched to the old jail about a kilometre away where we discovered Reception was housed. It was a dreadful-looking part of the prison. There was no running water or sewerage in the cells. It was filthy, and had the atmosphere of a Gestapo camp with barbed wire everywhere and armed warders on posts, just as we had seen in films about the Nazis.

A number of political prisoners were still being housed there, as well as common-law prisoners, and all one hundred of us new arrivals were put into one cell and locked up. Then, one by one, we were called out to Reception where particulars were taken of our names, parents' address and our sentence, and it was confirmed that we were all in the lowest category of prisoner, 'D' group; and it was then that we each received our prison number, and I learned who I was going to be on the Island – number 885/63.

After we had all seen the officer in Reception, we were told to strip for medical inspection. Many of us had health problems, but the doctor just walked past each one of us shouting 'Any complaints?' But when prisoners tried to step out to describe their illnesses, he and the warders simply rushed them back.

'I've got TB, I was receiving . . .'

'Get back, you're lazy.'

'I get terrible asthma . . .'

'Another work-shy. Get back.'

He didn't examine a single prisoner; he just walked along making rude comments and at the end of the tour declared us all fit for hard labour.

Next, we were taken to the stores where each of us was given a wooden spoon, a cake of blue soap, and a scrap of towel. African prisoners were given a cloth cap and sandals while the rest of us got a felt hat and a pair of shoes. A pair of shoes? They were shoes, but not a pair, chosen completely at random. Normally I wore a size seven, but in my hand I had a left size nine and a right size eleven. If it had not been so humiliating I would have laughed, it was like a comedy; but I was supposed to wear them, and I felt like weeping. Some of the others were even worse off, I could see them protesting, in vain, that they had two left or two right shoes.

Wherever we moved we found ourselves mixed in with common-law prisoners, many with scarred and battered faces, their eyes glazed, but their bodies muscular and physically tense.

'Watch out. We'll get you,' some of them threatened. 'Don't worry. We'll look after you,' others whispered.

A prisoner came up to us, moving quietly as though on his way somewhere.

'My name is Mandla,' he said softly. 'I've got something for you.'

We looked down and, from nowhere, suddenly saw in his hand a newspaper. We couldn't believe our eyes. It was the first paper we had seen in six months, and we grabbed it, eager to devour every word.

'Careful,' he said. 'Careful, keep it well hidden, if they find it, you'll get heavy punishment.' And then he vanished.

We also met up for the first time with many of our comrades whom we had not seen for long periods, as well as other comrades from various parts of the country whom we had never met before. They were very helpful to us, giving us courage and confidence in the Struggle, warning us that work on the Island was very hard, that we would suffer terribly and feel like killing ourselves at times, but that we would get through it, and must have strength.

EIGHT

Stones

There were more than a thousand of us in dirty, ill-fitting and scanty clothes, our caps looking strange on our hairless heads, and we marched in four silent columns across the Island to the old quarry.

Our feet were uncomfortable in the strange assortment of shoes and sandals, many of us barefoot, having lost our footwear in the scramble to collect them from the pile near our cell. It was a little after six in the morning, and we were off to work. No one sang. No one whistled. No one spoke. Four long columns, moving without a sound.

A house stood completely on its own, fenced in and guarded by an armed warder, and in the doorway we could see the figure of Robert Sobukwe, leader of the PAC, dressed in civilian clothing. The PAC chaps with us were very excited to be near their leader, but we were more curious than anything else. It was clear that he was in no position to greet us, nor could we greet him in any way, but he managed every now and then to move his head in such a way as to show he had recognised us as political prisoners. The warders shouted at us all the time to look straight ahead and not at him, it was forbidden, but we managed to get in sidelong glances.

A little further on we saw women chatting in little groups and children playing: we were excited to be approaching civilian life, the first we had seen in all the months since our imprisonment. As we trooped quietly past, the children started shouting at us: 'Kaffirs . . . coolies', and some even began to throw stones. One little boy of about five was standing on a small platform built in his yard, pointing a home-made toy rifle at us and yelling in his little voice: '*Kaffirs, ek skiet julle* – kaffirs, I'm shooting you.' We felt very bad to see these young kids brought up to hate us like that, and we could see them, the children of warders, growing up to be future warders themselves. We even saw little boys wearing tailored warders' uniforms, children's sizes, playing a special game of 'Prison Life'. Their mothers chuckled at the antics of their kids, and the warders escorting us roared with laughter in their crude way.

After we had trudged a good kilometre or so, leaving the scenes of civilian life far behind, we saw in front of us a huge man-made hole in the ground, on the sea side, with the most beautiful view of Cape Town across the sea. This was the quarry and, wherever we looked, we saw hard, grey granite rock dotted here and there with crude-looking zinc shelters and, spaced around the perimeter on raised platforms, six warders, each armed with an automatic rifle. We descended by pathways, and as we got to the bottom we were counted once again and ordered to work.

I picked up my first stone and placed it on a metal loop for balance. Then I started chipping as best I could. Splinters flew in all directions, I could not control the pieces, which pierced my arms and legs with agonising pain. I looked round and saw that virtually all the new prisoners were having the same problem; the wire-mesh protection was extremely irritating to our eyes and the hammers we used were worn out, with loose makeshift handles, totally ineffective.

We sat on small pieces of rock, about eight hundred of us in a huge circle, the wire mesh giving us a weird appearance, our hammers flying up and down, a pile of stones supplied by wheelbarrow in front of each of us, hard, granite rocks which we had been ordered to split into stones of small diameter.

We were absolutely new in the quarry and did not know what to do, but instead of explaining things to us the warders simply started lashing out with their rubber batons, sticks and pieces of rubber piping, calling us names, telling us how stupid we were.

Warder Delport, in charge of the work *span*, had a long rubber pipe, and his look alone scared us. He was tall and full of muscle, with a harsh red face and, as he hit out at us, he told us we each had to chop half a forty-four-gallon drum of stones by the end of the day – and if we did not, we would not eat the next Sunday.

It was blazing hot, even at that early hour in the morning, and sweat rolled down our bodies, but we could not rest for a moment as warders constantly walked past us, beating prisoners and shouting, sometimes aided by common-law prisoners who added their share of abuse and violence against us in a sycophantic way.

Fortunately Comrade Andrew Masondo, who had arrived a few months earlier on the Island, managed to make his devious way to us and assisted us in settling down to our work, giving us advice on the importance of standing together, and showing us what stones to choose and how to hit them so that they broke into slices which could more easily be smashed.

At about midday two common-law prisoners came along with an old rusty four-gallon tin full of water and scooped out one jam tin of water for each prisoner. When we asked for more we were told that this was prison and we were lucky to be getting what they were giving us; the containers were so rusty and dirty that we were put off drinking, but our thirst was immense and in the end we just gulped the water down.

The great majority of us were hammering away, chip, chop, chip, chop, endlessly, but about two hundred prisoners were attending to another task: getting more rocks ready. Some of them were pushing wheelbarrows, others were using fourteen-pound hammers or compressor drills to crack huge granite slabs off the quarry wall: first they would drill holes in the rock, then pound in giant metal pins with the huge hammers. Their timing was perfect – the men with the hammers would stand around until another had got the pin in position with metal wire, and then the hammers would rain down, one after the other, until cracks began to appear. Eventually a huge piece of rock would detach itself from the quarry wall and come crashing down with a tremendous crack. Sometimes a small neck of rock just would not break, and so the prisoners would place three or four massive logs into the crack, tie long ropes to them, and then, levering up about fifty prisoners on each rope, would pull in unison, until the rock finally split off and came pounding down.

In spite of all our ceaseless hammering, our arms worn out, our backs aching, by lunchtime none of us new prisoners had managed to produce more than about a quarter of the necessary quota, and even many old prisoners had not achieved the target. When the lunch bell rang we assembled four-deep to be counted again, then split off in twos to collect our food and sat around in a group while we ate our rations. There was absolutely no shade, but we were pleased at the break from the incessant hammering and talked quietly to each other and, exhausted, smoked what little tobacco we had managed to smuggle.

The warders, too, were eating. Some were sitting in a circle around us, but most were a little distance away in a shelter with tables and benches, and for the only time that day they left us alone.

The common-law prisoners sat on one side, and the political prisoners on another, and we began to hear lovely harmonies coming from the common-law prisoners. We ourselves were too tense to sing, but we enjoyed listening to the others, mostly singing old love songs without any meaning. One of their melodies, though, was to the tune of 'Galway Bay'. It started: 'Have you ever been across the sea to Robben Island, where the chain gangs break the rocks all through the day . . .?' The song went on to speak of warders beating prisoners, of the gangs amongst the common-law prisoners, and so on.

The bell rang at 2 p.m. and once again we were counted, then returned to work: back we went to the toil of breaking stones and back to the brutalities of the warders. By this time the sun was right over us and we were feeling the extreme heat of the day; we were a mixture of sweat, sand and dirt, and our heads and faces were greyish-white from the flying dust. Our faded khaki caps and black felt hats were covered with powder, and we hated our caps because every time a warder passed he would demand that we remove them, and then when we took them off, on the way back he would order us to put them back on again. Taking them off, putting them on . . . if a prisoner forgot to remove his hat, he would be beaten and told to show proper respect to the warder or, alternatively, the warder would himself knock the hat from his head.

Our arms ached. Our hands were blistered. Our backs were sore. Our necks were stiff. Our eyes stung. Our skin prickled. Still we kept on hammering, changing the hammer from one hand to the other; hammering and hammering without stop, all day, under the boiling sun.

By the 3.30 inspection, my pile of stones was nowhere near the required quantity, and looking around me I found that most of the other piles were just as small as mine. We had been hitting away from early morning, with one break only for lunch, and now Delport was coming round with a few other warders and some common-law prisoners carrying a huge drum, stopping in front of some piles and ordering the prisoners to fill the drum to prove how far short of the quota we had fallen. My pile reached just about halfway up the giant drum, and all Delport said was '*Kaartjie!* – Card! *Koelie, jy het nie gewerk nie* – Coolie, you didn't work. *Sondag sal jy nie eet nie* – Sunday you won't eat.'

I gave him my identity card and then saw him collecting the cards of all the new prisoners, as well as many of the old ones.

By this time blisters had come out all over my hands and I put the hammer down with its makeshift handle – just a piece of tree branch with the knobs and rough parts still on it. My whole shoulder was collapsing on me, my back was weakening, I had cuts on my arms and feet from the stone debris, the blood on them was mixed with sand, sweat and powder. The wire mesh over my eyes was most uncomfortable, but undoubtedly it saved my sight, although for those comrades who wore glasses it was hell.

I felt a really strong urge to urinate. I had seen other prisoners walking up to a warder and then going off to have a piss against a rock, so I took off my wire-mesh protection and went to the nearest warder with my hat in my hand.

'Excuse me, sir, I would like permission to urinate.'

His immediate response was the same as I had got on the day we arrived on the Island. '*God watter taal praat jy*, – God, what language are you speaking? *Ek verstaan nie daardie kaffirboetie se taal nie* – I don't understand that kaffir-lover's language. *En nog, ek is jou baas* – what's more I am your *baas*, not "sir".'

I answered in English that I did not understand Afrikaans and he refused me permission and ordered me crudely back to my place. So I returned and after about fifteen or twenty minutes' extreme discomfort I went back to him again; the response was exactly the same, and I returned to my work. The third time I went straight to a rock to urinate and while I was relieving myself the warder came dashing up to me, grabbed me by the neck of my shirt, allowed me to finish, and then dragged me off to Delport. There he reported that I was a '*hardebek koelie* – a hard-mouthed coolie', and I found myself facing a second charge that day.

When the four o'clock bell finally rang to mark the end of the work day, I could hardly stand up. My whole back was stiff. I could not straighten my fingers, my skin was stinging.

My eyes, throat and mouth were full of dust, and I had nothing with which to blow the dust out of my nose, only my short sleeves. I felt as though a massive load that had been on my back all day had been lifted, but still I could not move. It was as if the weight was still there. We were harassed by the warders to assemble, and the political prisoners all bunched at the back in mutual support, looking at one another and sympathetically asking how we all felt. Some of the more pleasant common-law prisoners came to us and told us not to worry too much because we would get accustomed to the work in time; we found that hard to believe.

A warder shouted 'Caps off!' We were counted, yet again, caps in hand in front of us, and then ordered back to the prison.

On the long, weary march back the prisoners who had managed to smuggle tobacco made little *zolls* and puffed away surreptitiously, blowing the smoke downwards. A warder would rush up to where he had seen the smoke, but by the time he got there the *zoll* had disappeared down the row and a little puff of smoke would come from somewhere else. The warder would demand to know where the cigarette was and we all looked at him with blank eyes, taking off our caps and hats as required, saying nothing.

We saw chickens scratching around, and people with tennis rackets, and also a large number of wild cats with bloodshot eyes.

All one thousand of us had to strip stark naked and stand in about ten lines in front of the warders. They waited until every one of us was ready, totally naked, with clothes over our arms, and then an officer ordered us to go, one by one, and hand the clothes over to a warder who would search them thoroughly, every fold and stitch. As he finished with each item he cast it randomly to the ground, not caring where it landed, and a general pile grew in which we could not identify whose things were whose.

Next, it was the turn of our bodies and we were commanded to do the *tausa*, and we saw the other prisoners going through the routine of leaping in the air, twisting round, clapping their hands over their heads, shooting their legs wide open and coming down bent over with their rectums exposed to the warders. Most of the prisoners in for ANC activities refused to follow suit. In my case a warder, thinking I was inexperienced, actually called a common-law prisoner back to show me how it was done, but I still refused. There was something particularly humiliating and degrading in the *tausa*. So as a compromise we just turned ourselves around and walked off. The common-law prisoners, however, actually seemed to enjoy doing the *tausa* leap which they accomplished with expert skill, landing with a great flourish of arms and legs and shouting 'My king!' They turned it into an artistic performance, and later we discovered they had another motive as well.

The guards would smack our naked bodies all the time with their batons and hoses, or just come up to us and kick us, even while we were trying to sort out our clothes. They were not especially angry, this was just their normal way of reminding us of their presence.

Then the three hundred or so of us who had had our tickets removed were ordered to march to a senior officer who said that we would not eat on Sunday because we were lazy and refused to work. As we ran in pairs to the kitchen, warders lined up all the way and kept up a barrage of blows until we grabbed our food, hitting us while we were eating. In fact, they kept on hitting us and hitting us right until the very moment when we were locked up at five o'clock.

Most of us simply unrolled our mats and blankets, lay down in our dirty clothes and rested our exhausted bodies, too tired even to use the two flush toilets that had replaced the buckets. We talked quietly and tried to sing freedom songs, and when the eight o'clock bell went for the end of the day we fell fast asleep immediately.

NINE

The roller

An enormous grass roller, the biggest I had ever seen, stood on a piece of soft, sandy land. It was solid metal, about two metres high, weighing a couple of tons, with an axle bar and handle so heavy that even two people could not lift it. In addition, there were long chains attached to each side, and a place for people to push from the back; it was much, much bigger than a steam roller, and about fifty of us were ordered to set it in motion.

We were the unfortunate ones who had been pulled out at random for work that day on the dreaded *landbou* (agriculture) *span* by Piet Kleynhans: one of the three Kleynhans brothers who were all warders on the Island. Tall and thin, powerfully built, clean shaven with crew-cut hair, he placed himself on top of the crossbar of the axle with a long leather whip in his hand and, even before we started pulling and heaving, we had the picture of a slave master driving his slaves to work.

I was put amongst those who were to push, and placed myself behind the jutting pieces of the axle itself, as Kleynhans ordered us to move the roller across the field. From the moment of the first shove we could hear him shouting at us to pull harder, and the whip cracked non-stop over our heads, on our shoulders, in our faces – everywhere. Warders passing by were vastly amused at seeing their colleague on the crossbar and begged to be given a chance to ride the roller themselves, but usually he refused, only occasionally allowing one of his mates to get a ride.

Holding the axle was extremely heavy work, especially for those in front, and we could only get the roller to move if we all pulled and pushed in unison, so we sang work-songs to co-ordinate our efforts, the music interrupted by the whip cracking overhead all the time. Other warders joined Kleynhans in screaming at us and cursing us, and many lashed at us with canes and hosepipes every time we passed them.

We went round in a large circle, round and round and round, from about seven o'clock that morning, heaving and straining, a continual agony, never once pausing, not even for a moment. Occasionally a prisoner would break away from the roller to have a quick drink of water or to urinate, but the roller never stopped. Sometimes the warders strolling along next to the roller would refuse us permission to leave, saying that we were lazy, and we simply had to contain ourselves until another opportunity arrived.

At one stage in the morning, one of the prisoners on the axle, Johnson Malambo, was pulled out of the group and accused by Kleynhans of being a *hardebek kaffir* (hard-mouthed kaffir). Apparently he had protested against the work and Kleynhans called out to two common-law prisoners doing light work nearby to dig a hole slightly away from where we were pulling the roller – prisoners would soon learn who was *baas* here.

Malambo stood near the place where they were digging, and each time we completed the long, gruelling circuit we saw that the hole was a bit deeper, with Malambo waiting quietly at its side.

Kleynhans got off the roller and was standing on the spot supervising the digging and we continued heaving the roller round and round without him, until after a while we noticed that the digging had stopped. Then we heard Kleynhans order Malambo

67

to get into the hole and, later, as we made the next circuit, we saw Malambo's head jutting out of the ground. Two common-law prisoners were shovelling sand round his shoulders into the hole and, by the time we got back, all we could see was Malambo's head sticking out at ground level. His shiny, shaven cranium looked as though it had just fallen off and rolled to the ground. We knew how baking hot the sun was and felt agonised for him. It was weird seeing that head lying there on its own, with stunned staring eyes.

Kleynhans climbed back on to the roller and the whip started flashing again, the warders laughing and cracking jokes. We moved round and round and round, the head always there. Some hours later, just before lunch, Kleynhans leapt off the roller and went up to Malambo. He was in a good humour, enjoying himself.

'*Kaffir, soek jy water?* – kaffir, do you want water? *Nee ek sal jou nie water gee nie, ek sal jou whisky gee, die beste whisky* – no, I won't give you water, I'll give you whisky, the very best.' Amidst gales of laughter from the other warders he opened his fly, pulled out his penis and started urinating on Malambo's face.

At one o'clock, after five hours of ceaseless rolling, we were told to stop work and assemble for counting. We detached ourselves from the roller and found our bodies so sore and full of pain that we could hardly stand, and when we got our food we fell to the ground and barely had the strength to eat. I had no appetite whatsoever and could manage only a couple of spoonfuls of mealie rice, and just dropped my plate.

Malambo was dug out and told to join us. He washed the earth off himself and sat next to us, not saying a word. His silence was terrible, and there was nothing we could say to him.

In the afternoon it was the same process again, pulling and pushing non-stop, going slowly round and round the cleared ground, with Kleynhans never tiring for a minute as he barked his orders and insults and lashed out wildly with the whip. At four o'clock, when we stopped, we had flattened the whole field. The walk back to the jail seemed as if it would never end.

TEN

'Look, chaps . . .'

'Jackets!'

We handed over our dirty jackets and received supposedly washed jackets in exchange: part of the Saturday morning weekly change of clothes.

'Shirts . . . pants!'

The problem was that the warder who came to our cell did not consider sizes, so we ended up with a crazy assortment: a big guy with a tiny pair of pants, a small bloke with a huge, torn shirt. It was like a lucky dip at Christmas time, but the worst thing was that the trousers still had bloodstains in the crotch, and many were almost worn through, and we never knew who had worn them the week before.

In winter we got an additional jersey, blue with a red stripe, the convict's jersey, but when we first got them they stank from having been stored away unwashed for six months. Nothing was ever clean, nothing was ever decent.

The shoes looked awful and were always battered and out of shape, well worn by the rain and hard work, by the time we politicals received them. The sandals were even worse; not only unshapely and worn out, but difficult to wear and soon broken. The result was that more than ninety per cent of the prisoners walked barefoot right through the year, moving softly on the ground, their feet toughening up.

Warders would stop us anywhere and at any time and suddenly demand that we strip, or we would go to the office and be ordered by some young warder to remove our clothes, or at work we would be made to strip or, when we went to hospital, we were made to strip. It was a simple expression of the power of the warders: they could tell us to take our clothes off and we had to obey, young and old. 'Take your clothes off!' We took them off. 'Get dressed!' We put them on again. 'Take your hat off!' We took it off. 'Put it on again!' We put it on again.

The Island had tens of thousands of seagulls flying overhead all the time, and not a day would pass without some prisoners getting bird shit on their plates, or on themselves. If we asked for another plateful we were told that it was not the prison's fault that the birds shat on our food, and we would get nothing more. Some warders would even ask what we were complaining about because it added flavour to the food and we were always moaning that it was tasteless.

The food was so cold that we had to pull a thick layer off the porridge and keep our eyes open for maggots while we were eating. It was always badly prepared and often rotten – even the bread.

The authorities provided only the bare minimum of food as required by the rules, to the nearest gram, and not a scrap more. It was never enough to start with, but the real problem was smuggling by the prisoners.

Breakfast was a plate of porridge with one spoon of sugar if we were African ('F' diet) and two spoons of sugar if we were Coloured or Indian ('D' diet). We also got a cup of synthetic soup and a cup of dreadful black coffee. The rumour was that the authorities took ordinary mealies (corn), dried and roasted them, mixed in some chicory and called it coffee, and whether or not

70

that was true, it certainly tasted like it.

For lunch 'D' diets got a plate of mealie rice and, three times a week, either dried peas or beans. 'F' diets got virtually the same, with the addition of a cup of *phusa mandla* ('strength drink'), a synthetic drink that was not bad, but was not really like food.

In the evenings the 'D' diets were supposed to receive a quarter of a loaf of bread and two hundred and fifty grams of vegetables, a cup of black coffee, a cup of synthetic soup and, four days a week, one hundred grams of meat. In reality we rarely got the vegetables, and never the full amount, and when we did get them it would be one type of vegetable for weeks on end. Carrots every night, or onions, until they went rotten. Instead of bread, 'F' diets got a plate of porridge, and they got only fifty grams of meat instead of one hundred per person. This is how it was, apartheid inside apartheid, down to the tiniest details, even in the heart of prison.

With this diet it was clear that even if there had not been smuggling, and even if the food had been of good quality, and even if it had been properly prepared, we would hardly have had sufficient. We were like cattle kept on spare rations so as to be lean for the market; bodies to be kept alive, not human beings with tastes and a pleasure in eating; in fact, even like different breeds of animal.

The African prisoners were lucky to get even half their fifty-gram ration of meat per week, so great was the smuggling. The kitchen was mainly staffed by common-law prisoners who would put the meat in pies which they would sneak out to their friends, sometimes with a thin layer of maize porridge on top to make them look like the normal meals.

We campaigned constantly for the common-law prisoners to be removed from the kitchen, but the authorities ignored our demands, and when a few political prisoners did manage to get into the kitchen they were predominantly PAC who had been discredited even among their own group and who did not stop the smuggling at all.

Nobody bothered to steal the maize meal, which was all we really had to eat, but highly prized items such as sugar, *phusa mandla,* meat, fat and bread were stolen all the time. The common-law prisoners would steal from stock in the stores, from food on the way to the kitchen, and have another go in the kitchen itself. The result was even less food for the rest of the prisoners. It was for that reason that the ANC prisoners agreed not to smuggle food; for some to eat more meant that others would eat less. It was different from stealing from the warders. The only exception we made was to permit smuggling of some of our rations to prisoners on spare diet in solitary confinement.

Unfortunately, the PAC refused to take a line on the matter. In fact, they refused even to discuss the subject amongst themselves, perhaps because some of their leading people were involved up to the hilt; this was a source of tension between us.

We would see the common-law prisoners behind us leaping in the air, twisting, clapping their hands, and so on; landing with their backsides exposed. It seemed impossible for them to carry anything on their bodies past the warders, but we knew that Mandla and about twenty others were running that risk almost every day to get us newspapers and tobacco. Exactly how they managed it we never fully knew. For our part, we continued firmly to refuse to do the dance, but it seemed that the common-law prisoners welcomed it because, by means of clever cries and praises and movements of the arms, they were able to distract the warders' attention and get objects through – even big ones. How they did it, we never exactly found out, but they must have directed their clicks and cries in one direction, while moving the objects in the other direction. We never ceased to be astonished – from under their armpits and out of their rectums we would see them take money, bags of tobacco, sausages, even canned food.

There was one chap who I saw place a tin of condensed milk in his arse, walk up to the warder, leap into the air, waving his arms as he spun and calling out loudly as he landed 'My king!', exposing his empty backside. Two minutes later he was pulling the condensed milk out of his rectum . . . without doubt, the greatest magician I have ever seen.

One day the warders came into our cells and gave us each an orange. The next day they did the same. Those were the only pieces of fruit we saw in ten years. Sometimes working in the quarry we would see large ships passing by and think of the Outspan oranges and Cape fruit bound for Europe.

The authorities replaced one day's issue of meat with fish. That could have been good if the fish had been properly cooked, but it was never properly cleaned, just thrown into the water to boil, and we detested it.

We were resting one evening just after lock-up when a member of the kitchen staff came running to the cell with a plate of smuggled food. He called out the name of one of the PAC prisoners, Joe Khoza. Khoza rushed forward, but so did half a dozen of his colleagues, and they all dived for the plate, some to eat the food, some to throw it away. Before long there must have been ten or fifteen PAC prisoners one on top of another, fighting and scrambling around the plate. We watched this mad scene from our bedding. Suddenly Sonny Singh pointed to the floor and said in an excited voice, 'Look chaps!' There on the floor we saw an eye, a complete, round, human eye!

One by one the prisoners in the scramble moved away. One of the more politically disciplined PAC chaps picked up the plate, dashed to the lavatory and poured the food down, and then we noticed that Johnson Malambo, a leading PAC member (the one who had been buried in the sand up to his neck), was rising from the group with his hand over his eye. One of our comrades picked up the eye and put it in a cup of water. Only then did Malambo realise what had happened to him.

We banged and shouted and cried to get the attention of the

night warder. He appeared after a long, long time and then refused to open up. We explained that a prisoner had lost an eye in an accident and he eventually agreed to call higher authority, but Malambo was taken to the mainland only on the following day by which time the doctor told him that it was too late to do anything.

Khoza was suspended from the PAC but, surrounded by a small circle of friends, he continued with his smuggling and, within months, was once more friendly with his colleagues. Although not fully accepted in their ranks, we saw him sitting in on their gatherings once more, and I always had an uneasy feeling when I looked at the long protruding fingernail on his right index finger.

ELEVEN

Quarry

The quarry was very old and we noticed that more and more water was seeping in. Delport tried to drain it, but it was clearly becoming dangerous and rumours started that the old quarry was going to be abandoned and a new one opened.

One day, instead of following our usual route past the warders' houses we were marched in the opposite direction. There was no civilian life on this journey, only wild bush and long grass. We saw buck running in and out, ostriches, rabbits galore, and a lot of bird life, including guinea fowl and peacocks.

After about half an hour we found ourselves on an open piece of land about forty-five metres from the small local airport runway, quite close to a shooting range. It was on the edge of the sea and the only rock we could see was in the water; nearby was an enormous nest of seagulls – there seemed to be millions of them.

The beach was totally exposed, without a scrap of shade. Just to lift the handles of the ancient wheelbarrows was an immense strain. Pushing against the sand simply drove the buckled wheels deeper and deeper into it. The poor condition of the rusty barrows made them barely manoeuvrable, and when the wheel struck a rock buried below the surface we would lose our grip and topple over with the barrow. The warders would rush over to lash out and swear at us for being stupid, and we would right the barrow, load up again, and carry on pushing. Just short of the sea we would be ordered to tip the barrow up and deposit the boulder and sand – exactly why, we did not know. It was a great relief to be pushing the empty barrow back, but we would not be allowed to stop for a moment, and only when we reached the loading zone would we be allowed, for the first time, to let the handles go.

The barrow was immediately filled again with a vast heap of sand and a huge boulder. Once more we pushed through the deep sand. It was back-breaking and frightening work and our arms, necks and bodies ached with pain.

There were about a thousand prisoners altogether in the quarry and we noticed hundreds of them with picks digging away at the soil and top rocks to make a large hole. Hundreds more were using spades to move sand from one place to another to load the wheelbarrows, while another large group transported sand and stones in half-section forty-four-gallon petrol drums which they held by specially attached handles. Gradually we became aware that we were excavating a huge hole covering about six football fields, and building a dyke to the sea.

Those who had picks were lined up in long rows on the rocky edge of the beach and, as their picks rose and fell, they sang a work song, the picks hitting the ground in time with the music.

The rusty wheel of my barrow squeaked as it ploughed its way along the beach. The body of the barrow was piled high with sand, on top was a large boulder and on top of that sat a warder, laughing, with his legs dangling over the side.

'Watch out, coolie, if you let me fall . . .'

I pushed with all my might, cursing the wheel for being so twisted, hating the soft sea sand and the stones hidden in it. The wheel jarred against a rock. I could not move it. The warder roared with pleasure.

'Push, coolie, push!'

The load was so precarious that I felt like tipping it over but managed to swing the barrow round and heave all my weight against it. The wheel began to roll forward, squeaking. From the distance I could hear the picks rising and falling, the sad songs of the prisoners, a seagull's cries overhead, and I managed to blot out the sound of the laughter coming from near my head by listening to them.

TWELVE

'Hosh'

The Big Five, whose emblem was a swastika, gave a salute with
an open hand and a shout of 'Hosh'; the Desperadoes, with the
hammer and sickle, used the Churchill victory salute; the Fast
Elevens; the Twenty-Fives – each had their own signs and cries.
There were many gangs on the Island and every common-law
prisoner belonged to one.

When we had first arrived the authorities had deliberately mixed
common-law prisoners with us in every cell, intending to degrade
us to the level of those hardened wrecks who had been in prison
all their lives, many serving multiple life sentences, prison being
their whole world. Sodomy, often forced, was common and assault
and murder were everyday matters. In fact, a murder would be
described in the same way that one would describe a soccer match,
criticising an attacker for missing opportunities with his knife.

The gangs operated in every jail in South Africa, so when a
new prisoner arrived all the others would wait for him to give the
salute and show the emblem tattooed by home-made needles on
his forearm. Each gang had an unwritten code of law enforced by
a King, who was the supreme commander, having under him a

Judge, Doctor and Lawyer. The authorities claimed officially that they tried to stamp out these gangs, but actually they encouraged them to keep the prisoners divided, and many warders became closely associated with particular gangs, virtually acting as their patrons in a strange relationship of mutual dependence.

Most of the prisoners were disfigured, their shaven heads covered with scars, their eyes bloodshot, their noses askew, their teeth knocked out, and their bodies full of tattoos, often obscene, such as a naked man on one breast and a naked woman on the other, the two being brought together by a special movement of the muscles. Prisoners came from all corners of South Africa and many were serving three, four or five life-sentences. Typically, a young man coming in with a relatively short sentence would be caught up in gang activity in prison which would lead to further long sentences for assault, attempted murder or attempting to escape and by the time they arrived on the Island they could have spent twenty years in prison with only the briefest of interludes outside. For many of them prison was their life, their single ambition being to escape. I never once saw the slightest signs of attempts to rehabilitate these prisoners.

There was continual struggle between the Big Fives and the Desperadoes to be the number-one gang on the Island, because the gang that was on top got the cushiest jobs, such as working in the warders' mess, as domestic servants at the homes of married warders, or in the prison kitchen or stores. The less fortunate gangs landed up in the quarry. Gangs often acted as informers against other gangs, especially if an escape was being planned.

The system of law applied by each gang to its members was rigidly enforced. Severe beating was regarded as a light punishment, and often death sentences were passed by the Judge and carried out by special executioners.

We would see the gang assembled in a corner of our cell where they would whisper quietly and tensely among themselves, sometimes for several evenings. They always occupied the best

79

spots furthest from the door and the toilets, and it was there that they would hold their trials, while we sat cooped up near the middle of the cell, close to the door and the toilets. Even when there were sixty of us and only twenty of them we found ourselves crowded into this little space.

We knew that something was afoot, in fact it kept us guessing, when they sat around their 'King' after lock-up and whispered to each other. We could never tell what was happening and although we were always extremely curious we were careful not to be seen taking any notice of their proceedings. Nor would we know what their decision was, or even if a trial was being held, until the sentence was carried out. Even then we did not know whether this was in response to a trial that had been held in our cell, or in another cell, or at the quarry. We did not even know what the offences were. One rumour was that gang members were accused of stealing the 'girl friend' of one of the leaders, or stealing gang property, or informing on the gang – either to another gang or to the authorities. Even though we worked all day and slept all night in their company, they kept such tight security that we never really knew what was going on; all we knew was that when sentence was passed, one or two people would be ordered to carry it out and another one or two appointed to see to it that the punishment was executed.

To the authorities he was just another prisoner, a typical demoralised *ja-baas* (yes-baas) type. But to us, Mandla, the common-law prisoner serving a long sentence for armed robbery who had helped us from the start, was a comrade. He smuggled in newspapers, tobacco, and even radios, and carried out his role brilliantly.

Once, when I was serving one of my many periods in isolation for allegedly being cheeky or failing to observe a lawful command, the authorities decided that instead of letting us sit idle all day, we should be forced to work; the result was that we were taken out of our cells and ordered to chop stones in the isolation courtyard, sitting some distance apart. We were mostly political prisoners but among us were two common-law prisoners, one working in the yard with us and another, Baaina, serving a sentence of solitary confinement and spare diet, and kept apart.

One day Baaina was brought into the courtyard for exercise. There were normally two warders on duty, the head warder and a young assistant, but at that moment the young warder was on his own and he was escorting Baaina from his cell for a half-hour exercise period.

We were in three rows chopping stones in the yard, not paying special attention to Baaina, who walked up and down past the row opposite me, getting closer to a corner where there was a pile of crushed stones with a spade sticking out of it. He continued to walk up and down and, without slowing his pace, picked up the spade and moved down the row opposite. We carried on with our chopping, not expecting any drama from Baaina moving close to us.

Coolly he lifted the spade with both hands and crashed it down on to the skull of the other common-law prisoner. We heard a crack and stopped work, horrified, while the prisoner screamed and raised his arms to protect his head. The spade kept going up and down, up and down, bashing his head and arms, blood splashing everywhere. The warder stood petrified. The prisoner kept on yelling but then suddenly he stopped, lost consciousness and fell to the ground in a large pool of blood.

Baaina straightened up, lifted the spade, pulled out his identity card and walked towards the warder who backed away, saying, 'Don't come here, don't come here.'

Baaina tried to calm him down and said, 'Don't be afraid, I'm coming to hand in my card and give you the evidence.' He was totally without agitation and quietly followed the warder to his cell.

We were returned to our cells and the victim was rushed to hospital. That evening someone asked Baaina what had been the problem. 'Five years ago,' he explained, 'there was a group of us planning a jail break from Bellville Prison, but at the last minute the authorities got wind of it, rounded us up and transferred us to Robben Island. We found out who had betrayed us and swore that the first one to get at him should do him in. He's been on the Island a year already and we were all waiting for the chance; today I was lucky. I managed to get sent to isolation, and there was the spade, so I did him in.'

Next day the victim came back to isolation with a huge bandage on his head; as far as he was concerned, nothing had happened, he was back in the swing again. Baaina was sentenced to six strokes for assault.

Some common-law prisoners were specially selected to bully us and inform on us, but we started picking out a few and began talking to them, pointing out that the life they had been leading was not correct, and slowly showing them that they had been victims of the existing society. We even started discussing politics with them, and the authorities realised then that their plan to mix us with the common-law prisoners was in serious danger of back-firing.

A prisoner took me aside and asked in a whisper if I had any soap. I said 'Yes', and showed him a little bar. He swiftly smuggled a bag of tobacco to me and, before I could examine it closely, snatched the soap from me and disappeared. I opened the bag and, under a thin sprinkling of tobacco, found dried grass.

THIRTEEN

A winter's day

It was a cold winter's morning, still dark, and prisoners who were suffering from tuberculosis, asthma, high blood pressure, epilepsy, fresh injuries from work or wounds from assaults queued, shivering, outside the hospital waiting for medicines. They were joined by prisoners with migraine, stomach ailments, toothache, headaches, colds, earache, and all the ailments of prison, each hoping to receive tablets, ointments, or other medicines.

The medical orderly came along: 'Yes, what's your complaint?'

'Terrible headaches, *baas*.'

'Get to work, you're lazy. Next!'

The next prisoner complained of asthma. The orderly bellowed, 'You were here yesterday, you come here every day,' and chased him into the cold as well. It did not take long for the vast queue of the Island's sick to be attended to.

We had our first meal of the day squatting in the yard. It was freezing cold and dark. We could hardly see what we were eating, and we were still breathless from our run to the kitchen and back to the courtyard, moving quietly so that the food would not be kicked out of our hands by one of the warders. We sat in fifteen or twenty long, straight rows with warders walking in between swinging batons in their hands to see that we did not talk or look around. We only had five or ten minutes to finish eating before being told to line up for work, and the first of us would move off, licking clean our only eating implement, a short-handled wooden spoon, and putting it in our pocket as the last prisoners were still arriving.

In the beginning, Indian and Coloured political prisoners were not prepared to accept differences in food and clothing, but the comrades felt that we should accept what we were offered because we were all demanding an improvement, and to voluntarily reject part of what we were offered would weaken the claim of the others. We shared our food, even though doing so was illegal but, unfortunately, we could not do the same with our clothing, so our comrades remained even colder and less protected than we were.

We thought we could see snow on Table Mountain. We were so cold as we sat in our short pants, short-sleeved shirts and worn-out jerseys that we could hardly raise the hammers. We were not allowed handkerchiefs so we wiped our damp noses on our jacket sleeves. An icy wind blew in from the sea, and even the warders shivered in their big khaki greatcoats, heavy socks and boots.

During the lunch break we squeezed together, trying to get the warmth of the body of a fellow prisoner. We could not even talk, and we got hold of some corrugated iron and used it as a windbreak, until Sergeant Delport ripped it away. It was such a cold winter we wondered whether we could possibly survive.

Our skin prickled in the chilly air, a thousand of us coming back to the jail after work and going through the daily routine of being searched. We lined up as usual in long single files, and the warders kept us waiting until every single one of us was nude, and only then did the search start. One by one we marched to a warder, our filthy clothes folded neatly over our arms, and handed over each piece of clothing for his minute examination. The warder ran his fingers down the seams and poked them into the pockets, looking for contraband, in our case for tobacco, news items and messages, in the case of the common-law prisoners for weapons and *dagga* (marijuana). After checking each item of clothing, the warder threw it behind him on to what soon became a large pile, and with five of them in a line doing this, there were short pants, hundreds of jackets, shirts and, later, socks and shoes flying over their shoulders. We dashed behind them to retrieve our things as best we could, pushing to get there before the common-law prisoners could help themselves to the best, and the whole process of a thousand prisoners dashing in a continual stream after the flying clothes, pouring down on their backs as they bent to snatch up their things, took only about fifteen or twenty minutes.

Back that night in our cells, dirty as we were, with stone dust in our nostrils, and thick powder in our hair and eyes, we did not bother to wash or change, we simply crawled between our thin blankets and wrapped ourselves as tightly in them as we could, keeping in as much warmth as possible.

FOURTEEN

Knee deep

The dyke entered the sea and curved round to form a breakwater with a road on top. When water began to seep in with the tide, huge concrete blocks were deposited on the sea side so that the quarry remained dry. The hard granite rock was now fully exposed where formerly the beach had been and most of us were ordered back to the 'Nip-line' – breaking stones. Some of us started again with the fourteen-pound hammers while the rest continued to move sand and large rocks out towards the dyke. Eventually everybody was involved in the quarry and, wherever one looked, hammers could be seen flying up and down, beating the hard stones, wheelbarrows carrying little mountains of sand to the Nip-line, fourteen-pounders cracking into the rocks and bringing down huge slabs of blue granite which landed with a mighty crash.

The warders did not permit the slightest sign of opposition to what they did. We simply had to take the blows and the abuse and not give the faintest indication of either suffering or anger.

One day, while manoeuvring my barrow towards the dyke, I put the handles down for a moment's breather. A warder named

Meintjies came up to me and gave me a hard slap with his open hand on my left ear – the one that had been injured during my torture. I became aware of a ringing sound and protested strongly at his behaviour, even complaining to Delport, the warder in charge.

In my cell later that evening, I noticed that blood was trickling out of the ear and next morning I reported the matter to the warders. I was taken to the prison hospital where I was examined by Dr van den Bergen who admitted me to the hospital for one week, and I was escorted to a temporary zinc structure with about twenty-five patients, ten of whom had beds and the others were lying on the floor.

A day or two after my admission, about two hours after being locked up for the night, the door opened and I saw a pale body come flying on to the floor of the hospital cell. When the doors were relocked I ran to the body and recognised my comrade Dennis Brutus lying there semi-conscious. (It was his letters to and from various international sports bodies that had been found in my house when I was arrested.) I called out his name and he opened his eyes and gave me a look of recognition, but he was in tremendous pain. He lay curled up on the floor and when I lifted his shirt I got a terrible shock. His whole back was red and blue and there was a deep gash right across his stomach. Although there were no marks on his head, his face was contorted with pain and he could hardly speak, just mumble; one of our comrades offered his bed and we made it up and carried him to it. I was the only one who knew him and the other prisoners crowded round to find out who he was. I told them about Dennis's work as a sports administrator, and of the campaigns he had taken part in to get racist teams from South Africa excluded from world sport, also that he was a schoolteacher and a poet.

The next day Dennis was able to tell us about his arrest, and we learned how he had come to have that gash across his stomach.

After his arrest, some time before, he told us, he had made a dash away from the police, one of whom had opened fire with a pistol, knocking him to the pavement right in the centre of Johannesburg, in fact at the foot of one of the giant skyscrapers put up by a mining company. He had been taken to hospital for major surgery – his life had been in danger then, with the wound freshly stitched and scarcely healed, he had been sent to Robben Island to serve his sentence.

There were twenty in his group, he continued, including many comrades well known to us: Billy Nair, with twenty years for being on the regional command of the MK in Natal; Curnick Ndhlovu for the same; and George Naicker with fourteen years. They were all ordered into the sea to pull out seaweed, and as they waded in knee deep they were mercilessly set upon by the warders who beat them black and blue with batons and rubber pipes, even going into the water themselves so they could hit out better.

Some of the prisoners had slipped in the water and were hit as they rose, there being nowhere for them to run and Dennis, who was particularly weak, was their main target, receiving more blows than anybody else, until he virtually lost consciousness.

Normally, Dennis had a rich, cultivated voice, he was one of the most articulate of all of us, but as he lay suffering on the bed he could barely get the words together; they came out in a groaning whisper, broken up and harsh, hardly making sense.

FIFTEEN

The Big Five

Sometimes in our cell we would see the twenty or so common-law prisoners separating themselves into their different gangs; the Big Five grouping together in one section and the Desperadoes in another, each having an intense caucus. Occasionally, a member of one would walk over to the other and we would wait tensely; he would give the 'Hosh!' and the Churchill salute and be admitted to the group where he would convey his gang's message and wait for a reply. The outcome could be anything: sometimes peace, sometimes war.

A small, tough-looking Desperado walked to the centre of the cell where he was met by a big, burly man from the Big Five. His shirt was stripped off, ready for action, and we crawled to our corners and sat very quietly.

All of a sudden these two chaps started punching it out. It began as a boxing match with each landing heavy punches on the other and both gangs cheering their own man on. They were two fit fighters who knew how to handle themselves. The smaller was much faster, but the larger dealt out heavier punches. Quite soon the first blood was drawn and now it was no longer a boxing match but a mixture of wrestling, boxing, judo and plain kicking, with the heavier chap all over the other. He kicked, hit and punched without stopping; beat the other man's head against the wall and then threw him, unconscious, to the ground with bloody wounds all over, only letting go of the body when it was totally still, and we were convinced that the man was dead. The Desperadoes were quiet by now, while the Big Five made a tremendous amount of noise in support of their man. The little fellow was dragged to his corner where his men washed him down and brought him back to consciousness. To our amazement, the next morning he was up and ready for work, laughing and talking as though nothing had happened.

The prisoner raised his arm and we noticed that his hand was wrapped in a towel, part of which contained a heavy object. He brought his hand down with a heavy blow on to the head of another prisoner, and even at our distance we could hear a cracking sound and see the blood spurting from the head. The victim dropped unconscious to the ground and the attacker calmly dropped the towel, walked up to the nearest warder and handed over his identity card. The man he had attacked was rushed to hospital, and a month later he was back in the quarry, laughing and re-integrated into his gang.

When he arrived at Robben Island as a convicted prisoner, Warder A— was a worried man. In his years as a warder he had been as cruel to the prisoners as any of his colleagues, calling them coolie, kaffir and hotnot (though in apartheid language he was Coloured himself), and beating and kicking them like the rest. So he knew how depraved prison life was, how the prisoners preyed on each other; the lies, the deceit, the violence. He was inside as a prisoner because one day four of his former classmates from school had been brought to his prison as political detainees and he had decided, unsuccessfully, to help them escape. Now he was on a three-year sentence and dreading being plunged into the world of dog-eat-dog that he had known so well.

He was amazed. He had never seen anything like it. He saw us sharing our little rations of smuggled tobacco or our few toilet things. He even began to call us 'comrade', without really knowing the meaning of the word.

Then one day he asked me if there were any communists in our ranks. When I asked him why, he said he just wanted to know. I pointed to three of the most senior comrades in our section who were all well known to have been communists, having been sentenced for taking part in the activities of the underground Communist Party of South Africa. He did not believe me; they happened to be the most gentle and helpful of all the prisoners, to whom most of us would go for advice – even he had done so once, little suspecting what their 'crime' had been.

He told me that at the warders' school in Kroonstad he had received and believed lectures on the evils of communism: that a communist would stop at nothing to achieve his aims and objects, that communists were brutes who had killed millions throughout the world. From his lecture notes, he said, he had come to the conclusion that all that the communists lacked was a pair of horns and a tail, they were the enemies of all mankind, and especially of the blacks in South Africa.

I reported this discussion to my comrades who encouraged me to have political discussions with this man, so I told him about the history of the ANC and what it stood for, about the history of the Communist Party in South Africa, and about the changing world as a whole.

On the eve of his release from prison he addressed a small group of us. He did not regret his three years in jail, he declared, they had been a greater education to him than the rest of his life put together, and on his release he would not attempt to get back into the Prison Department; he would work in the interests of the people.

Some time later we were pleased to receive letters from him

telling us that he was working as a social worker in Cape Town.

We learned that another group of prisoners, sent to Baviaans-poort, started openly having political discussions in the cells, but they had been too random in selecting people to attend and the authorities had soon got on to them, so they were returned to the Island with additional sentences. The majority of them came to us, and they, too, were totally transformed and integrated into a new kind of life.

One of the common-law prisoners who had escaped from the country returned to Johannesburg for his father's funeral and was arrested. After being charged and convicted for escaping and carrying on ANC activities, he came back to us on the Island, and we noticed how much he had changed. Before, he used to walk with the unique prisoner's walk, rolling hips, showing half his backside and clicking his fingers, but now he moved around just like us, and what was more, he no longer used coarse prison language, full of swearing and slang. In fact, he referred to us as comrades. He was among those who regularly smuggled news-papers to us and we regarded him as totally integrated into our community, a completely new person.

Gradually the authorities began to move the common-law prisoners off the Island. We heard that the first batch were sent to Leeuwkop prison where they organised a successful escape and sought out the underground ANC who managed to get them across the border to Botswana.

Eventually, all the common-law prisoners were gone, first to a separate jail, and then away from the Island altogether. A new batch came for a while, and we noticed that they would run away as we greeted them, or shield their faces, or turn round. We met two at the hospital and asked what was going on; at first they turned their heads away from us, but eventually they told us that they had been warned that we were evil communists and that they must not even look in our direction.

SIXTEEN

The white horse

They made us run the whole way to the quarry with Alsatian dogs at our heels, holding the dogs on a leash so close that we could hear the harsh panting behind us. The barking was loud and frightening and, on occasion, one of the dogs would manage to leap forward and sink his teeth into a prisoner's leg. Even though the injury was not usually serious – on one or two occasions other prisoners had suffered badly – the atmosphere was terrible and we never knew whether a dog would escape from his handler and really savage us. We felt the constant pressure to humiliate us, perpetually to reduce us to nothing in the warder's presence. They hated us and we hated them, it was quite simple.

One of our comrades, a big man in his fifties, was standing on top of a slab of rock attached to the face, towering above us a good six metres up. He was directing our pulling when suddenly the slab split away; we were horrified, we thought he must fall with the slab and be crushed by it, but he managed to wait until the rock was at a forty-five degree angle and then, with amazing timing, sprang away from it just before it hit the ground, landing on his feet with his arms outstretched as the huge stone slammed down, narrowly missing him.

The large wooden pole on which we were pulling slipped out of the rock and flew towards us at tremendous speed. Warder Meintjies appeared to be directly in its path and he stood paralysed as it hurtled at him. The log smashed the cap off his head but flew past, and for minutes afterwards he stood, silently transfixed to the spot.

Siva Pillay, who had been sentenced to eight years for ANC activities, had an argument with a warder after lunch, and later we saw him being marched off in the direction of Delport who was standing close to the shed. The warder and Delport took Siva into the shed. We saw him struggling with them and the next thing we knew he was hanging by his arms with his toes just touching the ground. To the warders this was a huge joke and they laughed in our faces and warned us that we would be next.

Siva stayed in that position the whole afternoon and was let down only after we had stopped work. He collapsed to the ground like an empty sack and was so weak that he could not move himself, so two of us picked him up and carried him back to the jail. Those comrades took him straight to the head warder and a medical officer to lay a complaint, but the prison officers waved them away; over the weekend a number of us – some from each cell – raised the matter with a visiting officer who had come around for inspection but he, too, refused to make a note of the complaint. Later, a group of us, myself included, asked for a 'letter' to the Commissioner of Prisons but were told that if we pursued the matter we would be charged under the prison regulations for making a frivolous complaint and that, unfortunately, was the end of the matter.

A big white horse, with a lieutenant astride, galloped off with a prisoner named Tshweni tied by a rope and running as fast as he could to keep up. Tshweni had got into an argument with a young warder and now we could see him in handcuffs being yanked along by a rope tied under his arms. The horse picked up speed and Tshweni raced desperately before falling over and being dragged along the ground; a trail of dust rose from the path as the horse galloped around the dyke towards the prison and eventually we lost sight of them in the distance.

Tshweni was put into isolation for several months so we did not see him for a while, but we were told that the lieutenant had dragged him through bushes and over gravel and that his body had been badly cut and his clothing torn to shreds. We felt that a protest should have been made about his treatment, but as he was a PAC person we could not intervene unless we could be assured of his co-operation.

One day, without explanation, the whole thousand of us were given picks, spades, wheelbarrows and *galas* (large iron staves) and told to start digging near the exit from the jail. We found ourselves excavating a trench about two metres deep and two metres wide, and soon realised that it was heading for the quarry. For the next three months we did nothing else but scoop out sand and stones. Some of the rocks were extremely tough and the work was as back-breaking as the chopping of stones in the quarry had been, but the warders never ceased chasing us with their batons, canes and hosepipes, some of them even climbing into the trench so as to be able to hit us better.

Hundreds of us with picks would stand in long, straight lines, our song rising in harmony with our work, drowning out the shouting of the warders and the barking of the dogs. Even when it rained we had to carry on digging the trench. We would stand dripping wet in the mud, knowing that when we got back to the cells we would have to sleep in our wet clothes and curse the warders, the Island and the whole vicious apartheid system.

Eventually the trench reached the quarry, and then, as suddenly as we had been told to dig it, we were ordered to fill it in again. It was rumoured that the authorities felt that the publicity would be too bad if it became known that the prisoners were forced to march to and from work each day along a trench. So the one and a half kilometre excavation, produced with so much sweat and suffering, was filled in once more with our sweat and suffering, and the common-law prisoners were instructed to build a wire cage over the route to the quarry, a new kind of tunnel along which we were, as before, chased by the dogs.

In the quarry we were put back on to breaking stones, and prisoners were regularly pulled out from work on some pretext or other and taken for punishment to a zinc shed where the tools and wheelbarrows were kept. As a security measure, the top half of the walls consisted simply of wire meshing so that the warders could see if any prisoner was trying to hide inside. But that meant that we, too, could look through the mesh and see the prisoners being punished. Siva Pillay was not the only one we saw; other prisoners too were suspended from a ceiling bar with their toes barely touching the ground, sometimes for one or two hours, sometimes for much longer.

One of my comrades – we called him 'Dip' – once said that the only time his heart was at rest was when he was locked up at five in the afternoon, knowing that while he was in his cell he would not be touched. But at 8 p.m. when the bell rang for us to sleep – the lights never went out – his heart started pumping as he thought about the next day. Would he survive it?

We all felt like that; during the first three years of our stay on the Island, each day had its quota of brutalities and torture and the warders seemed to enjoy seeing us suffer, for to them we were not human. They did not care whether we suffered or died, and told us straight out that they had more respect for the wild

96

animals on the Island than they had for us.

Every time a new group of prisoners came in, the warders' hostility increased, not only to the new prisoners but to all of us, and every time that Indian and Coloured prisoners arrived we of Indian or mixed descent would be called out and given especially rough treatment. This happened in mid-1964 when Neville Alexander arrived with six companions who had been sentenced to terms of imprisonment ranging from five to ten years for studying the possibilities of sabotage; the warders went for us for a good month afterwards, and made life hell for them.

Like most of the other prisoners, I was still unable to produce each day the required quantity of stones, but we had learned how to steal from the piles of the previous day to supplement our quota and so received fewer punishments; we were now seasoned prison workers, able to give support and courage to the new arrivals, and to preserve our own strength and morale.

SEVENTEEN

Chaos

It was chaos. Our relatives had travelled more than a thousand kilometres to visit us just this once, after months of thinking and worrying about us; there was so much we wished to say, and this was the one opportunity, but we were all shouting so loudly that none of us could hear anything, and the visit was becoming a disaster. On being told that someone was there to see us, without taking time to wash or straighten our clothes, we had rushed to the visiting quarters, a zinc structure divided inside by wire meshing up to the roof, with warders walking up and down between the two sections of meshing, about a metre apart, to keep us under surveillance.

We had to yell and scream to be heard on the other side, and the din was so great that as we begged our neighbours to lower their voices they begged us to do the same, but in no time we were all shouting at the tops of our voices again, repeating ourselves over and over, desperately trying to communicate.

We could see our relatives suffering, our mothers whom we knew to be usually soft-voiced and gentle having to shriek to convey the most elementary points to us, so we controlled ourselves, trying to give strength to the weeping visitors on the other side of the mesh.

Standing next to me was one of our comrades whose wife had given birth after his sentence; the baby, called Rivonia, was strapped to the mother's back, so he could see his child, and tears poured down the mother's face as she tried to speak.

My mother was also weeping and I shouted at her to stop, feeling terrible and on the verge of tears myself, but determined to make the visit a moment of mutual courage rather than a tragic occasion; I could see her all the time staring with shock at my hairless head. There were also warders walking backwards and forwards between us and our visitors, listening to our shouted conversations, interfering, telling us not to talk about anything but family matters, adding to the confusion.

Those of us who could not speak English, Afrikaans, Xhosa or Zulu, the four permitted languages, were particularly hard hit – they struggled above the noise with their limited English, shouting to family members who frequently knew even less English than themselves.

'Time!'

The half-hour seemed like ten minutes; we had managed to convey hardly anything, and many of us thought that the time had been deliberately cut short. We carried on talking for as long as we could, while being harassed to leave by the warders, and our relatives also kept shouting to us as they too were chased out the other side.

EIGHTEEN

Head Warder Delport

The prisoners who prepared meals for the warders would give them short rations, buttering the bread so thinly that one could hardly see that it was buttered at all, and cutting the cheese in razor-thin slices. So the warders would bribe the prisoners to give them larger helpings, offering them money or tobacco, or even relying on their common loyalty to a gang. Meintjies was with the Desperadoes, another was with the Big Fives and a third, rumour had it, regularly had sexual relations with members of another gang.

A large number of warders seemed to have grown up in orphanages, and to have received little education. Recruiting advertisements had promised them no military service, good accommodation, and lots of fun, but the only part that was true was exemption from military service. They were also offered study opportunities and free travel, which was partly true. Finally, they were told, off the record, that being a warder would give them a chance to keep the kaffir in his place. That, unfortunately, for us, was completely true.

Then there was another group of warders whose fathers,

mothers, uncles, aunts and grandfathers had all been in the prison service; they just went on locking people up from generation to generation, children of warders in control of children of prisoners; we had seen the next generation being prepared for our children.

Conditions for the warders were not good. They could leave the Island for only three days a fortnight and then only with written permission, and there was very little recreation for them: rugby, tennis, a bit of fishing, a clubhouse, a weekly film and little more. Seventy-five per cent or more were bachelors, and the only female company they could look forward to was the wives of the other twenty-five per cent, and their infant daughters – young girls escaped from the Island as soon as they could.

Two or three warders shared a single room, with eight in a common mess. Their hours were very long, starting at five o'clock in the morning and going on till five o'clock in the afternoon with only one hour off for lunch – and even that was usually taken while on duty. For ten days in a row they would work those twelve-hour shifts and then get only four days off as a break. Their next spell would be on night duty, either from four until midnight, or from midnight to eight in the morning.

They were always being harassed by their senior officers. If they came to work late they would be charged. If they were drunk they would be charged. If they failed to obey a command they would be charged (and some of the commands were humiliating, such as 'Run and fetch me some bread'). If they failed to salute they would be charged. If their shoes weren't polished or, even worse, their shoelaces weren't tied, they would be charged. They were bullied all the time. Their hair had to be close-cropped so that when they put on their caps there was no sign of hair at all. Their punishments were extra night duty, or a fine, or loss of free weekends, and we were amazed that they did not organise themselves into trade unions or some kind of body to protect their interests.

At the shooting range the target boards were referred to as *kaffir-kops* (kaffir heads), and we would hear the warders saying after practice, '*Jong, ek het die kaffir kop driemal geskiet* – man, I hit the *kaffir-kop* three times.'

The shooting team fared well in competition since they practised hard, and we looked forward to these competitions because we would often get the day off when they went to the shooting range; but we would hear the shooting with mixed feelings because, as much as we enjoyed time off work, we knew that the warders were becoming crack shots and that we or our comrades were the targets they had in mind.

Head Warder Delport never moved from the Island. He had a terrible reputation among the common-law prisoners who said that in his years of service – he was then in his forties – he had murdered many prisoners. Tall, heavily built, but not fat, with a bright red face, sleeves rolled up and a long energetic stride, he looked like a stereotype of the Boer farmer. He knew everything there was to know about quarries and always walked about carrying a piece of rubber hose about a metre long. He was a total terrorist who never lost a chance to beat us; he took pleasure in hearing prisoners scream and would order common-law prisoners to be taken to a shed where he would beat and beat them till they could cry no longer. One of the things that he especially enjoyed was standing on top of the pushcarts, loaded with sand and rocks, waving his hosepipe in the air and smashing it down on any prisoner within reach. He was the warder in command when Comrade Andrew Masondo, a former university lecturer in mathematics, who had helped us so much on our arrival, was set upon and had his shoulders badly injured.

Delport made no bones about his hatred of political prisoners, saying that it did not matter if we had university degrees, he was the boss. He was a slave driver. Under him, prisoners were hung from the ceiling and the worst atrocities took place, and for years we never saw him smile, not even when the warders were making their crude jokes; we would see him shouting at them or reporting them for the most trivial offences. The warders hated him as much as we did – even his family, we were told, stood in fear of him.

Sometimes Head Warder Delport would notice a warder missing from an observation post; he would creep silently up the ladder, move quietly in on the sleeping warder, carefully take off the man's cap, climb down and shout, 'Everything in order, Colonel!' The warder would leap up out of his sleep and start looking for his cap, and Delport would say sternly, 'I'll fix you up.'

If warders had the faintest smell of liquor on their breath he would report them. He really went for his colleagues, but mainly he went for the prisoners, and not a day went by without him laying charges against us so that by the weekend there would be hundreds of us going without meals.

Piet Kleynhans, who used to ride on the heavy roller cracking his whip over us as we pushed, had a younger brother almost as bad as himself; after a while they were joined by a third brother and, eventually, a fourth. The four Kleynhans brothers were hated by us and disliked by their fellow warders; they backed each other up in their brutality and formed a clique against the other warders. We campaigned constantly against them because of their inhuman conduct: they really behaved like Nazis in Gestapo camps, surpassing even the other warders on the Island. News of our campaign reached the outside world and Piet used to boast to us, 'You think you're important, I'm more important than you, my name is even mentioned in the United Nations and other important bodies of the world.' But in 1965 he was removed from the Island, and one by one his brothers followed.

NINETEEN

Mary

The large rock pool was infested with worms and a thick green slime lay on the rocks underneath.

'Clean it!'

Twelve of us were called out, with our spades, to drain the stagnant water, and as we started to work a strong stench of rottenness hit us in the face, the drops that splashed on our clothing making us stink. We plunged our spades into the water – insects skated on the surface – and scooped out as best we could, managing in half an hour to reduce the level considerably and further expose the slippery slime on the rocks.

'Take off your shoes!' Those of us with shoes took them off. 'Now get into the water and drain it all out.'

We looked down at the water. A few dead seagulls were floating on the surface and at the bottom we could see smooth slimy rocks and hundreds of pieces of jagged stone. We stood there, refusing to move.

'Get in!'

We stood still.

'I'm giving you a last chance, this is an order: get into the water.'

We protested that the water was filthy and dangerous and that we would cut our feet on the stones.

The warder was very young and very arrogant.

'Oh, so you're refusing to work?'

'No. We're not refusing to work. We're refusing to get into the water.'

'*Koelie, jy sal vrek* – coolie, you're going to die.'

That evening I was in a punishment cell, facing charges of refusing to work, disobeying a lawful command, and being disrespectful to a warder on duty. The cell was in a special isolation section called Koeloekoetz, a prison within the prison, which was used to house Nelson Mandela and other ANC leaders. The only items in it were a mat, three blankets, a little tin and a plastic bottle of water – and the next morning even they were removed, except the water.

It was not my first time in isolation and I knew that the chief warder would be round for inspection before breakfast, so when he came I asked him for a 'letter' to my lawyers, which he instructed the warders to give me. I later wrote to them setting out my situation and asking for someone to defend me at my trial at the prison, scheduled to take place in three weeks' time.

'Prisoner 885/63, you are charged with a breach of prison regulations in that on such-and-such a day you wrongfully and unlawfully refused to obey a lawful command. What do you plead?' The major looked sternly at me.

'Before pleading, I would like to have my lawyer present.'

'Well, your lawyer didn't come. Now what do you plead, guilty or not guilty?'

I refused to plead without my lawyer being present and asked for an adjournment to enable him to come, but the major refused my request and wrote that I had pleaded 'not guilty', ordering the trial to proceed.

My attitude was to refuse to take any part in the proceedings, but the warders lied so much that I was provoked and found myself cross-examining. My main line of questions was that we had not refused to work but that the command we had disobeyed was not a lawful one. I asked, 'If the warder had ordered us to murder a fellow prisoner, would we not have been entitled to refuse to obey?'

The major was irritated and in his summing-up he rebuked me for having taken up so much of his valuable time. 'You are showing the same sort of disrespect here that the witnesses complained of; if you receive a command, any command, you have to carry it out, and afterwards there are proper channels for raising the matter, but first you must carry out the command. You are cheeky and arrogant and a bad example to the others. You are clearly the ringleader, and your penalty will be four strokes' corporal punishment.'

That night I heard a voice shouting to me from across the yard, asking the result of the case, and I recognised the modulated tones of our leader, Comrade Nelson Mandela, first commander-in-chief of Umkhonto we Sizwe, who had been sentenced to life imprisonment at the Rivonia trial. I told him lightheartedly that I had been sentenced to four strokes, and he gravely and patiently gave me advice and encouragement for my ordeal.

Other comrades, Ahmed Kathrada and 'Mac' Maharaj, teased me about what would happen. 'Hey, Indres, by the time you get out of jail you'll be an old man. Now you'll have a torn backside as well, and no woman will look at you.'

For the next two weeks I waited anxiously in my bare cell: there was nothing to sit on, nothing to do in the cell the whole day long, only a Bible to read. We were supposed to have exercise twice a day for half an hour, but often we did not get it. The days were long and boring and I waited impatiently for the punishment, uncertain about my reaction, since up to then no political prisoner on the Island had been given lashes, and I was to be the first.

Every Tuesday and Thursday at Leeuwkop we had heard screams coming from the hospital yard where lashes had been inflicted, terrible screams, and I thought of them again and again as I waited. The prisoners had always yelled out 'Mama! Help!' – loud animal cries of pain – but I had made up my mind that, no matter how painful it was, they would not hear a squeak out of me.

✳

Right in the centre of the yard was the whipping 'Mary', a sloping wooden frame with leather straps at the top and bottom. In front, I saw a burly chief warder flexing his arms, and standing nearby were the major, Dr van den Bergen, and two or three other officials, with twenty or thirty warders in attendance.

Lying on the ground were half a dozen heavy bamboo canes with leather grips at the thicker end, and I saw the chief warder pick them up one by one to test them, flashing them through the air and bending them. As each cane whistled down he kept saying that he would make the coolie cry, and the warders standing around in expectant little groups talked loudly among themselves about how I would scream, waiting impatiently for the drama to begin.

One of the warders ordered me to remove my trousers; the doctor asked if I suffered from any serious ailments and when I said 'No' he pronounced me fit for caning. First, my hands were strapped high above my head and then, as I lay at a forty-five-degree angle on the frame, my ankles were tied. My pants lay on the ground quite near me and, under the doctor's supervision, cushions were strapped on my back and over my thighs, leaving only my backside exposed.

A medical orderly dabbed iodine all over the exposed part, and I heard the burly chief warder saying, even more loudly than before, that he was going to kill me that day, that I would have the scars for the rest of my life. He kept boasting about how efficient he was, with years of experience, and the other warders egged him on, almost hysterical with excitement.

In the mean time the doctor told me not to worry since it would not be too bad and would soon be over but even while he was talking I heard the whistle of the cane. Next moment it felt as though a sharp knife had cut right across my backside. There was no pain immediately but, suddenly, my whole body felt as though it had been given an electric shock. I grabbed hold of the Mary with both my hands and clung tightly to it.

The chief warder commented sarcastically, '*O, die koelie wil nie huil nie* – the coolie doesn't want to cry', and all the warders joined in the chorus. He went on to say that he would see to it that the next three strokes would land right on the cut; the medical orderly applied more iodine and this burned me even more than the caning.

The doctor continued to speak to me, saying that it had not been too bad, and that one stroke had already gone. While he was talking I again became aware of the whistle of the cane, but this time I heard a loud cracking noise, followed by a cursing from the chief warder that he had missed. There had been some pressure on one of the cushions, but that was all I felt.

The chief warder declared that that stroke would not count, but the doctor insisted that it would. The doctor then told me how lucky I was, and I heard the warders asking the chief what had happened. He told them that it had never happened to him before, but that he would make up for it with the next two strokes.

While the doctor was still talking to me, once again I heard the whistling sound. There was another loud smacking noise and I felt a stab of pain on the backside, but not too much pressure. I realised that the cane had landed mainly on the cushion, only the tip making contact with my flesh, and I heard the doctor shouting, 'Number three gone!' and the chief warder loudly muttering, 'Bastard. I've missed again.'

There was commotion among the warders who accused the chief of getting old and they told him that he was not doing his job properly. The orderly applied more iodine and the burning made my head spin; the doctor continued his conversation with me, repeating what he had said before.

The last shot came whistling down and cut me right along the very line of the first cut. That stroke was so painful that I was dazed, and strange shapes appeared in front of my eyes. I grabbed hold of the Mary and hung on to it as I tried to regain control of myself.

In all that time I did not speak or groan and, as the chief warder marched away cursing, I heard the warders commenting angrily about my refusal to cry. Once again I felt iodine being pressed into the wound, and the intense, burning made me totally dizzy. I heard the doctor saying that I had taken it well, and somebody loosened the straps. As my feet touched the ground I felt that I was going to collapse at any moment; everything seemed to be going round, and I heard the warder in charge saying abruptly that I must put on my pants and return to my cell. I asked which cell, and he indicated my normal one.

As I bent to pick up my shorts I could feel that I was going to go down. My arse was as hot as fire, and when the tip of my shirt touched it it added to the agony. Holding my shirt up, I managed to pick up my trousers and realised that if I stood any longer and tried to put them on I would fall to the ground, so I decided to walk away with my pants in one hand and my shirt held up by the other. The distance was about a hundred metres and I moved along it unconsciously, wobbling on my feet, my head spinning, past all the warders. I was determined not to show any sign of weakening, and the warders just stood and watched me all the way to my cell, waiting for me to drop. One of them opened the cell to let me in and I saw that, for some reason or other, the prisoners had not been sent out to work that day. As I staggered inside there was absolute silence and the prisoners waited for me to say something. Then, in the midst of my comrades, with no warders around to see, I collapsed.

The next two or three weeks I could hardly sit on my backside and at night I had to sleep on my stomach. The wound slowly healed but the scars remained for a long time, and to this day I still sleep on my stomach.

TWENTY

Holiday

We were enjoying ourselves, quietly singing revolutionary songs. Some of us were playing bridge with home-made cards, others were banging down draughts pieces on an improvised board, happy to have a day off work. A few days earlier, the cook had come running in: 'Have you heard? Have you heard the news? Have you heard the good news?' His face at the window had been radiant and we had leapt up to hear. 'Verwoerd is dead.* The pig has been stabbed.'

'How? What happened? Who did it?'

'Somebody went into Parliament and stabbed him with a big knife and got away.'

Now we were being given the day off as a mark of respect for the late prime minister, happy not to be shivering in the quarry; happy that the author of so much misery, the architect of apartheid, the arrogant man of granite, was being laid in the ground once

---

*On 6 September 1966 prime minister H F Verwoerd was stabbed to death by a parliamentary messenger, Dimitrio Tsafendas, as he sat at his desk in the House of Assembly.

and for all, and we were still alive.

The warders had been in real mourning. They had been really vicious to us. They had lost a father and had been truly shocked, as shocked as we had been delighted. They were not newspaper readers and rumours abounded: Tsafendas, the assassin, had been having an affair with Verwoerd's wife; Tsafendas was a Moscow agent, fluent in eight or ten languages, who had worked his way into Parliament; Verwoerd was not yet dead, he was being revived in hospital, and only when we got a smuggled-in newspaper two days later did we receive accurate information and were able to inform the warders what had really happened, about the dive-tackle in Parliament made by one of the MPs, a former Springbok rugby player, that had brought Tsafendas down after the stabbing and before he could make his escape.

As we dealt out the cards we speculated on who Tsafendas was, whether he was politically motivated, whether he had been used by dissidents within Verwoerd's own party, or whether it was a purely personal matter. There was lots of noise in the cell, heavy discussions everywhere; one theory even had it that the CIA had been behind the killing because they wanted a third force between Verwoerd and the ANC, so as to prevent a real revolution in South Africa.

A young warder appeared at the grille. '*Bly stil* – keep quiet, you're making a noise.'

We carried on talking a little louder, some shouting over their shoulders, 'Buzz off, man!'

'Who said that? Who said that? You'll lose your food.'

'Ah, fuck off, man!'

The warder stormed away and we carried on with our cards, our songs and our speculations, wishing that there could be more days like that.

TWENTY-ONE

'Carry on'

One day, coming back from work, just as we were about to enter the jail, I saw a knife flashing in the sunlight about two hundred metres away from me. A common-law prisoner was raising it – where he had got it from I do not know – and suddenly he was plunging it into the head of another prisoner. Blood came spurting out, there was loud screaming and we political prisoners scattered into the yard in all directions. Young warders, too, dispersed, but then regrouped themselves under command, while we political prisoners huddled in a corner, waiting for the inevitable reaction.

Warders ran to the common-law prisoners, waving sticks, batons, pipes, belts, anything they could get hold of, and started lashing out indiscriminately at all and sundry; even the stabbed prisoner was a victim.

Some warders then formed a circle round the prisoners, trapping them inside, while others ran in with weapons flying. We heard sticks cracking, batons splitting, and screams from all directions.

Prisoners, lying on the floor unable to move, were beaten and beaten and beaten. Blood was everywhere, prisoners ran this way and that to get out of the terrible circle. We were totally shaken by what was happening, not knowing what to do, trembling. A few warders with police dogs kept us at bay and extra warders kept arriving to take part in the beating, including many in casual clothes. One by one the prisoners were knocked to the ground, but the warders continued to hammer away at them, forcing them to get up so they could be knocked down once more.

The prisoners ran desperately to form a compact group of bodies so that it would be more difficult for the warders to get at them, those in front pushing and struggling in a continual motion of bodies to get away from the blows. The minute a prisoner was detached from the group he would be chased and beaten to the ground. When blood splashed on to the clothing of the warders they became even angrier and shouted, '*Wat maak jy met my klere?* – what are you doing to my clothes?' and hit the prisoners even harder as punishment.

After about half an hour the command came to stop. The warders ceased hitting, but carried on laughing and talking in an excited way, their sticks and other weapons now hanging at their sides.

The prisoners staggered away to assemble across the yard and about two hundred formed up in front of us. Blood was pouring from their heads; their clothing was torn to ribbons; their faces were unrecognisable. They were barely able to walk; unable to move their arms; moaning; crying. We political prisoners were absolutely shocked, stunned by what we had just witnessed, totally silent. The only sound was the crying of the common-law prisoners and occasional taunts from the warders, warning us that we could be next.

We were counted and then moved off to collect our food, but the common-law prisoners were so weak that they were simply driven to their cells and locked up, and the next morning a couple of dozen of them were taken to the hospital.

Often when going to work in the morning we would see common-law prisoners with bruises on their heads, hobbling and limping – sometimes even political prisoners like that – and we would learn that they had been set upon by the warders the previous evening in what was called a 'carry on' – that is, when the warders were given instructions to 'carry on' with their batons.

TWENTY-TWO

The tower

We were fast asleep in our cells; some sleeping naked, others fully clothed, when we were woken up by the sound of rattling keys and the door being violently opened. About twenty warders came dashing into the cell screaming at us to get up and face the wall. As we lined up against the wall with our arms stretched above our heads, they took up positions and ordered those prisoners who happened to be dressed to strip. They then searched every item of clothing, blankets and mats closely, throwing them all in a big pile in the centre of the cell as they finished, leaving us to retrieve our things before we could get back to sleep.

Sometimes they would come twice a week, sometimes not for months. On average, they raided us at night about ten times a year. It created problems for us: if tobacco was found in our possession we would be charged, if tobacco was found on the floor it would be confiscated.

Newspapers were our lifeblood. We ate, slept and dreamt news, and were in a constant war with the authorities over it – we to get it, they to keep it from us. Sometimes we even ate the news: once one of our comrades had a large newspaper cutting with him and

116

the warders were approaching, so he had no option but to stuff it in his mouth and eventually to swallow it.

As we got nearer to the concrete tower that guarded the prison – we were marching on our way to work – one of our group got ready for action. There were four towers, one at each corner of the prison: tall concrete cylinders about three storeys high, with internal staircases leading to a sentry post at the top, and the time to move was approaching. We knew it would require quick running, but it would be worth it – even the sacrifice inevitably involved, a sacrifice on behalf of the group.

The guard had been there all night, for eight hours at a stretch, with only his Belgian FN rifle for company. When he needed to pee he could urinate down a special pipe, but if he wished to relieve his bowels all he could do was to squat over a piece of paper and throw it out of the sentry-post window, and it was this that gave us our opportunity.

'OK. Go!'

Our comrade darted to the side, snatched up the bundle and within moments was back in our ranks. Walking along as though nothing had happened, with the rest of us giving him cover he wiped off the shit, read the newspaper quickly, and dropped it casually to the ground . . . mission accomplished.

A young comrade went to hospital with 'flu, and was turned away. The next day the same thing happened. On the third day he could not even get up, so some of his colleagues carried him to the hospital where they were told to take him away. They refused, leaving him lying on the floor of the dispensary, and even then he was given no treatment. Only when he was critically ill with double pneumonia was he rushed to the mainland. He died within days.

In the first months of prison we all lost weight quite drastically. Before I went in I weighed about sixty-eight kilograms, but by the time I got to Robben Island I was about fifty-two kilograms, and I never was able to get beyond this. In the mid-sixties they began to weigh us every six months, and we all noticed how we regularly stayed under weight. For some strange reason, however, about ten prisoners began to swell and put on ugly weight. Their arms became bloated as though they were filled with water. We could poke our fingers deep into their flesh. We never found out why this had happened.

TWENTY-THREE

The disc

The hammering of workmen at the other end of the isolation block made it easier for us to shout from one cell to another, but it also helped the warders to creep up on us unawares, so we had to remain careful.

'Ready?' The voice came from diagonally opposite, and I knew that there were ten other prisoners eagerly awaiting their turn. 'Coming!'

I heard a sliding sound and looked anxiously at the narrow space under the door of my cell. *Ting!* The noise seemed so loud, high above the hammering and the sawing from down the corridor. Damn! The disc had hit the metal post at the side of the door.

'No good. Try again,' I shouted, listening carefully for the tread of a warder's feet.

This was the most dangerous moment, when we could be caught in the act, without any chance of lying ourselves out of trouble. A few moments later I heard the cry 'OK, coming!' and this time the disc came sliding beautifully under my door, a thin thread of cotton trailing behind it. I took hold of the little piece of zinc and yelled, 'Let it come!' The thread was still slack. The noise down the passage continued. They were building a special isolation section within the isolation section, and we could make a pretty good guess who it was for.

'OK, pull!'

I pulled and the cotton tautened. Slowly I drew it in and could feel the faint resistance of something dragging at the end of it, and finally, I bent down, picked up the tiny parcel and gave it a little kiss – a brown-paper *zoll*.

Now came the difficult part. Getting tobacco in the isolation section was one thing, getting it alight was another. Normally I would use a flint hidden in my clothing and put a spark to a piece of charred cloth or to a scraping of the 1942 toothbrush, but all I had this time was a piece of the cloth in a little container and no flint, only a small stone.

I threaded the cotton through a second hole in the zinc, placed one end in my mouth, the other in my left hand, and held the container with the cloth next to the stone in my right hand.

'Ready,' I said to myself. 'Here goes.'

Pulling the cotton with my left hand and holding the end tight with my teeth, I got the disc spinning faster and faster, and gradually moved the stone closer. Got it! A spark leapt from the stone, but the cloth would not ignite.

I tried again and got more sparks, but somehow I could not manoeuvre the burnt cloth into the right position and never managed to get it alight.

The banging had stopped for a minute.

'Sorry, chaps, I can't get it going. Who else has got a light?'

A voice at the side said that he had a match, which meant that he had at least a quarter of a match and a piece of 'scratch' from the matchbox. We used to split our matches into four, and when lighting the little bits one had to be very quick to catch the flame – it was a real art.

Time was passing, there were a dozen eager smokers waiting

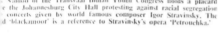

Naidoo of the Transvaal Indian Youth Congress holds a placard
e the Johannesburg City Hall protesting against racial segregation
concerts given by world famous composer Igor Stravinsky. The
d 'blackamoor' is a reference to Stravinsky's opera 'Petrouchka.'

Above left: *Indres Naidoo at a protest at the City Hall, Johannesburg, 1961*
Above right: *Indres Naidoo hugs his mother on his release from prison, 12 May 1973*
Below: *Indres Naidoo, Shirish Nanabhai, Moses Moola, Winnie Mandela, Berry Hughes and Khalil Saloojee at Transvaal Indian Youth Congress conference at Duncan Hall, Johannesburg, 1962* (Photographs: Mayibuye Centre)

Above: *Indres Naidoo on his release outside Leeuwkop prison, 12 May 1973*
Below: *Ms Anite Vervoort (Chairperson, Belgian Anti-Apartheid Organisation), Indres Naidoo, Toine Eggenhuisen, Major-General Aboobaker Ismail (Rashid) in Brussels, 10 October 1977*

Left: *Indres Naidoo at Free Mandela demonstration, Halle, GDR, 1988* (Pressefoto 'Freiheit')

Above right: *Indres Naidoo, Walter and Albertina Sisulu at Mayibuye Centre, UWC, 1996* (The Argus)
Below: *Newsmaker of the Year 1991: the Naidoo family. From left, Prema, Indres, Zoya, Kamala, Moggie, Shantie, Kuban, Murthie, mother Ama and aunt Thayanayagie Pillay* (The Indicator)

Above: *Swearing in of Senators: Lawrence Mushwana, Irene Mutsila, Indres E Naidoo, B J Nobunga and Bulelani T Nqcuka* (The Argus)

Below: *Gabi Blankenburg and Indres at his 60th birthday, 1996* (Miguel, Ab-Fab Photography)

for their turn, so instead of sliding the disc across so it could be criss-crossed to my neighbour I decided to wrap the *zoll* in my jacket and lob it across, which was quicker. The other method – swinging the piece of metal through the space at the top of the door – was too cumbersome; it was always hard for the guy next door to grab it as it swung past, whereas the jacket was easy to aim and easy to catch. So I rolled up my blankets, stood as high on them as I could, and got the jacket ready.

The banging had started again down the passage, and I listened for any sounds of approaching warders. If we were seen smoking in our cells it was not so bad because we could always destroy the cigarette while the warder was fetching the keys, or wrap it in some shit, where it would not be found, but there was no escape if the *zoll* could be attributed to us while being moved in the corridor.

'Ready?'

'Ready,' Came the response.

I stretched my arm out as far as I could, the jacket rolled tight in my hand, and was just about to throw when I heard the shout, 'Warder!'

Too late. I was caught red-handed. It would mean loss of meals, maybe another week in isolation, possibly even solitary confinement and spare diet.

After some delay, the cell door was unlocked and I saw why the warder had managed to creep up on us unawares; he was standing in his socks.

'Number?'

'885/63, sir.'

There was a look of triumph on his face as he padded off quietly, holding my jacket in his hand. I would get the jacket back, and I would also get my extra punishment within a punishment within a punishment.

Meanwhile, I was busy tying the half a *zoll* I had managed to save to the end of the thread. There was not much time left, and there were twelve anxious people waiting for their few puffs.

The hammering and sawing continued noisily. The special cell would soon be ready for Tsafendas.

TWENTY-FOUR

Asthma

Visitors to the Island were visibily impressed by the new hospital which had its own kitchen, lots of beds and a dispensary stocked with all the latest drugs. But the hospital kitchen was never used, since the prisoners got their rations from the main kitchen, and the drugs and antiseptics, for the most part, simply stayed on display until after their expiry date, when we would see the warders taking the penicillin and other drugs away for destruction.

Some of us managed to steal Dettol from time to time which we used for cleaning ourselves and, in fact, that was the only way we ever got any antiseptic. However, we did enjoy the beds in the hospital, and it was the only place where we could legally get hot water.

It was painful to watch the eyes of some of our comrades deteriorating from month to month, simply because they were not given glasses or because their glasses were not repaired.

There were big struggles over glasses. Prisoners with spectacles were not supposed to work in the quarry, so the attitude of the warders was either to ignore that rule and send the prisoners there, with all the dangers of rock splinters cracking the lenses, or simply to take people's glasses away. As far as the warders were concerned, glasses were simply an excuse for getting out of the quarry or, alternatively, were a way for people showing that they were 'clever'. The result was the opticians came very irregularly, once a year or even less.

*

We would be sitting in our cells and all would be quiet, when suddenly we would hear somebody gasping for air, shouting, 'Open the windows. Open the windows,' battling to get air into his body, with sweat pouring down him, even on the coldest nights. There was little we could do to help. There were many asthma sufferers. Some were given sprays, others not, and the doctor seemed to pick and choose whom to help and whom to shout at to go away.

One of our comrades would be sitting talking with us and the minute the conversation turned to police atrocities, prison brutalities or horrors of war his eyes would start rolling, he would scream and fall on his back, his limbs and body shaking. He would shout, 'Leave me alone, leave me alone, I don't know who did it, I don't know anything. Shoot me if you want to, kill me if you want to, but leave me alone.'

Never before had I seen people having fits, but in prison it was common for people to collapse to the ground and grind their teeth like this. We would lay him down, make a rough-and-ready pillow, and shove a spoon into his mouth to protect his tongue.

The minute he regained his senses he would be better and have no recollection of the episode. It was clear to all of us that we could never question him about what had happened.

When a prisoner complained of epileptic fits he would be prescribed a dose of castor oil or possibly aspirins, which were given for everything. It was extremely difficult to get any treatment for illnesses that did not have obvious physical symptoms. High blood pressure, piles and rheumatism were common, but the people suffering from them were almost invariably chased away without any attention; more often than not, visits to the hospital increased the suffering.

A visiting minister of religion opened his briefcase after the service, and in it lay a copy of the Johannesburg *Sunday Times* of that day. A comrade immediately went up to him and said, 'Father, may I carry your bag?' and before the minister could reply the bag was in his hand. Two other comrades accompanied him, talking to the minister, and the comrade with the briefcase opened it, took out the newspaper, and flung it to another comrade who was following, without the priest noticing.

A month later the same minister came, with the same briefcase; in it we found another newspaper, and once more our comrades managed to lift it from the bag.

Thereafter for six months, the priest came once a month, and once a month he left without his newspaper. Unfortunately, one day the commanding officer ordered that he be searched. At first the minister refused, but eventually he submitted, and the newspaper was found in his bag. We never saw him on the Island again.

One night we all knew that Sonny Singh had a whole copy of the *Cape Times* under his blankets, and the warders were searching. One got closer and closer and we all waited tensely for the moment of discovery, but as he got to the man next to Sonny the command was suddenly given to stop the search, and Sonny was safe.

We would be sitting around having our meal and he would shout out our names slowly, one after the other, keeping us on tenter-hooks, and we would leap up, feeling wonderful, and dash over.

It was Saturday afternoon: the day for letters from our family.

125

At first, the prisoner in charge had come around only once every two or three months with a small bundle in his hands. But as the number of letters we were allowed increased from one every six months to two or more a month, the container got bigger.

All our comrades would be as excited as we were, and make friendly joking comments to us. We would take the letters back to the cell and after lock-up would sit on our bedding, take out the letter and read it many times over. That evening our comrades would leave us alone with our letters as we tried to make out as much as possible from them, but the next day the letters became public property. They would move from hand to hand and sometimes we would not get our own letter back for weeks, after all the prisoners had devoured its contents.

Even the most trivial item of news was devoured, discussed over and over again, and analysed from every possible angle. 'Prince So-and-so in Europe is to marry Princess Such-and-such.' We discussed such items with full gravity, arguing about how it would affect our struggle.

Not for one minute did we stop smuggling newspapers and if the authorities accused us of that offence, we never denied it. In our opinion it was a crime to deny us knowledge of what was happening around the world, not just the political events but the social, cultural, sporting and scientific happenings as well. The intention of the authorities was to cut us off completely from the outside world, to break us down. We, on the other hand, never once gave in. If we spotted a newspaper in the possession of a warder we would be sure to get it into the jail by hook or by crook within a short time, even if it were locked in a desk or a van.

From time to time we managed to smuggle in small transistor radios – our biggest prize, and also our biggest danger. The main problem was to find good hiding places and to arrange access so that we could tune in at news times, but our problems did not end there because the batteries would run out, a terrible moment, and it might take months to get replacements.

TWENTY-FIVE

Tsafendas

The partition blocking off the two end cells in the isolation block was now complete and we waited with considerable curiosity for the arrival of Verwoerd's killer. Even though we knew that his action had solved nothing, and we now had Vorster instead of Verwoerd with more violence, more torture, more repression than ever before, we felt lots of sympathy for Tsafendas. He had a sort of mad courage and had rid the world of a tyrant whose racial plans had caused untold misery.

I was in isolation on the day that Tsafendas arrived. Security was very tight and we were kept locked in our cells all the time, but that evening we decided to shout to him. 'Hello there, how are you?' He remained quiet. 'Welcome to Robben Island, you are among friends.'

He returned our greeting cautiously but did not commit himself, and in the next few days, while I was still there, we never succeeded in getting into real communication with him.

Not long afterwards he was moved,* and all that remained

---

*Tsafendas, finally declared insane, was committed to a mental institution for life. He died in 1999.

was the blocked-off cell, and his name: whenever we wanted to warn off somebody from some action, we would say jokingly, 'Watch out, I'll Tsafendas you!'

TWENTY-SIX

Maadu

We were sitting in the yard, staring intently at the letters in the hand of the prisoner; joking to hide our nervousness and trying to guess from the envelope, the stamp and the small glimpses of handwriting, whether there was one for us.

The prisoner looked down, taking his time, lifted up the letter and shouted out, as though announcing a prize at a fair: 'Justin Sithole.'

Justin Sithole jumped up, a grin on his face, his companions patting him on the shoulder as he put down his plate and ran over to collect his letter.

Another letter was taken from the pile. The prisoner looked at it. We waited anxiously. 'Indres Naidoo.'

I leapt up, my heart filling with pleasure, my mates congratulating me. I walked over slowly – as slowly as the prisoner called out our names – and could tell already from the handwriting that it was from my family. I glanced down at the envelope, trying not to reveal my impatience, and then, sitting down again, I carefully pulled out the pages, my fingers fumbling a little. There were thick black lines everywhere, blotting out the words. I read 'We have been to the funeral of — and it was a very sad occasion.' I felt desperate; from my expression my comrades could see that something was wrong, but did not ask.

Later, back in the cell, the doors locked for the night, I held the letter up against the light and tried to make out the words faintly visible behind the censor's heavy lines. 'Fi . . .' I could just about see '. . . er'. Fischer! Bram Fischer! I went cold and passed the letter to a comrade for him to look, hoping that I had been mistaken.

We all went into a deep depression and began to compare letters to see if there was confirmation. Gradually we were able to work out what had happened: Paul Fischer, young son of our comrade and lawyer Bram Fischer, imprisoned for life, had died of a long-standing disease.*

I placed my letter in the pile that I had preciously hoarded, and re-read some of the others for comfort. I especially enjoyed those from *Maadu*, full of teasing and provocation. *Maadu* . . .

Once I had decided to write to an old friend and comrade, whose husband was on the Island with us, and told her that I would be so old, so grey and so blind by the time I left prison that no girl would even look at me, did she perhaps know of an old cow who would be willing to write to an old bull like me? A couple of months later I received a letter in an unknown handwriting from a person who described herself as someone with lumbago, heavy glasses, false teeth and a rubber bust, and who signed off as *Maadu* – the Tamil word for 'cow'. And so our correspondence began.

I picked up another letter and quickly put it down. It read, 'Dear Indres, How are you these days?' Then followed black lines all the way through until the last line, left uncensored; 'Love, Sheila'. Sheila Weinberg; both her parents were in prison for furthering the aims of communism, and here she was taking the

---

*Paul Fischer died in Cape Town on 27 January 1971 at the age of twenty-three. The prison authorities would not allow Bram Fischer to attend his son's funeral.

risk of writing to me on Robben Island.

I re-read one letter after the other from my precious pile, re-living their contents and re-living the experience of opening each one, lost in thought about the people outside.

TWENTY-SEVEN

The Brigadier

Brigadier Aucamp, the man in charge of security on the Island and in all jails, was our most dangerous opponent. He was shrewd and cunning; the most powerful man on the Island, and he loathed political prisoners. There were stories about him all the way from the Island to Pretoria, where he was stationed.

According to prison regulations it was the commanding officer who should have been all-powerful in every prison. In reality, it was Aucamp who ruled wherever there were political prisoners; he was the one who had the final say; four or five times a year he would come down to the Island, and even the commanding officer would run around smartly to get things in order for him.

When we demanded to see Aucamp he would avoid us, but when we least expected to see him he would come: pompous, arrogant and hateful. He was always in plain clothes; short and plump, with a wrinkled face; he never smiled, was never polite when he talked, and when we complained about assaults and brutalities he would say sharply, 'I ordered them. Next complaint?' When we complained about the quality and quantity of the food, his harshly spoken answer would be, 'You are lucky to get food, in your *pondokkie* [shanty] you would get nothing . . . Next?' If we said anything about the lack of clothing, he would tell us rudely that the money came from the white man's taxes and when we tried to argue that we, too, paid taxes he would scornfully reject our statements out of hand.

Aucamp ordered many of us to be locked up in solitary confinement and on occasion ordered baton charges. Once, when we were in conflict with the authorities, he demanded to see me.

'What's your name?' he asked.

'Indres Naidoo.'

'How long are you serving?'

'Ten years.'

'How many years have you completed?'

'Six.'

'You'll never leave jail. Get out!'

We were convinced that he was a member of the *Broederbond* (the secret Afrikaner society that controlled the government), and was carrying out *Broederbond* policy against political prisoners.*

Aucamp was a member of the Prison Board that was supposed to monitor our progress and make recommendations for parole or promotion to a higher classification. Although first offenders usually started off in 'B' group, the second highest grade, we were classified in 'D' along with the hardened habitual, common-law prisoners. Only when we had completed a third of our sentences could we be upgraded, and we were never considered for parole, however good our behaviour had been. Even when we managed to reach 'B' group, and some even 'A' group, the usual privileges – contact visits, radios and newspapers – were withheld from us, and behind it all was Brigadier Aucamp. He knew nearly every prisoner inside out, having informers in various places on

---

*The *Afrikaner Broederbond* was an organisation established in 1918 to promote the political, cultural and economic interests of Afrikaners. After the National Party came to power in 1948, every prime minister and state president up to 1994 was a member of the *Broederbond*.

133

the Island – we knew at least three among the PAC prisoners.

Each time we saw him he looked a little more sick, but somehow, in spite of rumours that he was about to retire, he always came back. As far as we were concerned he could have come straight out of the Gestapo. We hated his guts, he was the source of all our misery, and when the rumour strengthened that he was very sick, we could not wait for him to die.

✳

A warder had been dropped from the Robben Island rugby team, even though it was obvious to him and all who knew the game that he was the one good player and all the others were hopeless. (The team, incidentally, played in one of the lower Cape Town leagues – and was beaten every week.) So a prisoner working in the kitchen told him to consult Natrarial Babenia, the prisoner who could see into the past and the future.

We warned our comrade Babenia, and he instructed the kitchen staff to collect as much information about the warder as they could. A week later the warder told Babenia of his difficulties and Babenia asked to see his palm, telling him all the while about his problems with love and other difficulties in life. The more Babenia revealed, the more information the warder came out with himself, and eventually Babenia was able to explain it all: the warder's problem was that he was just too handsome and popular, that was his trouble, and this made the rest of the team jealous. The warder was so pleased that he gave Babenia some tobacco and told his colleagues about this prisoner with the wonderful, mystic powers. Babenia soon had a large clientele and never ran short of tobacco, or hot water.

We had a saying that if you wanted a kick in the face you should go to Spy Thirteen since one of his favourite sports was suddenly to shoot his long leg up at you and catch you on the point of your chin with his shoe. He was the one who had warned me to speak Afrikaans and call him 'baas' on the day of our arrival on the Island, and I was always in conflict with him.

We knew that he was working for Brigadier Aucamp as security man on the Island and was in charge of the whole system of informers. On occasion he would attend to our complaints; at other times he would not. He was very sly. He tried to show me that he was a friend but, in fact, he was often very brutal.

When he left in 1965 he was replaced by Chief Warder Fourie, a young, conceited warder who, like Spy Thirteen, was not popular among the warders because not only did he spy on us but he spied on his colleagues as well.

The commissioned officers, whether single or married, had beautiful houses, well furnished, in an elegant section, with gardens and lots of prisoners to act as domestic servants. They were well paid and had reasonable working hours; many of them even had departmental cars to get them round the Island. Their recreation and sporting facilities were separate, and once, when I was in a painting *span,* I had an opportunity of working in the village and could see the officers playing bowls on beautiful greens and tennis on lovely courts. I helped to build a mini-golf course for the officers, though I never actually saw them using it, and could not help contrasting their luxurious facilities with the miserable facilities available to the rank-and-file warders.

Even in the clubhouse they had a separate section for drinking and socialising. Their families, also, had better facilities and privileges, and we heard from some warders that off duty and outside formal socialising, the officers never mixed with the rank and file, and the same applied to their families.

The non-commissioned officers were less well-off; some mixed with the commissioned officers, but most formed their own group.

Finally, the rank-and-file group of ordinary warders was divided between young prison-school cadets and old recruits who had come into service without any training. These last were regarded as the lowest of the low, they were not given uniforms and were trained 'in service', which in reality meant nothing more than being trained in how to push us around and how to swear, shout and beat.

One of Aucamp's most trusted and loyal officers was Major Kellerman, who arrived on the Island as a captain in 1964 and soon got himself into the position of second-in-command. He was a real sadist. My first clash with him was in early 1965 when I went with comrade Reggie and others to collect stationery from the office. It was not even his office, but he passed loud remarks about coolies being parasites who needed to be put in their place. We looked at him and he turned directly to us and demanded to know what we were staring at. Before we could say anything he declared that we were only fit to be locked up, and walked away.

Kellerman had been the officer in charge of my trial for disobedience, and by 1966 he had become a major and was commanding officer for the Island. At that stage he would come on inspection and receive complaints. He came round regularly, gave us a good hearing, spoke tactfully, and always found our complaints to be unjustified. He was less arrogant than before, but much more shrewd, and was the longest-serving commanding officer, staying until 1969.

His period saw a lot of hardship, but also a lot of improvements, brought about by pressure from prisoners as well as from external sources such as world opinion and the Red Cross. One thing I must grant him: he was always ready to come to us to defend his position, unlike Colonel Steyn, the first commanding officer, who only inspected us once in six months and then ordered anyone who had stepped forward to make a complaint or a request to be locked up immediately.

Warders' wives would get on the boat to Cape Town and never return. Many warders themselves would desert when taking their leave, or resign from the service the day their contract period was over. Salaries were low for the rank and file, and life was filled with boredom. We used to learn from the warders or from common-law prisoners about which warder was sleeping with which warder's wife, and would notice that Warder X had disappeared from duty to be told that he had been caught in bed with Warder Y's wife and given a 24-hour transfer.

Head Warder Delport, as the man in charge of the quarry for years, knew every little detail about how to run the quarry, how to force the maximum amount of work out of the prisoners, and how to beat us for the slightest failure of performance.

He broke many backs and fractured many limbs during those years, yet despite his total dedication to the Prison Department and the system, he remained only a head warder. He was a complete teetotaller who carried out instructions absolutely with no questions asked, and who demanded the same of those working under him. Nevertheless, he stuck in his rank while others less dedicated were getting promotion over him.

He was hated by every prisoner, political and common law, because he drove us beyond what was possible, setting targets of work beyond human achievement, and then thrashing us for non-compliance. But that was not the reason why he did not get on in the service. The reason was a new Prison Department policy of encouraging in-service education, and he just could not pass his exams.

A couple of warders – it is better not to mention their names – did not actually refuse to carry out instructions, they just held back a little, and we got to know who they were. They would keep to a corner when a 'carry-on' was ordered, somehow managing never to strike us.

Warder Z spoke politely to us and referred to us by our full names, and even secretly passed on a packet of cigarettes from time to time. He was a very pleasant fellow and would say, 'Chaps, remember me.' Our attitude was that we would remember him, but the PAC's attitude was 'Fuck you, you're just one of them.'

There were two or three more like him who showed some signs of human feeling and who clearly did not approve of the treatment being handed out to us. They were all rank-and-filers – we never once noticed an officer reacting in that way – and would call us '*kêrels*' (chaps) when the others always said '*kaffirs*', '*koelies*', '*boesman*', '*hotnot*'. They never lasted long on the Island; they just did not fit in, and were soon transferred.

TWENTY-EIGHT

'The People's Flag'

One day a warder saw me blowing my nose and confiscated the cloth I was using on the grounds that I was not authorised to have it. I had a perpetual cold, my nose ran continually and I was constantly sneezing. Van den Bergen always told me it was simply the damp climate I was not used to, but when my chest got bad he considered sending me to Cape Town, although he never gave me tissues. We used to wipe our noses on our sleeves, on our jackets or on any piece of cloth we could get hold of. I had two scraps of white cloth that I would use for that purpose and then wash out later on. Now I had lost one of them and decided to take the matter up with the commanding officer and demand the right to blow my nose.

'Yes, what is it?'

I explained the problem of my nose and added, 'Either my cloth should be returned, or I should be allowed to buy a new one, or the authorities should provide me with one.'

He dismissed me.

One by one in the days that followed, the rest of the comrades requested the right to blow their noses.

'Prisoner 885/63, this way.' I followed the warder to the office. On the table was a coarse piece of red cloth, the result of two weeks' campaigning. 'Prisoner 885/63, this is your issue, look after it; we haven't got money to throw away, this is taxpayers' money.'

I walked out, elated with my prize. Next day, every prisoner received a little scrap of handkerchief.

With dust everywhere and the chronic colds we all suffered, we had to wash out our hankies practically every day, and at times they could be seen hanging out to dry: patches of coarse bright-red material lodged between the bars of every cell, rows and rows of them stretching throughout the prison. The authorities accused us of flying the Red Flag and recalled every one of the red hankies, giving us soft khaki ones instead, and at last we could blow our noses in peace.

TWENTY-NINE

Doctor Rubbish

A prisoner due for release after serving six years developed a serious stomach ailment, but the authorities refused to attend to him. The doctor had chased him out of the surgery on a number of occasions, and this comrade openly accused him of being a fascist so the doctor reported him and he was locked up in isolation for being rude. Soon afterwards, he was taken seriously ill and the authorities had to remove him to the mainland for treatment, but it was too late and he died. We heard through the grapevine that his stomach had been totally empty of food because of his disease.

Many warders in the hospital were rude, they were in a position to make life very difficult for us, and they kicked prisoners out at will; they were usually the ones who decided whether or not one saw a doctor. Even when the doctor or dentist was visiting, the warders used to control us and stop us from speaking out about our problems, so it was difficult to get an illness attended to.

At first we were not supposed to get toothache at all, but after a couple of years we were entitled to get toothache once every six months, because it was then that the dentist came. Extractions were free but anything else was regarded as a luxury, so the prisoner had to pay out of funds sent by his family for any fillings, cleaning or dentures.

On the whole the dentists were quite reasonable. One in particular was very concerned about the political prisoners, always asking after the health of Nelson Mandela and the others whenever he had the chance, and one thing we were quite sure of: none of the dentists were in the prison service – they treated us like human beings.

Some of the prisoners who worked in the hospital showed us some sympathy, and one of them even became quite expert at attending to the sick. In a friendly way we used to call him Doctor Rubbish. One night he did a really good job when one of our comrades tried to kill himself by cutting a vein in his neck; Doctor Rubbish stitched him up at the hospital, and the next day the doctor said that the stitches had saved the man's life.

He was a real fighter, not only against prison and apartheid, but against asthma and fits. He constantly demanded treatment but was always refused, both by the warders and by the doctor who insisted that he be locked in isolation for being lazy and pretending to be ill.

Eventually, he was removed from Robben Island as a trouble-maker and taken to Leeuwkop Prison about a year before his release. We heard that he was locked up in isolation and given a rough time for the rest of his sentence.

Every single prisoner at some time or other participated in smuggling newspapers. The authorities discovered all the methods mentioned in this narrative and put a stop to them, but there were many more which they never found out about, and which must remain secret.

The chief Dutch Reformed Church minister on the Island, who was also the official prison chaplain, was nicknamed Zambia because he had once worked in that country, and was extremely hostile towards the African states and towards the liberation movements in southern Africa. But we enjoyed going to his sermons because he would always tell us about 'terrorist activities' in this or that place, how many had been killed here or captured there, and so he would keep us informed about the progress of the armed struggle.

There were also warders who rushed to give us bad news, such as when Bram Fischer was arrested in November 1965, in their attempt to show us that we were wasting our time with our political beliefs.* In that way we could fit together many pieces of information and break the news isolation.

The warders always enjoyed finding tobacco, it was like catching a fish, but they got really excited when they came across a piece of newspaper.

'Chief, chief, look what the kaffir's got!'

A scrap of paper could result in anything from two weeks' spare diet in isolation to three months' solitary confinement.

The Island's rubbish dump was a valuable source of news. One comrade working there was caught on his way back from work with a few newspapers and sentenced to fourteen days' solitary confinement on spare diet. A few days after his release, he was found again with some papers and given the same sentence. A few days thereafter, he was found with half a sackful of papers, and for the third time in two months he went into isolation.

We got our newspapers to a central point where a group of us would read them and memorise all the articles of interest: political,

---

*Bram Fischer was arrested on 11 November 1965. He was sentenced to life imprisonment on 9 May 1966.

143

social, cultural, scientific and sporting, remembering as much as possible of all the details. Each of the readers then transmitted that information to a further small group who in turn disseminated it to another group, and so on.

The beauty of it was how we managed to memorise so much. A newcomer would struggle to remember twenty items, but within a short time he had learned many ways of doing so. For example, I would first take items dealing with South Africa and count how many articles there were on the subject; then how many articles there were on Africa as a whole; then Europe, Asia, America, and so on. Then, when disseminating the news, I would remember that I had read ten items on South Africa, five on Africa and so many on the rest of the world, which helped in recalling the actual contents.

We reported mostly during our lunch breaks. 'Comrades, today we have twenty-five items . . .'

In fact, the items would become so embedded in our minds that we would remember them in the greatest detail and, even when we had our monthly news review and analysis, we would recall just about every item for the whole month.

We had to read as quickly as possible and then find a way of disposing of the newspapers, so we tried burning them in our cells, but that caused a lot of smoke.

Next, we tried tearing the newspapers into little strips and flushing them down the toilet – something that we did not do too well at first, because we made the strips too big and blocked the sewerage which meant that a volunteer had to push his arm in and pull the strips out. Getting rid of four newspapers, bit by bit, flushing, flushing, flushing, could take hours, and attract attention.

We also had to be careful to tear the papers softly, especially at night when the jail was absolutely silent. But we overcame that problem by soaking the newspaper before tearing it.

At times the spot searches by the authorities would put us in a jam. We would swallow cuttings and hide the newspapers where we could, or throw them out of the window. But time and again we were caught.

One day they found a crudely made key on Saddick Isaacs and, searching him further, came across a little transistor radio. That was the first time they had found a radio on a political prisoner. They marched him off, together with four companions, with huge smiles of victory on their faces. We heard later that they had each been sentenced to six strokes with the cane, and that Isaacs also had an extra six months added to his sentence.

Next day we were kept in our cells, and when we went to work again the day after, the whole area had been turned upside down; stones had been moved, tools were scattered everywhere and the ground had been dug up. The little radio that we ourselves had hidden had disappeared.

THIRTY

Obsession

One of the prisoners had an obsession: he would pick up seaweed and store it in the cell or at the quarry, together with pieces of metal, zinc, cork and wire. There would be a raid and the warders would walk off with everything, and he would start collecting all over again.

Months would pass and we would see him sitting in the cell after lock-up, carving the seaweed and cutting holes in it with little home-made tools. Every now and then he would raise it to his lips and blow and we would hear strange sounds coming out. With glue and paper he added wire and reinforced part of the seaweed.

The warders would raid the cell again and stamp on this strange-looking object, and he would start all over again, shaping out a new piece of seaweed, adding string, cork, wire, paper and tin. Slowly we could see what was emerging from his imagination – a saxophone.

He would blow and blow, getting different crude sounds out of it, slowly improving the tone while we all waited patiently to see the finished product.

More than a year passed before he managed to buy a saxophone reed from outside, and then a totally new sound emerged, much richer and more varied.

The instrument was ugly, it lacked the power and grace, as well as the glitter, of a true saxophone, but we loved it almost as much as its maker did.

He never stopped perfecting it, trying to make it more beautiful with silver paper, and working incessantly on the sound, getting it closer and closer to that of the real thing, and when visitors came to the Island the warders would take them with great pride to see the amazing saxophone produced by their policy of encouraging artistic expression amongst the prisoners.

THIRTY-ONE

Tribute

'Comrades and friends, this is a sad occasion for all of us. We are paying our last tribute to the beloved ANC leader and President, the late Albert J Luthuli, who died a violent death earlier this week. Will everybody please rise for a minute's silence.'*

Every man in the cell stood up, each one next to his bedding, head bowed. There was total silence, just faint sounds of singing from the distance.

'*Wat maak julle hier* – what's going on here?'

We heard the sharp voice of a warder at the window, but we ignored him and he went away.

'*Amandla!* – Power!' The chairman gave the clenched fist salute.

'*Ngawethu!* – To the people!' we answered with salutes, while the PAC chaps remained silent.

'Thank you, comrades and friends.'

---

*Albert John Luthuli was elected President-General of the ANC in 1952. He was awarded the Nobel Peace Prize for 1960. On 21 July 1967 he was struck by a train while taking a routine walk on a familiar route near his home at Groutville, KwaZulu-Natal. He died from his injuries on the same day.

We sat down on our bedding, arranged around the cell against the walls.

'Comrades and friends, as you all know, our president was killed by a train on his farm in Natal where he had been restricted by the racists. Whether that was really how he died, or whether he was murdered, we do not know, what we do know is that we and Africa, and all humanity, have lost a great leader, winner of the Nobel Prize for Peace, renowned throughout our country and the world for his great contribution to the struggle for peace and justice.

'Our late comrade President always inspired us by his gentleness and calmness, by his tremendous dignity and courage, by the way he stood ever ready with the people, ready to make any sacrifice on their behalf, ready to lead them in any struggle.

'I will now call upon comrade George, who worked closely with him for many years, to say a few words.'

At the end of the memorial service some of our comrades led the anthem and we stood with arms raised in clenched-fist salutes, while the PAC chaps stood with the open palms of their own salute, only joining us in singing the anthem when the music and words coincided with their version.

'*Amandla!*' Our fists shot higher, '*Ngawethu!*'

The PAC guys remained silent, but were respectful.

THIRTY-TWO

The Geneva Men

One day we saw a large, middle-aged man walk in with the commanding officer and other officials. We knew that he was not a prison official from the way he walked and talked, even from his clothing. He spoke English to the officers, who clearly treated him with respect, and we tried among ourselves to guess who he was. A journalist? A Member of Parliament? A judge? He was too refined to be a member of the Prison Department.

He smiled at the prisoners, nodding his head to them, showing a kind of interest that was clearly different, and as he toured the prison, he tasted the food, examined the clothing, and had a good look around.

Only weeks later, through the grapevine, did we hear that he was a Mr Hoffman from the International Red Cross. I must say, we were pretty sceptical about the visit.

Twice a week, a doctor from the mainland was supposed to check the kitchen and general hygiene, and to attend to the medical needs of the prisoners. I might be wrong, but I doubt whether Dr van den Bergen went to the kitchen more than three or four times in the seven years that I knew he was visiting the Island. All he did was examine prisoners who were referred to him, and he did so in such a way that we all hated going to the hospital. He shouted at us, swore, accused us of being murderers, and told us how lucky we were not to be locked up in other African countries. We were always struggling against him, complaining to the prison authorities.

One prisoner went to the doctor with severe migraine headaches. The next thing we knew he was being locked up in an isolation cell in the hospital. When he did not get any food the following day he asked what was happening and was shown the doctor's prescription: 'No food for four days'.

Sometimes he ordered a good dose of castor oil for a complaint such as rheumatism, saying, 'It is all your fat that is causing you troubles.'

Every day, as we marched to the quarry, we would see a little progress in a large hall being constructed by the building *span*. Eventually it was finished and we were anxious to see the inside of it. In fact, we demanded to be allowed to eat there instead of out in the yard, but the authorities refused, saying that we would only dirty it.

So every day we would pass the large, empty building, occasionally managing to peep inside: it was built in a vast rectangle, with a series of toilets installed at the far end, rows and rows of wooden benches in the centre, large windows on the sides, the walls beautifully painted in pastel blue at the bottom and cream at the top, and varnished wooden bars making a lovely crisscross pattern under the roof.

It was our building, prisoners had built it with great precision and attention to detail, but we were not allowed in it.

A smuggled newspaper informed us that Mr Hoffman of the Red Cross had published a report strongly critical of conditions on the Island, to counteract a misleading statement put out by the regime that he had in fact reported favourably on our treatment.

We were elated, and affectionately began to refer to him as the Geneva Man, even though some months had passed and we could not even remember very well what he looked like.

THIRTY-THREE

Strike One

It was Head Warder Delport who precipitated our first major act of defiance. We had been seething at the constant brutalities and humiliations, near breaking-point on many occasions, and we often speculated about how we could fight back. The head warder not only produced the final impetus, he gave us the form that we needed.

It started quite spontaneously. A common-law prisoner was dishing out the food as normal – while we queued for our helping – laying out the plates and filling them with their portions. We had been waiting patiently in our long queue: Coloured and Indian prisoners in front, African prisoners behind, and all of us were very, very hungry.

The food had arrived late and we watched as he dished up hurriedly to make up for lost time. The rule was that we could take our plates only when all the food had been laid out, one plateful for each prisoner, in long, long rows. He moved down the rows, first filling the plates for the Indian and Coloured prisoners and then working his way through the plates for the African prisoners.

There was not enough, the food ran short. About a hundred plates remained empty, and the prisoner went up to Delport, expecting, as usual, to be sent back to the jail for more. 'Reduce the "F" diets.'

The prisoner was astonished and stood his ground for a while. 'Reduce the "F" diets.'

As the prisoner started scooping back some of the food from the full plates, murmuring began amongst us. Some said, 'Don't take the food, we can't take the food.'

Two prisoners walked up to Delport. 'Sir, we wish to . . .'

'Get back, you either take your food or leave it.'

That remark incensed us and brought us all closer together.

The trusty prisoner held out two plates in his hands, ready to give them to us as we filed past. '*Gaan vat jou kos* – take your food.'

We 'D' diet prisoners in front were ordered to march; our rations had not been affected. We moved forward, came to the outstretched plates – and walked right past. Every single prisoner followed us in the same way – a long, grim file of prisoners, all refusing the proffered food.

As the last prisoner went by, the trusty was still holding the initial two plates in his hands, with the hundreds of others lying unclaimed on the long, rough table.

We sat down in the enclosure, forming little groups, to discuss the position. Many of us said how hungry we were, but all of us were determined not to eat. 'It's your bloody business if you don't want to eat,' Delport shouted. 'I don't care a damn, but you'll still do my work.'

'This is it,' we began to say. 'We must keep it up.'

We felt that we had started something that we just had to continue, but there was also fear of what the repercussions might be; the reaction from the authorities, and concern about how we would be able to get word to the outside world.

We knew the authorities would completely seal off the Island,

and we knew of baton charges and of mass assaults. Would they react in the same way? We had heard of force feeding in British jails, and of prisoners dying as a result. We were also greatly worried about whether we could rely on the PAC prisoners to stand with us and, finally, of the physical limitations of a hunger strike. How long could we stand it?

The general view was that, come what may, we had to take a stand sooner or later, and this was the time. Our political feeling far outweighed our personal reservations and we prisoners in for ANC activities decided firmly to lead the hunger strike from then on. (In future I will refer to ANC or ANC prisoners to mean prisoners convicted of taking part in ANC activities.)

At two o'clock, Head Warder Delport arrived and, totally unconcerned, barked that this was our last chance to eat, and if we didn't want our food that was our business, we could get on with our work.

We assembled to return to work in absolute silence; the plates remained on the table; the food on them cold. When we recommenced chopping stones, the pace did not slacken at all.

Delport and the other warders walked up and down, telling us all the time that it was our stomachs, not theirs, that were going short; that they knew that kaffirs and coolies really only wanted a full stomach and nothing else.

Just before four o'clock, Delport again approached us to take our meals but we simply carried on working, and when he came to measure our piles of stones at four o'clock, he was able to take the tickets of only a few of us.

On the way back to the prison we spoke once again about the hunger strike and managed hurried consultations between ANC, PAC and other prisoners. ANC people in whom we had special confidence instructed a number of us to move to the front line so that, on arrival at the prison, we would be among the first to be stripped and searched and, therefore, be the first to take our places

155

in front of the evening meal queue.

There were suddenly other prisoners, from other *spans*, inside the yard eating when we arrived, and they looked up, astonished, as, moving forward in twos, we walked straight past the kitchen window without collecting our meals. Some clearly felt guilty, others began throwing their food away.

The authorities ignored them and ignored us, but junior warders walking between us started passing rude remarks, Warder Meintjies, being one of the most vocal, jeering at us that we would get nowhere, we were simply being stupid, we were the ones who were suffering, not them. He told us, 'As far as we are concerned you are doing us a great favour because the Prison Department will be saving food, so we won't have to use up so much of the white man's taxes.'

Those of us with tobacco smoked more than usual in the cell that evening, which in itself became a point of dispute because some felt that we should cut out smoking as part of our strike. But the majority view was that, since we were smoking illegally and the tobacco had not come directly from the authorities, we could carry on. Lots of us laughed at ourselves at the ridiculousness of taking action against the authorities by depriving ourselves of food.

Then, just before the eight o'clock silence bell, the comrades in our cell gathered in a corner and we started singing freedom songs. We could hear similar singing throughout the rest of the jail. The hunger strike was on, and we were determined to see it through.

The next day, Friday, the authorities opened each cell individually and made us file in separate sections past the breakfast food. We formed our little queues, moved forward, and again refused to take anything – everybody, the entire jail, even those who had eaten the previous night, walked past.

That morning we worked in the quarry as normal. At lunchtime the food was already there waiting, no delay this time, the plates piled high with mealies, beans and mealie rice, looking tasty and covered with appetising fat. We had never seen such food on the Island. We filed past once again, unwavering in our decision.

To our astonishment we saw about twenty-five PAC prisoners, under the leadership of Selby Ngendane, a member of the national executive, stopping at the table to pick up their plates. They comprised one of the many factions amongst the PAC prisoners and were commonly referred to by their colleagues as the 'Katangese',* because of their separatism. The group sat eating on their own and when someone asked why they were breaking unity they declared emphatically that they absolutely refused to take part in a hunger strike 'engineered, planned and dominated by the communists'.

Work proceeded as normal. We had got word out that everyone must work as though nothing special was happening and that, at all costs, we must refuse to be provoked by the warders, even if we were insulted or called '*kaffir*', '*boesman*' or '*koelie*'. We had to exercise the utmost self-restraint, that was the instruction. However much we might be pulled and pushed about, we had to discipline ourselves and not react in any way.

The warders were agitated. They walked tensely around with batons in their hands, looking for the first opportunity to assault us and cause confusion, but the comrades were magnificent in their restraint. We continued to produce the full quantity of work required, some working with the big hammers, singing work songs, others pulling huge rocks with ropes, pushing wheelbarrows loaded with stones or sand, or working with pick and shovel, while the great majority of us just chopped stones as normal. At that stage every single political prisoner, with the exception only of those in the isolation and Swapo sections, was in the quarry. We sang to ourselves, talked and laughed; nervous, but in high

---

*Upon Zairean independence in 1960, the mineral-rich province of Katanga seceded and proclaimed itself a republic.

spirits, wondering all the time what would happen.

We issued a further instruction: the sick and very old should take food, which included about twenty comrades with suspected TB, severe asthma or epilepsy, and one comrade mentally disturbed. All of them except one turned it down. An old comrade suffering from asthma spoke for them. He said that if the rest of us could go on hunger strike, so could they. He wanted to know how long we intended to keep it up – we could not answer – and insisted that they, too, were part of the campaign for improvements, and in the end we managed to impose our decision only on one comrade, a very sick man suffering from a number of complaints, and then only after tremendous pressure.

That evening our plates had a number of vegetables, the porridge was steaming hot and looked mouth-watering, the soup was thick, and we could see bits of vegetable in it. The twenty-five 'Katangese' took their portions and were sent to a cell on their own, and our unfortunate comrade was placed with them. Once more we just walked past. Nobody broke ranks.

After locking-up time, we sat in little groups in our cells singing songs, mostly freedom songs, and giving the impression that our hunger had disappeared; only water passed our lips. Some of the comrades started cracking jokes: 'It's OK for us guys, we'll soon be out and eating roast chicken, it's you chaps we're worried about, how many years can you keep it up?'

'Don't worry about us, we'll also be out soon.'

None of us had the slightest doubt that we would be liberated before our sentences were over.

Then the news came through that the comrades in the isolation section, led by Nelson Mandela, as well as those in the Namibian section, had joined the strike. We were thrilled, and sang with even more intensity than usual.

Saturday morning was the same procedure, with all of us walking past the baking hot porridge, the rich, thick soup, and the steaming coffee on the breakfast table.

At lunchtime there was a variation: instead of all filing out together we were taken out, cell by cell, in small groups, past food more delicious-looking than ever: piping hot, attractively dished up, even with scraps of meat in the bean stew. There was no doubt about it, the best food we ever had on Robben Island was the food we never ate.

In the afternoon there were more warders than usual, many of them armed, and we could see FN rifles at the ready on each of the concrete towers. The warders were extremely provocative to us, even ruder than normal, pushing us around incessantly and calling us every name under the sun; but still we filed past the food, still we maintained our self-control, and still we refused to eat.

The next morning, as we were preparing for inspection, the whole prison in an extremely tense state, our sick comrade suddenly rushed over to us.

'Please, please,' he begged, 'let me join you. It's hell with those guys, they actually enjoy the eating. I can't bear being with them a minute longer, they never stop passing terrible comments: communist this and communist that.'

We had a quick consultation.

'Comrade, you must be brave,' we told him firmly. 'You are too ill to go without food. We don't want your death on our consciences; you must live, you must live to see freedom. Go back to the cell; and take your food; we're sorry to force you to do this, but it's the only way.'

Sadly he went back to the cell, and we felt really rotten about what we had done, even though we knew we had been correct.

No one came for the usual Sunday inspection that day – we were in fact even tidier than usual – but at about 10.30 a.m., time for lunch on Sundays, we saw the kitchen staff prisoners running rapidly towards the cells, carrying large wooden trays. A lieutenant walked into our cell, looked around, and then shouted, ' "B" diets, come out!'

Nobody stepped out, but we were amused at suddenly having

been promoted to 'B' diet.

' "B" diets, step out!' he repeated.

When no one moved he ordered the Indian and Coloured prisoners to lead the way and, outside, we saw food really spectacular by Robben Island standards: mealie rice soaked with fat, carrots, cabbage and tomatoes – which we had never seen before – cooked in meat gravy.

' "B" diets, *vat jou kos* – take your food.'

It was so childish, we laughed inside, but gravely we walked forward, looked at the plates, and filed back into the cell, the plates uncollected.

That evening many of us began to complain of feeling weak. The singing and the joking continued, but the question was, how long would we be able to carry on. We were also wondering if the outside world knew about us. Visits and letters had been stopped and we felt particularly isolated and abandoned.

On Monday, the fifth day, when we assembled to go to work we could feel our strength failing. We hardly said a word, we were more serious and when we marched to the quarry our pace was slow. The warders noticed that and passed comments, but did not really force us to speed up; even Delport, usually the loudest voice of all, was quiet.

The journey across the Island, normally one of half an hour, lasted almost an hour and at the quarry, in spite of instructions to work normally, we worked very slowly, probably producing less than a quarter of our normal quota. Delport, however, was spending the whole day out of sight in his little office, and the junior warders did not push us as they walked up and down, although they continued to throw insults and abuse.

Lunch came; no one took it.

During the hours of work, as we slowly raised our hammers and lolled over our stones, we discussed whether it was correct to continue the hunger strike and, if so, for how long. Until death? And how would the world know?

160

On our painfully slow march back to jail we saw the chief warder arriving in his little panel van. He rushed at the prisoners, picked out about a dozen at random, threw them into the van, and drove them off to isolation.

We refused supper.

On the sixth day our progress to the quarry was even slower, we shuffled along at a snail's pace, and when a number of prisoners collapsed they were picked up by the authorities and driven to the isolation block for refusing work.

In the quarry we sat listlessly in groups, totally without energy, hardly pretending to work. Some of us keeled over and the warders piled us on to wheelbarrows, three or four at a time, and pushed us up to the isolation cells, letting the barrows hurtle down a steep slope on the way and laughing uproariously as they saw the bodies tumble off. That was the only sound to be heard: laughter, and clanging metal; we were totally silent.

Our discussions became very serious: some felt that the authorities would let us go on endlessly, that the outside world knew nothing, otherwise by now world pressure would have had its effect, but by far the majority of us were in favour of continuing. For many, hunger had disappeared and we felt that we could go on indefinitely; we recalled the long periods endured by martyrs such as Mahatma Gandhi, as well as the hunger strikes successfully conducted by our comrades in the white women's prison after the Sharpeville massacre a few years earlier. We felt that, whatever the consequences, we could not give up.

After lunch, the number of prisoners collapsing increased and, with the sun blazing over our heads, there was an uneasy feeling that many of us had reached the end, we were all very, very weak.

It was about two-thirty or three o'clock when we saw the officials' truck in the distance, coming towards us. A stone-cold silence fell over the whole quarry and we all turned to watch it approaching. Was it coming to us or was it going to by-pass the quarry? Many of us were certain that it was coming to us, which could have only one meaning: they were coming to negotiate. We had won.

But what if the truck drove past? What if we were making a mistake?

Closer and closer it came, and it pulled up right next to us. Major Kellerman, then deputy head of the prison, climbed out and stood angrily in front of us, looking as large and powerful as a granite rock; his staff stick under his arm, determination written all over his face. There was heavy tension in the air.

'I don't care two hoots if you eat or not.' His tone was very arrogant. 'It is your stomachs that are going hungry and you won't achieve anything by your stupid action.'

Then suddenly his voice changed. 'Well, what are your complaints?'

The words were hardly said when he was blasted with complaints from all sides; we began to speak loudly, almost all at once. 'We demand the immediate end of assaults.' There was a great buzz, everyone spoke at the top of his voice. 'We demand more civil treatment.' . . . 'We demand to be recognised as political prisoners.' We were all standing around him and shouting. 'We demand that every prisoner receives a copy of prison regulations.' . . . 'We demand that we be given better and warmer clothing.'

One of our comrades was sitting on a large pile of stones, yelling, his arms gesticulating. 'We, too, are human beings, we, too, have feelings, we, too, have families. The people of South Africa are with us, the whole world is with us.'

It was impossible for Kellerman to maintain his arrogance in the face of our strength, and he put up his hands. 'All right, all right, you elect three or four people and let's have a proper discussion.'

Within minutes we had nominated six prisoners to represent us and they marched off with Kellerman to Delport's office. We waited expectantly for their return, wondering what was going on inside the office, why it was taking so excruciatingly long.

When they came out, about three-quarters of an hour later, we could see victory on their faces. 'Gentlemen,' they said, 'we have agreed to call off the hunger strike. Major Kellerman has undertaken to investigate all our complaints. All those in favour?'

Our hands shot up, we had renewed energy, we were unanimous in our acceptance, overjoyed.

That night we could not manage all our supper. The plates were piled high, higher than they had ever been, but the hunger strike had left us weak and our stomachs were unaccustomed to food.

For the next few days the food remained good. The number of assaults fell, and the warders' attitude to us was better, but something that worried us a lot was that we were unable to communicate with our comrades in the isolation section or with our Namibian comrades who were still carrying on their hunger strike, refusing to believe the warders when they said that our strike was over. We learned that when Nelson Mandela was asked how he could take part in a strike when he did not even know what it was about, he had replied, 'Don't ask me. Ask the prisoners who started the action.' But now we had finished, and he was still carrying on.

Even the prisoners in the special punishment cells were still refusing to eat, each sitting on his own all day with plates of uneaten food piling up at his side.

Finally, all those prisoners were persuaded that the strike had indeed ended, and the first large scale hunger strike on the Island was over. How permanent would be the gains, we did not know. But whatever the authorities did to us, they could never take away our sense of victory or our sense of power.

Some time later the so-called ringleaders of the strike were in fact each sentenced by a visiting magistrate to six months' extra imprisonment, and the food gradually returned to normal, so that once more we could barely eat it. Yet somehow the atmosphere on the Island was never exactly the same as it had been before.

THIRTY-FOUR

Stars

We were surprised one day when the commanding officer came
to the quarry and asked us if we wished to see a film. Surprised?
No, we were astounded, and said absolutely nothing. He repeated
the question and asked us if we had lost our tongues. A few
prisoners replied meekly, 'Yes, we would like to see a film', and
he then told us that at eight o'clock that evening we would all be
taken to the hall to see a film.

On the way back from the quarry we debated whether the film
show would take place, wondering whether it was one of their
tactics to try to demoralise us. Many of us did not believe that we
would see a show that evening and, when we were locked up at
five o'clock in our cells, the discussion was quite animated. We
felt anxious because the usual routine had been interrupted and
we did not know whether to make up our bedding as usual. We
went nervously to have a wash, and we tried to smarten ourselves
up, straighten our clothing and smooth our hair, but still we
laughed at ourselves and said we were wasting our time, there
would be no movie that night.

Just before eight o'clock, the warders came and we saw

prisoners filing out of the other cells in twos. It was the first time in four years that we had been outside at night, under the moon and the stars, and we were beside ourselves, looking up continually as we crossed to the hall, enjoying the night air, enjoying the darkness, enjoying the thrill of seeing the stars, really seeing them, not as littls specks barely visible through barred windows, but as a beautiful pattern directly overhead.

Commanding Officer Kellerman stood at the entrance to the hall with two men we had never seen before, and as the prisoners filed past he spoke to us in an unusually polite manner.

'Hello, Naidoo,' he said to me. 'How are you?'

I was taken aback, but replied that I was well, thank you. Then he asked Sonny Singh, who was next to me, how his head was after treatment for a skull fracture. Sonny replied that it was much better, thank you. The major explained to his two companions that prisoners got medical treatment on the mainland. He was putting on a good show.

We saw a big Western movie; it was terrible, and we loved it. We were a lively audience, responding enthusiastically and noisily to the action. We lit up our *zolls* and the warders tried to stop us from smoking, saying that, even outside, people were no longer allowed to smoke in the cinema – we simply did not believe such a ridiculous story. We carried on smoking. The warders were visibly unhappy, they did not like to see us watching a show, they liked even less to see us sitting comfortably with our legs crossed and enjoying a smoke.

Halfway through the show Kellerman addressed us. He said that we would be allowed to play sports such as soccer, cricket, tennis and table tennis, that we should elect a committee of five to liaise between the prisoners and the authorities, and submit signed minutes of all meetings to the authorities.

We could not believe our ears.

On the way out, the commanding officer asked us if we had enjoyed the show and bade us good night, and the warders suggested that we should 'stand nicely and walk well, chaps'.

We talked for hours amongst ourselves about that rubbishy film, recalling other films we had seen with the same actors, re-telling the story and discussing the incidents over and over again.

The following day we were introduced to the two visitors for the first time; they told us that they were from the Red Cross in Geneva. I was among the first group that saw the Geneva Men and we raised with them all our complaints about food, clothing, work, visits, medical treatment . . . everything.

They said that they knew this was the first film that we had seen and they told us that the projector had been donated by the Dutch Reformed Church of South Africa, and that only two other prisons in the country had projectors. They added that they were trying to negotiate to come at least once a year and would make certain recommendations to the authorities, but that their powers were limited. We found them sensitive to the realities of our situation.

THIRTY-FIVE

The Major

Major Kellerman noticed us all looking out to sea and saw what we were staring at: a large injured seal, a real giant, sitting on a rock about two hundred metres away. He climbed up the observation tower and took the warder's FN rifle. We saw him taking aim for a long time before he finally shot. The seal fell dead.

About twenty of us ran out to pull it in, and we noticed that the bullet hole was right in the centre of the forehead. The warders came up, and in their subservient way congratulated the major on his fine effort.

Kellerman asked us who knew how to skin a seal. Immediately my hand went up. I looked around and to my consternation saw only the hand of comrade Dip, who clearly had the same idea as I. Anyhow, we were able to select about six prisoners and Kellerman, who had groaned when he had seen my hand go up because he and I were always clashing, warned us not to damage the skin which was very valuable.

I was really worried, never having skinned a seal, or any animal, before, but we put our heads together and decided that the only thing to do was to slit the seal down the middle. Cutting a dead seal open was far less strenuous than working in the quarry, and we were amazed to see the amount of fat and meat inside one animal. Fortunately, we were able to get the skin off with hardly any damage, and we took the fat and the meat for ourselves. The fat we boiled down in one of the 44-gallon drums; and for months in the cold winter we were able to smear it on our exposed skins to help us keep warm. We also boiled a portion of the meat in sea water and cut it into chunks for the prisoners, feeding the whole quarry – all eight hundred men – and still having plenty over to take with us to the jail and give to those who had worked elsewhere. The next day we boiled more and fed everyone all over again, but by the third day the meat was too putrid, and we threw it into the sea.

'Gentlemen, gentlemen, a hearing, please!' That was the normal way of making announcements in the lunch hall. Prisoners carried on eating and talking; they were a little tired of trivial announcements, such as: 'Gentlemen, gentlemen, please; have you seen my spoon?'

'Gentlemen, gentlemen please!' Zola Ngingi, our comrade, stood on a bench, clapped his hands for attention, and started talking. He was a quiet person, serious, and got an immediate hearing. 'I call for nominations for the Prisoners Recreation Committee.'

The PAC chaps were taken aback. It was their own fault; after the major's announcement we had suggested a general meeting to elect two representatives from the ANC prisoners, two from the PAC, and one from the 'others', but the PAC men had refused, telling us to wait. We had waited – one, two, three, four weeks, and still no answer.

People jumped up to make nominations. Two ANC prisoners had their names suggested and agreed to be candidates. Someone put forward the name of a PAC prisoner. He refused. One 'other' was nominated – he accepted.

As the PAC people refused one after the other, the meeting became a bit noisy, and a senior warder climbed on to the bench and shouted, 'Can't you people even organise a meeting properly? I'm now taking over the chair.' There they stood on the bench, Zola on one side and the warder on the other, taking nominations. In the end one PAC man, Anthony Suze, accepted – or, rather, he did not decline – and was declared elected by the warder.

The result was: three ANC representatives, one PAC, and one 'other'. But the following day Suze apologised and told us that he would have to resign, so we added another name and submitted the list to the authorities.

In spite of their ignorance, the warders never doubted for a moment that they were totally superior to us. They would tell us that we might be lawyers, or Nelson Mandela, or have a BA degree, but we were still kaffirs, and a kaffir was a kaffir, and that was all.

Nearly all the warders had been given nicknames by the prisoners, partly so that if we spoke about them they would not know who we were referring to. Cofimvaba, one of Aucamp's men on the Island, got his name from a little village in the Transkei where he had once lived but he got to know his nickname and used to love walking up and down saying, 'Yes, Cofimvaba is here, shut up, Cofimvaba is here.'

He was an eccentric fellow, detested not only by us but by many of the warders as well because he pushed and bullied everybody and never had a decent way of speaking to anyone, not even to his superiors. He was completely preoccupied with himself, as though he alone knew how to do things properly. He never walked, he always rushed along at near running speed, and instead of sending more junior warders to grab or shout at a prisoner, he would move across, however far it was, to do the job himself.

The staff stick that he carried in the early years of our stay on the Island never lasted more than a month. He would hit out at prisoners anywhere and if a prisoner attempted to complain or lay a charge against him he would get in a charge first, saying that the prisoner had assaulted him, and he could always count on half a dozen warders to confirm his story. Later, when the staff sticks were taken away, he would often get the political prisoners to come into his office and then assault them with anything that happened to be lying around.

Cofimvaba hated my guts; whenever he saw me he would flare up and shout and, most of the time, whatever I asked for he would automatically refuse. In fact, he, Kellerman and Delport had been the major figures in the trial that had led to my whipping.

Once, when about twenty political prisoners were locked up in isolation, Cofimvaba personally led a group of fifteen to twenty warders who went from cell to cell at midnight, ordering each prisoner to strip and then beating the hell out of them one by one with batons. Our protests came to nothing, even though one of the prisoners was a hunchback with TB of the spine.

Cofimvaba never hesitated to beat up prisoners; even after instructions had been given not to assault prisoners, he just carried on beating us up in private. He was so full of himself that even the warders suffered at times. One young warder brought one of our comrades to Cofimvaba saying that the prisoner refused to call him *baas*.

'What's your name?' Cofimvaba asked.

'Van der Merwe.'

'Oh, your name is Van der Merwe, your name isn't *Baas*?'

'No.'

'Then why the hell should he call you *Baas*? Get out of here, get out of my office.'

The comrade started smiling.

'And what the hell are you laughing at? Get out, get out.'

Film shows always started and stopped at the will of the Prison Department. We could not select our films, having to make do

170

with showings of films that were already being brought to the Island for the warders; more than that, we had to pay half the cost, which could have been one of the reasons why we got films at all.

At first we got commercial films, but then pro-apartheid propaganda began to arrive, and we were really in a spot! Many comrades felt that, as a matter of principle, we should refuse to watch them, while others argued that any contact with the reality of the outside world was important. Just to keep in our heads the images of our country was important – its landscape, its houses and trees and roads and people, but, more important still, we had to keep in touch with the way the enemy was directing his propaganda. This was in fact exactly the same argument we used to have about propaganda literature – we were allowed to read *Bantu, Inkubela* (Homeland), *Fiat Lux* from the Indian Affairs department, and *Alpha* from the Coloured Affairs Department, and the majority felt that we were sufficiently mature politically to read this rubbish without being corrupted by it.

In the end we did not have to take a final decision on whether or not to boycott the films, since the authorities stopped forcing them on us. Perhaps they were anxious to get our contributions to the films that they were hiring for themselves, we never knew.

Sometimes, especially on a lovely summer's day while we were pushing barrows through the sand or chopping stones, we would see something moving around in the water, and all of a sudden we would notice water shooting up – and there would be a whale. We saw whole schools of whales playing this way and that, as well as porpoises and dolphins jumping and sporting. We loved watching them, it was a change of scene, something free and playful; a little happening that made an enormous impression on us.

THIRTY-SIX

Rumbles

There was almost complete silence all around, and opposite me came the regular breathing of a comrade fast asleep after a heavy day's work in the quarry. It was all quiet after the eight o'clock bell. Some comrades were under their blankets, some were studying hard for the approaching exams, while I was sitting on my bedding, leaning against the wall, totally absorbed in the revolution that was unfolding in Jack London's *Iron Heel*.

From far, far away, far in the distance – seemingly from hundreds of miles – came a strange roar. I had never heard anything like it before, it seemed to be advancing very rapidly from the mainland and getting louder and louder and closer and closer.

I had hardly put my book down to listen when the sound was right on top of us and the whole cell shook. It was as if a giant was standing outside, busily shaking the whole building; the bells that were hanging in the courtyard started ringing wildly, and in the cell itself pandemonium broke loose.

Prisoners jumped up; some started screaming, others ran towards the door, some ran to the bathroom. My immediate reaction was that there had been an explosion in the boiler at the nearby kitchen. I jumped up quickly to look out of the window to see what had happened, but the noise had started fading away towards the sea and was becoming quieter and quieter as it receded.

The jail was buzzing. We could hear people talking in the other cells. Someone said it was an earthquake, and most of us accepted that. I ran to collect a geography book from those studying the subject and opened it at the section on earthquakes, but before I could read anything the same strange sound started again from the mainland side.

When it hit us for the second time there was chaos. Prisoners screamed loudly, some jumped on to the broad windowsill and hung on to the bars, calling out frantically to be released, while others dashed to the door, trying desperately to pull it open with their hands. Naked bodies ran past, some with blankets hastily pulled around them. I sat waiting, alert to see if there were any cracks in the wall or ceiling through which we could escape; people around me were crying.

The second wave of sound and trembling was much milder than the first and once again passed rapidly out to sea.

We were all very restless, waiting to see what would come next. Someone started a rumour that giant tidal waves often followed earthquakes, completely submerging islands in their path, and we started discussing what we should do if that were to happen, or what we would do if the ceiling collapsed on us – it was solid concrete; the walls were thick, the doors were made of steel with double-locks with an extra massive iron grille inside, and the bars in the windows were nearly three centimetres thick; we felt totally trapped.

I looked in front of me and saw my comrade lying there, still fast asleep. Some of us started laughing, and soon nearly everyone was laughing and teasing each other, especially those who had run to the door and windows, asking what they had expected to do.

173

My comrade woke up and wanted to know what was going on, what time it was, what had happened. We were so amused that we began to laugh uproariously, uncontrollably, which puzzled him even more.

THIRTY-SEVEN

Five stars

Helen Suzman, at that time the solitary member of the Progressive Party in the whites-only Parliament, came to visit us in the company of other MPs. The visit was disappointing because we didn't seem to get through to her. We would raise matters, in a lengthy discussion, and she would say, 'But this is prison, it's not a five-star hotel, you know.'

We felt let down, knowing that she had made a stand in Parliament on our behalf; however, when the smuggled newspaper of the next day arrived we saw the headline with delight: ' "Grim, Grey and Dead Place", says Helen Suzman.'

The minute smoking was made legal, a number of the heaviest smokers gave it up and, in fact, became the most vocal in the campaign to curb the rest of us. The first legal smokes came on my birthday – which, incidentally, was also the day on which Swapo launched the armed struggle – and soon we would find as many as half the cell lighting up at the same moment, especially when the eight o'clock bell went at night. Those of us who had money from our families would buy our full quota of cigarettes and pipe tobacco and share it with those who had nothing. Between us we commanded a big majority and were always able to vote down resolutions aimed at controlling our smoking, so that in the evenings the cell would be filled with heavy tobacco fumes which would only slowly disperse through the bars as we slept.

We decided to campaign energetically on the issue of our defencelessness against earthquakes. We raised the matter with the visiting officer, then with the commanding officer, and then we demanded a letter to the Commissioner of Prisons, stressing how vulnerable we were in the face of natural disasters, asking to be moved to the mainland. We wrote letters and petitions on every occasion. It was one of our most deeply felt petitions. We never forgot that earthquake, for that is what it had been.

The Xhosa word *nyakima,* meaning 'earthquake', was a household word among us. Anything forceful became '*nyakima*', and later when we were allowed to play football and someone made a powerful shot at goal we all shouted '*Nyakima! Nyakima!*'

One comrade from Swapo, who had been shot in the leg in one of the first battles to liberate Namibia and whose wound had not been properly treated, arrived on the Island with his leg amputated. The authorities made him a stump: a heavy, crudely fitting piece of wood that lifted his whole body to one side and made walking so uncomfortable that he managed better with crutches. The Red Cross fought on his behalf and after a long battle succeeded in getting the authorities to allow him to have a proper artificial leg fitted.

One day a cook came to me in the quarry to say that a newly arrived comrade, Michael Dingake, was asking for me. We had already heard about his sentence, and on returning to jail, after collecting my food, I walked past the group with whom I normally ate and shouted in a loud voice for all to hear, 'Michael Dingake!'

Everyone was shocked to see me behaving like one of the warders or one of the *agterryers* (trusties), but Michael flung up his arm.

'Here I am,' he shouted.

We rushed towards each other and embraced. We had no more than ten minutes alone but within that short time he packed in a lot of personal information. We planned to meet again the next day, but he was taken off and placed with the leaders in the isolation section. We never had a real chance to speak again.

So little happened on the Island or, rather, so little happened that we were allowed to write about, that finding something to say was quite difficult and we never got much pleasure from writing. We wanted the contact, but with hardly anything to communicate we would throw it away and destroy our few painfully put together thoughts.

It was not very often that the Commissioner of Prisons, Brigadier Steyn, came to the Island and when he did he did not always see us. We found him uninterested in our situation, always very arrogant towards us, always telling us to be more grateful to the Prison Department for what it was doing for us. 'Outside you used to eat *pap* (maize),' he would tell us. 'Now you are getting real food; outside you used to sleep like tramps in water pipes, here you have blankets; it is not a five-star hotel, you know.'

When new prisoners came in we used to gather round them at night in our cells and get as much news out of them as possible. That was really the best news we could ever get because it gave us inside information on the activities and whereabouts of our comrades – some inside the country, others in exile. So we managed to keep relatively well informed about our struggle and also about our comrades: who had married, who had died, who had got divorced, who was in prison.

We were particularly encouraged by the news we got of the work being done in the outside world by various anti-apartheid bodies who were keeping the world informed about our conditions on Robben Island. Many names became familiar to us: Canon Collins of the Defence and Aid Fund, E S Reddy of the UN Unit on Apartheid, Leslie Harriman of the UN Special Committee, Ethel de Keyser and Abdul Minty of the British Anti-Apartheid Movement, and others; these were household names to us, if you can use that term in a prison.

Our morale was greatly boosted to know that we were not being forgotten; that the names of our leaders, like comrades Nelson Mandela, Walter Sisulu, Govan Mbeki and Ahmed Kathrada, as well as comrade Toivo Ja Toivo of Swapo, were known and honoured throughout the world.

Many of us lesser-known prisoners learned that we had been specially adopted by groups of Amnesty International, and although in itself that did little to bring about an end to apartheid, it was a great morale-booster for each one of us who was adopted.

We were also particularly pleased to hear about the interest which the World Council of Churches and international trade-union bodies were taking in our struggle, particularly in calling for an end to investment in South Africa.

THIRTY-EIGHT

Warder Smith

The few common-law prisoners who did odd jobs on the Island would run after Head Warder Delport, polishing his shoes and calling him *baas*. They would be on their knees pleading with him to let them do him services and he would carry on with his work, ignoring them or kicking them away, or ordering them to take off his shoes and kiss his feet, which they would do.

He never succeeded in getting a political prisoner to stoop so low and we noticed that our different behaviour was beginning to have an impact on him. For example, he would say to a common-law prisoner, 'Kaffir, fetch me some coffee', and the prisoner would jump to it, saying 'yes, my *baas*', then run at great speed to the shed and back, saying 'My king, here's your coffee.' Delport would pay no attention to him while he poured out the coffee or while he stood submissively with the flask in his hand, asking if the *baas* would like some more.

In our case, we paid no attention to him when he called us *kaffir*, *koelie*, or *boesman*. He would say, 'Naidoo, go and fetch me my coffee.' I would walk at a normal pace, bring his coffee, pour it out, and leave him without saying a word.

Most of the senior officers had a very low level of education, much lower than that of many of the political prisoners. Gradually we saw changes and an intake of young graduates who were rapidly promoted would be resented by the old-timers who would say, 'I've been in the Department for thirty years and I'm still only a head warder, while this young person is already a colonel.'

It would be a common sight to see someone like Head Warder Jordaan, in his late fifties, always red-nosed and smelling of drink, listening to someone like Major Visser, twenty years younger, calling him *oom* (uncle), but expecting him to stand smartly to attention.

Often the warders came to work with black eyes, or with patches over their eyes, or with their arms in plaster. They fought among themselves all the time and we used to make comparisons: there were ten of us to each one of them and in all the years I can count exactly how many fights we had, exactly five, while they would have five fights a month, at least. Their behaviour as a whole was as low as you could find. They swore, not only at us but at each other, all the time. They stole from each other and carried tales to their superiors. No one knew whom he could trust.

One thing we noticed was that the four decent warders on the Island never got decent jobs or promotion. Warders would do almost anything to become section heads, or to be placed in charge of a *span*, or be made a storekeeper, but to get those positions, they had to inform against other warders and treat the prisoners as badly as possible. The result was that the worst warders got the best positions, and the best warders never moved.

There was absolutely no sense of comradeship among the warders. They would all shout and scream at us, but even that was as much to catch the eye of their superiors as to express their real feelings.

Head Warder Delport knew that a number of us were studying. In fact, he knew us better than any other warder. He would jeer at us, 'You might have a BA, but you'll always be a kaffir [or a coolie, as the case may be].' He was very arrogant about the fact that he was white and we were black so that we would never be his equal. When we used to take study notes to the quarry to read during the lunch hour, he would steal up on us and confiscate them and soon we would see them on the fire.

One of the political prisoners, Donald Matangela, would suddenly drop on to his haunches, put his hand to his ear as though holding a receiver and say in a military voice, 'Come in, come in; receiving you loud and clear. Enemy troops approaching.' If we asked him what he was doing he would get up and walk away without a word, as though we had interrupted a top-security conversation.

He was a young man who, after being sent abroad by the ANC for military training, had deserted camp and returned to South Africa where he had been arrested and sentenced to eight years' jail. When he arrived on the Island some of our comrades were rough with him, convinced that he was an agent sent to spy on them and in fact he admitted under pressure that he was – though that might not have been true.

He was isolated, partly by us and partly as a result of his own strange nature. For example, when we were given dry mealies (maize) to eat, he would finish his dish and then look around for leftovers. If we offered him some of ours he would reject it. Similarly, when we asked the kitchen to give him an extra portion on a special plate, he would turn it down, preferring to collect whatever remained in the other prisoners' dishes and wash it under a tap before eating it. Sometimes he would hoard enough mealies from lunchtime to give himself a second dish at night. Once, when I offered him part of my lunch, he said angrily, 'You want to poison me?' The fear of poisoning was quite common amongst all prisoners, but he carried it to extremes. Donald was physically fit, very tough and with military training, but he was never sent out to the quarry, just kept as a cleaner in the yard. One Saturday when we were all taken back to our cells after lunch Donald remained behind, still eating. We heard dogs barking and a commotion outside. We rushed to the cell windows and saw about ten warders and four dogs setting upon him. Batons rained down all over his head and body and the dogs snapped at him. He moved bravely, trying to shield his head with his arms and calling out, though not crying or pleading, for the warders to stop beating him and for them to call the dogs off. We also started to shout from all the cell windows, 'Stop it, stop it.' But the attack continued for a distance of about two hundred metres to the office.

Later we learned that in the presence of other warders Cofimvaba had beaten him up very badly. When we heard this we all protested strongly and a number of the comrades even went as far as writing letters to Kellerman, demanding an explanation, but Kellerman replied that we were making a false complaint and that in any case the matter was already being investigated.

A few weeks later, Donald Matangela was charged with attempting to assault a warder, Cofimvaba, and sent to solitary confinement for one year. Not long afterwards, still looking fit and strong, he managed to slip out of the jail yard with a team working in the village. Cofimvaba spotted him and rushed up, asking what he was doing there. Donald straightened himself up and said in a firm voice, 'I don't speak to junior officers. Call your commanding officer!' Even Cofimvaba had to laugh, but he put Donald back in a truck with a warder and returned him to the prison.

All was quiet in the examination room while we scratched away at our answers – thirty or forty of us and four or five warders. Suddenly, after about half an hour we would hear a warder storming out shouting, *'Vok dit man* – fuck it, man.' Others would leave more quietly after about an hour. When the results came out we heard on the grapevine that we had fared very well while the warders had almost all failed. Cofimvaba (Lieutenant Naude) used to taunt them: 'The terrorists are doing well, what's the matter with you?' They used to reply that we prisoners were lucky because we had almost nothing to do all day but read, while they really had to work.

Head Warder Duiker, a more mature person who gave the appearance of intelligence and understanding, used to have long discussions with the prisoners in English, which was quite unusual. His work was more specialised: he was in charge of a building team of about twenty to thirty political prisoners. But even he would hit out at us; a tall, tough man weighing about ninety kilograms, he used sticks or whatever else he might have in his hand.

One Saturday afternoon, we were all moving in single file to the kitchen to collect our lunch and he was standing there with a piece of rubber hosepipe in his hand. As we passed him he suddenly struck out at us, one by one, and I happened to be one of his victims. I stopped and demanded an explanation; and his explanation was to give me a few more cracks and tell me to get going.

The following day, when Major Visser came round on inspection, I stood out and made my complaint and showed him a big bump on my head. The major wrote it all down in his Complaints Book and promised to attend to the matter, and on Monday Cofimvaba took more particulars from me, telling me all the time that I was wrong, that such a thing had never been done before, and that I would be sorry.

For a long time I heard nothing but, months later, when my mother came to visit me, she said that she had received no letters from me and asked how I had been treated. I managed to tell her that I had in fact written and that I had been assaulted.

About two months later I was summoned by Cofimvaba, who wanted to know if I had been assaulted and, if so, when. I reminded him and he checked in the Complaints Book, where he found the complaint but, to my surprise, showed me that next to it was written 'Prisoner has decided to drop the matter', with his signature attached. I denied that I had made that decision and a day or two later I was locked up in isolation.

Not long thereafter, a young Cape Town attorney came to see me. He was very sympathetic, took a long statement, and discussed what could be done. I was in favour of bringing an action, but he felt it would be difficult to prove and argued that I had already made my point that we would not tolerate that sort of behaviour. I believe that he was among the first lawyers to visit the Island, which itself was a big gain for us, so I left the matter alone.

Major Visser, by the way, had only been in the Prison Department for six years, having previously been a school principal. He was almost certainly a government supporter, and defended the Prison Department, but he always gave us a hearing and soon became the one to whom we went with our complaints. We had first met him at Leeuwkop Prison where he had been a lieutenant; then he had preceded us to the Island as a major in charge of our studies; eventually he left as a lieutenant-colonel. Later we heard that he had been made responsible for all prison education and was a brigadier at the Pretoria headquarters.

One day a long, sleek plane flew very low over the Island and we all went into a buzz about Concorde, discussing this its test flight, the number of passengers it could carry, its speed, its cost and the problems of getting it launched. We noticed a number of warders listening intently, eager to find out about the plane.

The same thing had happened when the United States aircraft carrier *Roosevelt* had passed the Island on a goodwill visit to Cape Town. There had been a knot of warders eavesdropping on us to find out what was going on. But our biggest audience of all had been when the Americans had first landed on the moon – the warders simply knew nothing, and looked to us for information.

Smith never walked, he always ran and was always grinding his teeth. He used to tell us about his car in Cape Town. One day it would be a Chev, silver-plated, the next a gold-plated Lincoln, and so on, and every day his girl friend had a different name, and every day he was getting married to her. Once he told us about his degree from Stellenbosch University, and when we asked him what it was, he said 'BA'. We asked what his subjects were and he said 'Nature Study' – a junior school subject – and afterwards we all called him 'Nature Study'.

He was the only one who did not laugh when I told him my Van der Merwe joke: Van der Merwe had lots of headaches and eventually had a brain operation. The surgeon took out the brain, but then the phone rang. It was the surgeon's girl friend, and he forgot about his patient, and when he looked around he saw that Van der Merwe had gone and the brain was still there. So he put the brain in a fridge, and a year later, when he was walking down Adderley Street in Cape Town, he bumped into Van der Merwe again. 'Hey, Van der Merwe,' he said, 'where did you go? I've still got your brain in my fridge.' Van der Merwe replied, 'Don't worry, man, I've got a job as a warder on Robben Island and I don't need it any more.'

When we told other warders that joke they would come back at us: 'Hey, you terrorists, you're so stupid you'll never defeat us; when you want to throw a hand grenade you take out the pin, count one, two, three, four, five on the fingers on your left hand, then place the grenade between your legs and count six, seven, eight, nine on your right hand . . . BOOM!'

Anyhow, we used to tease Smith, especially when he was bragging about his latest sexual pleasures with his girl friend, changing her name and her personality each day. But the other warders were really nasty to him. We would tease him: 'Smith, no girl will ever look at you,' and he would tell us how big his penis was, but his colleagues would order him about like a dog to fetch something or the other, perhaps a prisoner, and he would look around, startled and then run off at great speed to do what he was told.

We often saw him with black eyes or scratches on his face, and he would tell us that he had got into a scrap with a colleague and beaten the daylights out of him. Smith was small and light, but compact, and we learned from other warders that he was, in fact, a good fighter.

Frequently he would be put on post duty and we would feel especially threatened to see him, and others like him, standing there with rifles. We organised comrades in various cells to write to the commanding officer demanding that Smith and the others be recalled from sentry duty, but in response the authorities warned us that they would charge us all with insulting a member of the staff and with making a 'frivolous complaint' – a common charge. A month or so thereafter, however, he had disappeared from the scene.

Although the Prison Department, after heavy struggles on our part, had reluctantly agreed to our studying, they put every obstacle in our way, especially financial, insisting that our families pay in advance, and not in instalments as we requested.

What helped us a little was an old ruling of the correspondence section of the University of South Africa that prisoners pay a greatly reduced fee; but far more important for us was the support we got from the International Defence and Aid Fund. For many years the Fund, under the guidance of Canon Collins in London, had been sending money to pay for lawyers and help the families of prisoners. Now they came to our aid by paying our study fees. So it was a great shock when one of our smuggled newspapers brought us the news that the Defence and Aid Fund had been banned from operating in South Africa.

The warders boasted to us that we were now finished, that our organisation had been banned, and that we would never get money for studying any more. 'When you were outside,' they told us, 'you slept in gutters, you had nothing, now, because you're prisoners and you had this organisation you were able to study, but that's all finished.'

Fortunately, money kept coming. First NUSAS, the National Union of South African Students, sent funds for our fees and books, but soon they too were forbidden from doing so. However, somehow or other, our families were able to send the necessary cash, we never knew where they got the funds from, and we never asked. Even when the University of South Africa announced that the special concessions to prisoners were being withdrawn, we somehow managed to find the required fees, and we continued to get better exam results than the warders.

THIRTY-NINE

Space trip

Warders lined both sides of the pavement, blocking off curious pedestrians, and we were bustled in our handcuffs between them and into the luxurious foyer of the giant, modern Medical Centre. Miraculously, we were right in the business heart of Cape Town; four of us, requiring medical treatment, amongst the first prisoners to be sent to the mainland.

People who tried to get into the lift were driven away and we were taken up to one of the top floors where we were rushed out of the lift, through an open door, and into the doctor's surgery.

It was like walking into a treasure house. There were magazines and newspapers everywhere and the warders were too embarrassed in front of the nurses to stop us from reading. The nurses were lovely and went out of their way to be pleasant to us, and we smiled when they were around but whenever they left the room the warders would shout at us to stop reading, and our faces became blank. As soon as the nurses returned, smiling at us, we would start smiling and reading again; they even brought extra magazines for us to look at, what a feast, while the warders scowled.

The two big items that filled almost every magazine were Vietnam and the first landing on the moon. We had already heard of the moon-landing through the grapevine but now, for the first time, we were seeing pictures of Neil Armstrong in his space suit. It was marvellous and we could not help thinking that while man was landing on the moon our conditions in prison were still so primitive. The warders glowered as we read every detail and soaked up the words and the pictures.

The nurses and the doctor spoke to us in a friendly way and, through the window of the X-ray room, we could see the greatest marvel of all: a newscast in lights. Our faces lit up. The very latest news was being flashed across a screen on a nearby building and all we had to do was to turn our heads subtly so as not to draw the attention of the warders. Never had patients been so slow in doing what they were asked, so reluctant to be treated. We stalled for time as much as possible, but we eventually ran out of pretexts and found ourselves being taken away again. Our spirits sank as we entered the lift, and the warders became more jovial with each other and arrogant towards us.

When we got downstairs the prison van was not there. The warders did not know what to do, and began to look glum. There we stood, the four of us, in long prison pants, khaki shirts and white jackets, with close-cropped hair and clean-shaven faces, smiling. How beautiful everything looked, just beautiful. The people seemed so well dressed, with such beautiful clothing; beautiful cars moved up and down in a busy, beautiful world. Everything seemed to be on the move, it was just too beautiful and too busy for us to take in properly, but we loved being there. Our eyes darted from one side to another. We were elated and kept drawing each other's attention to the different marvels we were seeing; we just could not stop talking to each other and greeting the people whenever and however we could. And smiling.

The warders stood there, increasingly grim-faced, trying to shut us up with their staring, furious at the delay. It was clear that the passers-by recognised us as being from the Island; how, we did not know. But they stopped and talked about us in loud voices so that we could hear them and feel that we were the centre of attention. Some were even daring enough to come really close to us as a way of indicating their support, and it gave us a good feeling: messengers, drivers, the black working people in general almost universally finding some way of signalling their support for us. But they were not the only ones. Casually dressed white students with long hair; elegant shoppers; even some of the wealthy drivers of huge luxury cars gave us a secret sort of backing. There were a few hostile stares from some of the whites, but not many. For almost an hour we stood in that wonderland of movement, our eyes filled with excitement and our hearts swollen with the support we could feel from all sectors of the people of Cape Town. The warders kept glancing angrily at their watches and looking frantically up and down the street, waiting for the van, and their discomfort and grumbling was an additional pleasure for us.

Eventually, the Black Maria arrived, and our faces began to freeze up, while once more the warders began to smile.

FORTY

Strike Two

We decided to launch another hunger strike. The warders had been entering the isolation cells, sometimes with dogs, and severely beating the prisoners, so the small number of us entitled to buy sugar purchased all we could and slowly created a reserve. Then we declared that we were going to refuse to take any meals until the authorities promised to put a stop to violence against the prisoners. This time the strike went much more easily for us. We took two tablespoons of sugar each day and found that we were maintaining our strength. For one, two, three days the authorities refused to react; four, five, six days. We could have gone on much longer but, eventually, they came to us and after consultations we called the strike off. The assaults stopped immediately and, although conditions generally remained harsh for a long time, we felt that we had gained a great victory.

Occasionally, senior officers of the Prison Department would come to the Island, but we never got anywhere with them, always feeling their hostility and lack of interest. Nevertheless, we took a decision to speak to anyone who came to us, to make our point on every possible occasion, though it took real discipline on our part to meet the commissioner and the others, knowing their hatred of us and knowing how little we could expect from the interviews. We prepared ourselves very carefully whenever we had advance warning, and had a general line ready for surprise visits. In particular, we prepared ourselves not to respond when they reminded us that we were not in a five-star hotel.

We read with great pleasure, in one of the smuggled news reports, that when the South African Commissioner of Prisons had gone to Stockholm to attend an international conference on standard minimum rules for prisoners, there had been strong demonstrations against him. He had not been able to answer questions about Robben Island put to him by journalists who clearly knew more about conditions on the Island than he did, and had generally made quite a fool of himself.

We were tired of stealing stones to supplement our pile, and there were never enough anyway, so we decided that we should all work normally, continuously, the whole day, and produce whatever quantity emerged and no more, even if we lost all our meals.

When Delport came to measure the piles of stones he was amazed to find that every prisoner had in front of him far less than the specified amount. He collected about a hundred prisoners' cards at random, telling the prisoners concerned that they would be deprived of meals for the weekend.

The prisoners decided that they would challenge the deprivation of meals, and use their right to be tried by a visiting magistrate for refusing to work, even though that carried the risk of severe punishment, including corporal punishment and up to twenty-one days on spare diet in solitary confinement.

Eventually, about two dozen of the group found themselves in front of a magistrate from Cape Town, and with the aid of a lawyer succeeded in proving that the quota system was arbitrary and unjust and had no legal basis.

The quota system was dead. Getting a trial was a victory, having a lawyer was a victory, winning the case was a double victory. We specially enjoyed seeing how annoyed the warders got when they observed the lawyers – well dressed and cultivated, obviously people of importance – speaking to us courteously, using words such as 'rights', and generally conversing with us as though we had something useful to say, and were not just ignorant *kaffirs* and *koelies*.

Once when I was in isolation, a newly arrived prisoner passed by with a batch of Swapo comrades and, stopping at my cell, read my name on the door.

'Are you a brother of Shantie Naidoo?' he asked.

'Yes.'

'That's wonderful.'

He introduced himself as comrade Benjamin Ramotse, who had been kidnapped from Botswana by the South African security police and put on trial for organising the return of guerrillas. Shantie had been great at the trial, he said, refusing to give evidence against himself or Winnie Mandela, Joyce Sikakane and others accused of carrying on the underground activities of the ANC. He told me that I could be proud of her and that whenever he had the chance he would try to stop by my cell to pass on further details about her own trial for refusing to give evidence.

The authorities began to give us X-rays and picked up a vast number of TB cases, between fifty and one hundred a year. Those patients were then segregated from the rest of us and received reasonable treatment, usually for a year or two, and as the years went by the number of TB cases dropped quite markedly.

We were given some form of injection every year, but we never found out what it was for, because the authorities never bothered to tell us . . . we simply received it.

As secretary of the Film Society I was able to accompany the films even when the prisoners in the isolation section had their special showings. I looked forward to the trip even more than to seeing the films because it gave me a chance to be with our leaders and pick up their strong spirits.

Comrade Nelson Mandela stood out because of his size, the very way he carried himself: full of confidence, dignified, every inch a leader. Then there was Comrade Walter Sisulu, deep, thoughtful, choosing his words carefully; fatherly, and yet some-how always making the youth aware of the great role they had played and still had to play. Comrades Govan Mbeki and Ahmed Kathrada gave enormous encouragement in their own ways, and Comrade Mac Maharaj was always bursting open, full of energy, among the first to give a welcome, full of good humour.

Unfortunately, however, a separate hall was completed for the isolation prisoners, and they were given totally separate showings, which meant we lost contact again.

FORTY-ONE

The Green Berets

When the prisoners came from the quarry on a Friday they would always look up to see if the hall windows were covered with blankets. If the blankets were there, everyone would come rushing to me in my capacity as secretary of the Film Society – a most ineffective body, by the way – to find out what would be playing the following morning.

We filled the hall with great excitement. The film starred John Wayne, and promised us lots of action and lots of opportunity to cheer and boo. Whatever our tastes might have been outside – where good films were rarely released for black audiences – in that hall we wanted to see action, and lots of it, to have the chance to laugh and shout, to let go after being controlled, controlled, controlled all the time.

There were double blankets all over the windows, and the projectionist stood at the back, next to his big machine, waiting for the lights to go off, his right hand ever ready to come up and censor any scene he might consider undesirable.

The lights were dimmed, and the movie began with lots of

loud music and drama. We read the title as stirring music pounded into our ears: *The Green Berets*.

The film moved along at a good pace, slowing down only for rather feeble scenes of conversation. At one stage we noticed a woman's dress ever so slightly disarranged, and the projectionist's hand shot up; the screen was blacked out and we started shouting, 'Take your hand away. What's happening?', but he ignored us until the scene was over.

At an important stage of the action we saw Vietnamese soldiers and guerrillas taking over a village; they hauled out their flag, ran it up a mast, and as it started flying, we all spontaneously burst out cheering and clapping – every single prisoner in the hall. In the thin light we could see the warders staring at us in amazement.

Later, when we filed out of the hall in our hundreds, buzzing with the action we had seen, we noticed that the warders were still shaking their heads and some told us openly how ignorant we were, that it was a simple film and we did not even know who the *skelms* (villains) were and who the good guys.

Whenever there was an issue of new clothing, whenever the jail was cleaned up and the food improved in quantity and quality, whenever the warders started speaking civilly to us, we knew that the Red Cross was on the way and we felt pleased, even though we knew that the moment the visitors left, conditions would return to the Robben Island 'normal'.

One of the Red Cross visitors once asked us if we thought it worth while their coming, or if nearly all the improvements were taken away as soon as they left.

'Yes,' we answered to both questions, definitely yes. They were our eyes and ears and must keep on coming. They represented some contact with the outside world, with a different set of values; and what was more, even to have two weeks' improvement was an advance, and conditions were slowly becoming a little less brutal.

FORTY-TWO

Joe

We were lined up to go to work when I saw a group of new prisoners; I was shocked to notice among them Joseph Morolong, whom I had known from Congress circles some years before. We had not heard of his arrest and sentence. All we knew was that in the early 1960s he had been banished to a hut in a remote semi-desert area of the Northern Cape.

I snatched a chance to dash to him and give him a quick greeting, and on the following day when he joined us at work, I set about pumping him for news.

Word had filtered in about the time that our soldiers had entered Zimbabwe with the intention of making their way to South Africa, and we were all buzzing about this. We even sang songs to mark the occasion, our spirits were very high and we used to say to each other, 'Umkhonto is coming, Umkhonto is coming.' We were thrilled to have Joe with us to bring us up to date.

'Tell us everything, Joe, everything; how are our boys doing in Zimbabwe?'

'What?' he responded. 'Our boys in Zimbabwe? What are they doing there?'

'Didn't you know? MK soldiers of the Luthuli Brigade are fighting in Zimbabwe on their way down to South Africa.'

He was amazed, he had heard nothing. So we also told him what we knew about the war in Vietnam, about the struggles of Frelimo and MPLA, in Mozambique and Angola, about Swapo, other news from Zimbabwe, and world events in general . . . he could not hear enough. We also told him about comrades outside who had died, who had got married or divorced.

Then it was his turn. He told us about his years totally alone in a hut, restricted to an area of one square kilometre, in which he had been the only human being. Once a week he had been permitted to go to a nearby village to get rations and mail, and after some years he had met and fallen in love with a local schoolteacher. At times he would slip out of his area of banishment to be with her and on one of those occasions he had been caught by the police. When they searched his hut they had found two old copies of *New Age* and *Fighting Talk*, two journals of our movement which had been legal at the time of his banishment but which had been banned thereafter. He had explained to the court that he had kept those papers because he had nothing else to read during all those years, but whenever he had felt particularly isolated he would get them out and read them again.

Joe quickly integrated himself among us. His sentence, for breaking his banishment order and for possession of banned literature, was three years, and we noticed how, in that time, he was putting on weight and becoming increasingly animated. We could see him coming alive; even during the endless smashing of stones in the quarry he radiated new energy, he enjoyed conversations and always had a point of view to contribute; it was a pleasure to have him around.

Then slowly, we noticed his energy beginning to fade away. He started losing weight and became increasingly withdrawn.

'Joe, what's the matter? You've become so silent these days, what's going on?'

'You've got to understand, comrades, soon I'll be released.'

Saying goodbye to comrades always had an element of sadness to it, but we never felt sadder than when we said farewell to Joe, on his way back to banishment.

FORTY-THREE

The Castro way

Suddenly the authorities conducted raids throughout the jail and in our places of work, turning everything upside down. About fifteen or twenty of our people were arbitrarily taken away and locked up in isolation. Among them, I remember, were comrades Steven Tshwete, Ebrahim Ismail and Dwaba.

Warders started abusing and assaulting us, and tension built up in the prison. When we demanded an explanation for this crack-down we were simply told, 'You know why.' Later, we were informed that the authorities were claiming that they had found knives, axes and other dangerous weapons that we had made illegally in our place of work with the idea of the ANC and the PAC using them against each other.

That came as a tremendous shock to us. We vehemently denied the allegation, and we even demanded to be shown those so-called weapons that we were supposed to have made. Brigadier Aucamp, who often came to the Island at this time, kept saying that we were planning to attack each other. Then another, rather different story was put around: that we had been planning an attack on the warders. Even when the Red Cross came that year, the authorities kept on with that allegation. In fact, we knew nothing about the weapons and told the Red Cross so, suggesting that they demand to see them. As far as we know, the weapons were never shown, and as far as we were concerned, they had never existed.

Occasionally a judge would come, but generally they were of little use, hardly spending any time with us and not making any real contact. We never heard of any particular results coming from their visits, though there was one English-speaking judge who seemed genuinely concerned. If they did ask us about conditions and we made our complaints, we knew in advance what their reply would be: 'This is not a five-star hotel, you know.'

The new visiting section consisted of about thirty cubicles in which we spoke to our visitors through panes of glass. I was much more fortunate than most of my comrades, many of whom had hardly any visits and some of whom had none at all during the ten years I was in prison, mainly because their families were too poor to afford the long train journey to Cape Town and, occasionally, because their families did not even know their sons had been imprisoned.

For example, one of our comrades who, without telling his parents, had slipped out of the country to receive military training in Ethiopia, had been captured on his return through what was then Rhodesia, handed over to the South African police, and tried and sentenced to twenty-two years, without his family knowing anything of what had happened to him. He tried desperately to get in touch with them by writing, but without success, and the only correspondence he ever received was a tiny Christmas card sent by his sister, which he treasured and kept with him all the time.

More close comrades came in and although we were sad that

they had been captured, we were excited to see them, to give them support, and to pump them for information about the world, about their trials, about the struggle, about the war in Vietnam and the increasing resistance of the American people to it, about the continuing struggles in Angola, Mozambique and Guinea-Bissau, about Zimbabwe and Namibia, about every little corner of our country. How was So-and-so? Who had died? Who had married? Who had children? Who had changed jobs or moved to another town? We interrogated them relentlessly for hours and days on end.

We were allowed to receive photographs, about four each. They were especially precious to us and, like our letters, quickly became 'prisoners' property' and would often circulate for months before we got them back.

Every time a new batch of prisoners arrived I wondered, with some excitement, if my friend Michael Ngubeni would be among them. I had read in a smuggled newspaper of the trial in which he and other comrades, like us, had been led into a trap by a police agent and had been sentenced to twelve years' imprisonment for attempting to blow up a police station.

One day, when I was peeping out of the window at a new batch of prisoners, I saw him there.

'Mike, Mike!' I shouted.

He turned round and waved, and the following morning I managed to work myself next to him at breakfast and pump him for news, first about his own trial and then about our comrade Marius Schoon who had been sentenced with him and sent to Pretoria Prison, where the white political prisoners were kept, then for news of friends and relatives back home. He barely had a chance to eat. After the meal he was separated from us, but two days later we made contact with him again, and this time we filled him in on our experiences and advice on what to expect and how to survive.

When individual prisoners were assaulted, or very sick ones were refused medical treatment, we would campaign on their behalf. We would go *en masse* to the chief warder. Once, there were hundreds of us around Cofimvaba, who kept shouting, 'I'm not scared of you. I'm not scared of you,' as we drove our point home loudly. It was those campaigns that had resulted at last in a number of comrades being sent off to the mainland for medical treatment.

We often demanded that each prisoner be given a complete set of the prison regulations, but never once did we get them. All we received were occasional extracts dealing with such matters as how prisoners should behave and what punishment they could expect if they stepped out of line.

We were coming quietly out of the hall after lunch one day when we saw, through a gate about a hundred metres away, scores of warders armed with batons chasing and beating common-law prisoners. The prisoners were dashing frantically around the yard screaming, dogs were straining on their leashes. We stopped dead still in our tracks and spontaneously started to shout, 'Stop it! Stop it!'

We were terribly agitated by this inhuman conduct and some warders tried to push us away, but we stood our ground and refused to move, even when they threatened to baton us if we did not move. Other warders blocked off the gate with blankets, but the screams continued.

Next day, at inspection time, we moved forward one by one, dozens of us, to complain to the visiting officer about what we had seen. He was very arrogant and told us that it was none of our business, we did not know the circumstances, and we were not the ones who had been beaten up so what were we worried about; he even cut the inspection short.

A few days later, we asked for the opportunity to write to the commanding officer and raised the matter with the chief warder, and the following weekend we made another attempt to complain. Eventually, a promise was made to investigate the matter, though we heard nothing more about it after that.

When the Red Cross visited the Island a few months later, we spontaneously raised the question with the Geneva Man, as the central point of our list of complaints, and the Geneva Man promised to investigate.

We never heard anything directly, but months later the visiting officer complained very crossly to us, asking what we meant by raising matters with the Red Cross that were no concern of ours and getting warders into unnecessary trouble.

From time to time we demanded that we be allowed to make written petitions to the commanding officer and listed our complaints. We were firm in our general position: the petitions must reflect our basic political demand that we be unconditionally released from prison and, pending that, we demanded the status of political prisoners. Only then would we attend to other aspects such as food, clothing, medical attention and recreation.

Getting the official paper on which the petitions had to be written was itself a battle, taking up to six months each time as we struggled on against refusals and constantly being referred to someone else. When we finally got the paper we would appoint a team to draft the petition and present it on our behalf, and sometimes an individual would demand the paper to submit a complaint in his own name as, for example, I did over the handkerchiefs.

Getting a petition sent on to the Commissioner of Prisons or to the Minister was almost impossible. In most cases it would be blocked by the commanding officer, but on three or four occasions we did manage to get past him, and it went all the way to Pretoria.

The most eagerly awaited newcomers to the Island were the

comrades from the first trained batch of ANC guerrillas, the Luthuli Brigade, who had been captured after seeing action in Zimbabwe. We crowded round them, pumping them for every detail of the battles, of their training, and what kind of weapons they had used. Soon we were singing, to the tune of the 'Banana Boat Song':

Take-o, take-o
Take the country – the Castro way.
Take-o, take-o
Take the country – the Castro way.
Give him a bazooka, and a hand grenade-o.
Take the country – the Castro way.

Those comrades did not stand a chance. We wanted to know everything about the external mission of the ANC, what it was doing, how it was organising training for the armed struggle, how many offices it had opened in different countries of the world.

Each of us had special people we wanted to hear about. 'How was Uncle JB?' . . . 'How was Uncle Moses?' . . . 'How was Doc?'

We wanted to hear stories about our acting President, General Oliver Tambo, who epitomised the unity and continuity of our organisation, and to learn about how he and his colleagues were mobilising our forces outside the country. In particular, we loved hearing about the especially eloquent way in which he was always able to express to the world the passions and longings of the people of our country, and proud that we were represented in the councils of the world by such a dignified voice.

More, always we wanted to hear more, about our successes abroad, about the way in which all the different elements in the Congress Alliance were being welded together into a single force, the ANC. We counted off the number of places where the ANC had opened offices: Dar es Salaam, Lusaka, Algiers, Cairo, Addis Ababa, London, Moscow, New Delhi, Stockholm, Havana (there was a rumour that the car licence of our representative there was ANC 1), Toronto. We tried to imagine what each one was like, the many languages, the streets, the people – so different from South Africa. We heard about our youth studying in famous and not-so-famous universities in various parts of the world, training to be doctors, engineers and scientists, ready for the reconstruction after liberation; about publications of the ANC being sold all over the world; about solidarity actions against visiting sports teams and trade missions from South Africa. Few of us had ever left South Africa, but our imaginations and the little bits of information we received gave us a vivid picture of many people in many parts of the world, working in many different ways for a common goal – the end to apartheid and the liberation of our country.

FORTY-FOUR

View

About eight of us were handcuffed together and put in the prison boat for the journey across Table Bay. Fortunately, there were large portholes in the below-deck section and we could see the skyscrapers of Cape Town getting larger and larger as we got nearer.

I was extremely excited – even though I had a bad pain in my chest – to be going to the mainland for an X-ray, looking forward to seeing something of the outside world again. The sea was calm and we had space to move around. We all kept our eyes glued to the portholes waiting to get a look at Cape Town, our excitement mounting as we got closer.

The boat pulled into a special enclosed section of the harbour reserved for the Prison Department and we had our first good view – of common-law prisoners loading and unloading the Prison Department cargo boat, with armed warders standing around everywhere.

We were barely off the boat when we found ourselves sitting in the back of a closed prison van speeding along the highways across the foreshore of Cape Town into the suburbs and out of the city, getting our second view – the sides of the van. There were just two little peepholes at the back and we took it in turns to stand there and stare at the precious world rushing by.

Whoever's turn it was would give a running commentary. 'Hell, there's a beautiful woman there, she's wearing a red skirt, it's so short you can see right up it. There are three of them now.'

Meanwhile the rest of us stared at the walls of the van.

'Oh, what a beautiful highway, four lanes going each way, look at that fantastic Chev, look at that colour, burnt orange, the driver is just as beautiful as the car. Hey, look, there's the University of Cape Town on the right, what a beautiful building.'

We watched our comrade watching the world. 'How do you know it's the University of Cape Town? You've never been there!'

'Of course it's the university. It looks like a university, it can't be anything else ... Hey, there's a poster. The *Cape Times*, it says something about Vietnam ... I can't read it.'

'You bloody fool, an important thing like that and you're looking at girls' legs!'

We made a short stop and had our next view – Pollsmoor Prison. Eventually, when we reached Westlake Chest Hospital, we were rushed out of the van by the warders, who tried desperately to stop us from communicating with the nurses and patients. The X-ray machine looked at us, and we looked at it.

Soon we were speeding our way back again in the prison van, one lucky prisoner only at the peephole. We stopped once – at Roeland Street Prison – but were quickly back at the prison boat, and now we got our first really good view of the day – Robben Island.

FORTY-FIVE

Rangers and Bucks

The Warder placed the ball in the centre of the field and ordered the game to begin. We were not there at the time; we were sitting fuming in our cells and only heard about it afterwards. The two teams of PAC players set about it, kicking the ball lustily, imagining where the touchline would be, imagining the sound of the referee's whistle.

It was not so much that the PAC had actually decided to accept the authorities' offer – one game a week for twenty-two players – but that they had been unable to control their soccer-mad youth. As far as we were concerned – the 'others' were fully in agreement with us on the issue – either every prisoner had the right to recreation, or none should accept, there was to be no breaking ranks.

When the warder felt that the game had gone on long enough he shouted that it was over, picked up the ball and took it back to his office.

The players returned, breathless and excited, trying to tell us about the game, totally insensitive to our feelings.

Eventually we won the right for football for all.

The PAC prisoners continued to boycott the Recreation Committee, even though their one football game had not been followed by others. So the rest of us, ANC prisoners and 'others', decided to go ahead with our plans without them.

At exactly 8 a.m. on a Saturday morning the cream of the ANC football followers ran on to a small field between the Isolation Block and B Section. Wearing blue prison jerseys were Rangers, captained by Comrade Jacob Zuma who was serving ten years; the Bucks were in khaki prison shirts, under the leadership of Comrade Curnick Ndhlovu, who was serving twenty. I was the referee and, after giving the two teams a talk on discipline and fair play, I signalled the game to begin.

Almost all the thousand prisoners on the Island – except those in the Namibian section – were watching. One large group of spectators buzzed with excitement, talking enthusiastically among themselves and speculating on who would be the good players and who had just been the big talkers. They quickly gave affectionate nicknames to the players: *Nyakima* (earthquake) to one of the good strikers, Mau, Guluva, and so on. Those were the ANC and a number of 'other' prisoners.

The PAC prisoners watched silently, making occasional critical comments among themselves, which we could just about pick up; from their point of view, the whole game would be a fiasco because the ANC knew nothing about soccer, were not sincere in putting on the game, and without the PAC would get nowhere. Meanwhile, watching through the bars on the high strip windows in the Isolation Block were the faces of our leaders: Nelson Mandela, Walter Sisulu, Mac Maharaj, Andrew Masondo, and others.

The game started scrappily. Not many of our comrades were soccer players, they were more used to rugby, and even those who had played were unfit and out of training. Some had not touched a soccer ball for ten years, and at first everyone was just running everywhere, kicking the ball wildly without any plan or direction. Some even missed the ball completely and everybody laughed, including me, even though I was the referee.

Comments started coming from the crowd: 'Kick the bloody ball!'

We could hear excited shouting from our comrades in the isolation section: 'Shoot at the goals!' . . . 'Open your eyes, ref!'

Comrade Mac Maharaj's voice was the loudest of all.

'Handball, ref! Open your eyes, ref!'

The remarks from the PAC spectators, especially the younger ones, some of whom had played professional football, were openly hostile. 'What do you know about football?' and, when a player got hurt, 'Take him off the field!'

But gradually the game settled down and became more enjoyable for everybody. Players began to show more control of the ball and to position themselves better, and although there were no really good moves, the prison population clearly began to enjoy the outing. The Bucks were beginning to show superior skill when suddenly a prisoner waved a clock, borrowed from the kitchen, and shouted from the touchline, 'Half time!'

The second half went very smoothly, producing much excitement. Many of the spectators were watching football for the first time and they were beginning to see the value of the game, even though the standard was not very high. There were not many shots at goal, but when there were there was great excitement; in the end the Bucks ended up as the winners, by a small margin. The players came off the field, exhausted. Many had just stood around, out of breath, during much of the match, but our feeling was one of elation because the outing had been a success and had opened up great possibilities for the future.

For the rest of the week the match was the main topic of conversation among the comrades. We talked about the highlights of the game, laughed over the funny bits, but mainly discussed how we could raise the standard of play and improve it as a recreation for everybody. We also argued about how we could get the PAC to stop their boycott.

*

We were not surprised when Anthony Suze came to us and asked if he could put up a team against the Bucks the following Saturday, saying there were just twelve of them ready to break the ice.

When the time for the game arrived I ran on to the field as referee, ready to signal the team on to the field, when suddenly we found twenty-two PAC players already on the ground. I left the field and joined the comrades in the Bucks team, still waiting on the touchline. There was no doubt about it, the game was good, much better than ours had been, but we were not happy about the way it had gone ahead, and felt tricked. After the match Suze apologised to us and said he had not been aware of the second team, but asked us to be patient because the next day the whole PAC would be discussing the matter. As far as he was concerned, there was a group of them that would play soccer, whatever the decision. We told him that, for our part, we would get two of our men to resign from the Football Committee to make way for two PAC prisoners.

The next day we watched the PAC meeting in heated groups. Clearly there was a big struggle going on; at times we could hear raised voices, tempers were beginning to fly; we sat quietly, wondering what the outcome would be. At the end of the day a jubilant Suze informed us unofficially that, after much pushing and threats from him and others, the PAC had decided to play soccer for a trial period.

First, we had eight teams in the Makana Football Association, so named after an African leader of resistance who had died a century before, trying to swim to freedom from the Island. Four of the teams were composed of PAC prisoners and four of ANC and 'other' prisoners, and we had a committee consisting of two PAC prisoners, two ANC, and one 'other'. Shortly after that a Referees' Association, a Constitution Committee and a First Aid Unit were also formed.

The teams began to buy boots, then jerseys – there were some striking colours. A ninth team joined which was made up of a mixture of ANC and PAC people left out of the other teams; although pretty weak players, they were always popular because of their spirit. We were unhappy at the division between ANC and PAC clubs and suggested that our players simply went and joined theirs, and in turn a couple of their players joined ours, and soccer became integrated. Within months we had twenty-six sides in three divisions, and the main problem was getting enough time to put on all the games, as well as getting the conditions improved. We took the organisation of football very seriously, modelling our competitions and administration on international rules.

Soccer was undoubtedly a major talking point in the prison and did a lot to bring the prisoners together, the standard becoming very good and providing great entertainment for all of us. We had league and knock-out competitions and matches between specially selected sides, and the games went on right through the year. As secretary of the MFA, I was commonly referred to by all the prisoners on the Island as Mr Assoc, and from then on that was my name.

Training was vigorous, even though confined to the cells. The players did heavy exercises five days a week; ball control; had intense discussions on tactics and pre-match talks. We often debated whether it was worthwhile doing the exercises on such a poor diet, but we went on with them nevertheless.

A special problem we had was that we used to exercise in the toilet section, and if we blocked off the toilets the other prisoners would complain that they could not perform their functions; if we did not, we had to do our deep breathing under conditions that could only be described as extremely unfavourable.

Choral music was very popular amongst the prisoners, especially when sung in the African languages. Choirs ranged from ten to fifty and they sang, illicitly, in the cells; shutting up when ordered to do so by a warder and then starting up again later that night or the next day. Mostly they sang in several parts and were very good. Sometimes they were sensational, like the group that sang the 'Hallelujah Chorus' one December: fifty beautiful voices resounding illegally through the cell. But to me the most exciting of all were the songs specially composed on the Island, semi-political songs about life in South Africa; I do not sing particularly well myself, but will never forget the loveliness, the sadness and the strength of those special Robben Island songs.

Word got around that one of the books on the students' reading list in the newly opened library had interesting information on Vietnam. So prisoner after prisoner queued up to read it, until the authorities decided that if we were that interested, it had to be subversive and hostile to the cause of the free world, and that was how President Eisenhower's *Mandate for Change* came to be banned.

A tea chest with a stick and a long piece of fishing gut made a good bass. Plastic bags stretched across tins or wooden boxes made reasonable drums, and the wind section consisted of dried seaweed of different sizes and shapes. That was our impoverished band, and although the instruments could not be hidden and were always being destroyed, new ones could always be made and the band kept on playing.

We put shows on at the weekends; everyone had to do something; sing, recite a poem or at least tell a joke. Some of us were very shy and would sit down in confusion when only halfway through a piece, but the audience was always supportive. 'Give him a brush. Give him a brush,' we would shout and rub our hands together as though brushing something. Clapping was illegal. The concerts themselves were illegal and from time to time warders would shout through the window, '*Bly stil* – shut up. Stop this nonsense.' Others, however, would stand and listen for hours.

We were allowed to receive real musical instruments from our families, and before long we had a band consisting of saxophone, trumpet, clarinet, flutes, harmonicas, penny whistles, and many guitars. Some of the players had never owned a musical instrument before, but they learned very quickly and one of our comrades, a professional musician, had a wonderful gift of being able to make lovely sounds within hours from any instrument put into his hands.

Many prisoners took up music seriously, receiving tuition from other prisoners; some even studied theory through the university correspondence courses. We had many composers on the Island and the band would play modern jazz, popular tunes and other pieces composed by their own members.

It was Christmas Eve in the jailhouse, and I had a great success. We were singing and reciting and telling jokes till well after the bell had rung, when I was called upon to present my item. I walked dramatically to the front of the cell, insisted on absolute silence, flung my arms out wide, opened my mouth, gestured energetically and moved my lips as though I were singing – but did not let out a sound. My hands and mouth were constantly in motion, and the prisoners stared at me, amazed, waiting to hear something. After a few minutes I took a deep bow and said, 'Thank you very much, gentlemen, you have just heard "Silent Night".' There was an immediate roar of laughter and I got a big round of brushes.

FORTY-SIX

The play

We were chopping away at the stones, dust flying everywhere, the sun hot overhead, and a group of us talking quietly.

'Hell, man, we had a lovely show last night, it was fantastic.'

'Oh, so that's why all the commotion.'

'Yes, man, Michael Kahtla and company put on a show called "Che".'

'Che?'

'Right, it was fantastic, man, a real tribute to the guy. They showed this group of guerrillas waiting in the bush for a convoy – the convoy approaches – they move forward. But what they don't know is that they are being ambushed themselves. Some got shot and Che lies there and says, "Comrades, move, the struggle continues." They did it beautifully, man, and made wonderful speeches; we gave them lots of brushes!'

We asked if it could be put on in our cell and how many people took part, so that we could switch the numbers in good time, sending the right quota to the actors' cell to make up for their absence. The comrade agreed to ask the actors to come to us in a few days' time.

The play was the talk of the quarry, and even some of the PAC chaps, who had been sitting in their own section of the cell pretending not to be interested, had been captivated by it, in spite of themselves. Their enthusiasm did not surprise us because although their own plays were well acted, they offered so little: pieces like 'Animal Farm', and sketches about suffering and oppression in South Africa, never showing the way forward, never giving them courage to fight, or showing a way out. We used to look at their plays – they had some talented actors and the singing was always beautiful – but in the end we always felt empty. Our own plays inspired us, even if the acting was not of a very high standard: poems by Brecht, plays by Gorky and Chekhov, sketches from our own struggle. They united us, inspired us, made us warm to each other, and part of a struggle for freedom that was worldwide and was winning its own victories.

We selected eight volunteers to replace the expected actors and waited impatiently for the day to arrive for the performance of 'Che'. Two evenings before the scheduled performance, six warders burst into our cell, turned over the blankets, destroyed blackboards, scripts, notes, anything they could find – months and months of work – causing havoc. Through the open door we could see that Michael Kahtla's cell was also being gone over, and the next day our comrade sat next to us in the quarry.

'Sorry, chaps, they destroyed the make-up and the props, there's nothing left. It will have to be put off.'

FORTY-SEVEN

The right to sing

The PAC attitude was that the ANC was nothing, had no leadership, no policy, that Mandela was finished, that the ANC was controlled by whites, that it was dominated by the Indians who wanted to colonise South Africa to help India with its excess population, that it was run by Moscow, and that it spoke about 'the workers' when South Africa had no workers, only slaves. What was this word 'comrade', they wanted to know; there were only sons and daughters of Africa, no comrades.

Whenever we had stood in line to receive our clothing, stark naked, with our dirty things over our arms, they had commented that that was exactly how in Mao's China the people would receive their clothing. We heard them telling their people that Ben Bella had 50 000 men ready to invade South Africa, that Nkrumah and Kenyatta also had men ready to liberate the country. Then, the next day, we would hear one of their top leaders giving a long, serious talk on etiquette; on which side of your lady to walk in the street; how to peel a banana; how to take your leave from table.

They would talk about the right of Africans to be themselves.

'If we want to sit down stark naked in Eloff Street with flies on our penis and play ping-pong, that's our business.'

When they had numbered a thousand and the ANC only thirty, they had jeered at the thirty of us; saying that soon there would be no ANC at all. Yet, even as the years of underground resistance had begun to change the proportions, more and more ANC comrades coming in, while PAC prisoners were being released (their units outside being inactive), and we outnumbered them several times over, their leaders still never lost their arrogant, ultra-confident attitude. 'Vietnam? What's Vietnam to us? We're not interested in foreign struggles. Never, never trust the ANC, never try to work with the ANC, go it alone, go it alone.'

One thing, though, I must give them. When it came to singing they were tops, they sang beautifully, and quietly, with lovely harmonies and lots of repetitions, and we could listen to them for hours.

Suddenly all choirs were banned. We never heard why and campaigned bitterly for the right to sing, but the ban was never lifted and the singing stopped, even in our cells.

Politically there was never any chance of uniting with the PAC; their whole philosophy was totally opposed to the ANC vision of a truly liberated and non-racial society. They were hopelessly organised and penetrated by informers, split into a dozen factions. They had no coherent strategy; they simply reacted emotionally to situations. But we were all prisoners together, had daily contact with each other and had to get on together socially. So we encouraged discussions about sports and about cultural activities, not only those on the Island but in South Africa generally and internationally.

It was not an uncommon sight to find a group of ANC sitting with PAC, talking earnestly and cracking jokes about everything except politics. The PAC had begun to accept that the ANC was, in fact, the force on the Island, and showed a willingness to discuss certain matters with us, such as campaigns for release and better conditions, though we still had differences: for example, we insisted, as a matter of principle, on starting petitions with a demand for unconditional release and only then would we go on to press for improved conditions, while they felt that the demand for release was too unrealistic and that we should simply ask for better conditions.

Some PAC people even came over to us and asked to join the ANC group, but we explained that prison was not the place for us to have them enter our ranks, especially if it created bad blood and two groups, and that it was really after their release that they should take such an important step.

Others started to struggle inside the PAC group to overcome the hostile attitudes to us and after a while it became clear that they were in the majority. Many factors contributed towards their changed outlook: the struggles which we had led on the Island, the arrival of some trained ANC guerrillas able to speak of highly skilled preparation in socialist and African countries, of battles in Zimbabwe and South Africa, of an organisation with structures and programmes and international backing. Even the smuggled newspapers constantly spoke of the threat of ANC 'terrorists' without mentioning the PAC at all or, at most, speaking of it as a moribund organisation.

Now that nearly all the common-law prisoners were gone, and now that ANC and PAC prisoners were integrated in sporting activity, the main social division was: rugby or soccer? There were enthusiastic rugby players, mainly from the Cape, and equally fanatic soccerites, mainly from the Transvaal and Natal where soccer was the dominant game. One particular problem was over the use of the ground, but after a while we sorted it out, usually having alternate days for the two sports. Also, most of the players who played the one also played the other, and we taught each other the skills of our respective games, so that some keen soccerites emerged in the top rugby teams, and vice versa.

When I ran on to the field for my first rugby game in 'C' Division, having been totally devoted to soccer for months, a big cheer rang out from the spectators: 'Mr Assoc, you're on the wrong field!'

I was playing fly-half, very confident because I knew the game inside out, having watched many top teams. Within minutes the ball came to me. I ran it a few metres and then, as an opponent (also new to the game) rushed at me, I leapt into the air and gave a beautiful swing pass, just as I had seen it done by famous fly-halves of bygone years. Before I reached the ground I felt a bullet-like head crashing against my ribs and the next thing I knew I was flying through the air and lying flat on my back.

The crowd was laughing and yelling *Gau* ('country bumpkin' in Xhosa). It was also a joke to me, except that I was not able to get up and eventually had to be carried off the field. We were still joking about it, but the pain got worse and I was taken to hospital. Diagnosis: one broken rib.

I played again, but it took me six months to summon up the courage. That time I played fullback, without any incident.

One of the special pleasures for us at football was hearing the enthusiastic cries of support from our comrades in the isolation section. We could just about make out their faces between the bars of their high windows, but from the voices we had no doubt who was shouting! 'Kick the bloody ball, man!' (Comrade Mac), or 'Good move, well played!' (Comrade Nelson Mandela).

Clearly, they were all enjoying themselves, but one day, as we ran on to the field, we looked up to the windows for our customary support and saw no one there – only black paint. The windows facing the field had been completely painted over and there was total silence; we carried on the game, but with much less pleasure than usual.

The authorities told us that we could build a second soccer

field on an open piece of land within the prison yard, and every Saturday and Sunday hundreds of us worked at digging and levelling the ground, pulling out rocks and weeds, making goal posts and nets and, finally, laying lime to mark the touchlines of an international-size field. We also built a volley-ball court.

The authorities simply refused to supply us with cement, so we quietly went ahead and levelled out the ground and slowly started stealing what we needed. Every week we would snatch a little. cement and gradually extend the surface – we were building a tennis court. We must have stolen at least fifty bags when, after six months, the court was ready, and then all we needed was a net, which we made from fishermen's nets washed up on the shore near the quarry.

Whenever visitors came to the Island, the authorities would be sure to show them the fine tennis court which they had provided for the prisoners . . .

Many prisoners had never seen a table-tennis game before, let alone held a bat in their hand, but hundreds learned, and learned quickly. Before long, we had people trying out all sorts of new ways to hit the ball and get it to spin. It was the most popular game on the Island, and although at first I was among the best players, to be honest, by the end of the year I was lucky to hold my place in 'C' division.

The final of the table-tennis competition aroused immense excitement. For the third year running the match was between Comrade Brian Zola, in his early twenties – small, energetic, flexible, running here, there and everywhere; you could see he was a physically fit man – and Comrade Mike Fhishla, nearing forty years old – tall, steady, mature, using all his skills to force errors from his opponent.

Fhishla smashed the ball with such force and direction that we would already be scoring up the point for him, when Brian, falling

222

on his back, flicked the ball up as it was about to touch the floor and we would see it back on the table. In the end, age counted, but we really admired the skill and maturity of Fhishla; he played a beautiful game.

Hundreds of spectators watched, and the PAC people did not even think of themselves as PAC – they were just prisoners watching along with us.

A handful of us started a Bridge Club and within months we had taught about a hundred and fifty players, all playing the same few conventions, organised into three divisions; they included a sprinkling of PAC members, but were mostly ANC and 'others'.

Chess grew as rapidly, from even smaller beginnings – Reggie was virtually the only good player to start with – and here there was even more extensive PAC participation. We had bridge competitions and chess competitions that were keenly disputed.

Draughts competitions were fought out with enormous noise. Pieces would be banged down aggressively with loud shouts of 'My cow is eating your cow!' or 'I've got your sister now!', and lots of fantastic sayings in Xhosa and Zulu. In fact, so enthusiastic were the games that it became a standing joke that draughts was the most dangerous sport on the Island and required spectators to wear protective headgear and armour.

The players liked playing only with large pieces so that they could really crash them down on the board; that was part of their psychological warfare, and one of our comrades, a really skilful player who was just too quiet, too calm, always lost to weaker opponents because they would unnerve him with their cries and distractions.

FORTY-EIGHT

Strike Three

The warders, in their heavy greatcoats, froze as the wind whipped across them, and we, in our jackets, shivered continuously; our noses running, our fingers frozen and painful, our lips so cold we could hardly talk to each other. One by one we picked up our stones and hammers and moved to the protection of the huge dyke. It was so calm against the wall that we could take off our jackets and shirts and enjoy the sun, but if we moved just three or four paces away, the freezing wind would hit us again, so we stuck to our shelter.

Delport was clearly unhappy about our being warm and, after angrily watching us for a while, he walked right up to where we were, his face redder than usual, his hands in his deep coat pockets – it was particularly windy that day – and very coolly instructed us to pick up our stones and move upwards on to the dykes.

We rejected this, we refused to move, so he repeated the command – we stood our ground. Delport grew more and more agitated, gaining a kind of pleasure at seeing us openly refusing to obey a command since, as far as he was concerned, we had been having our own way in the quarry for far too long; now we would see who was in command. 'Move back!' We stayed put, hammering away at the stones.

'I repeat: move back to your proper positions.'

We continued to hammer.

'I am repeating, for the sixth time, move back to your work positions.'

We remained where we were and he stormed away, his hands still deep in his pockets, his face flushed and tense.

About half an hour later we saw Cofimvaba coming to the quarry. He walked right up to us and without another word ordered us to pick up our stones and move to the top of the dykes. By that time we realised that we were heading for a major confrontation, but we maintained our position. Cofimvaba began to run from one side to the other, poking us with his stick and threatening individual prisoners.

'Do you think you run this jail? This government is too soft; we give you a finger and you take a whole damned hand.'

He strode to his van and drove off, and not long after we saw the commanding officer's van approaching with four or five other vans loaded with warders and dogs. Major Kellerman, accompanied by Cofimvaba, walked right to the centre of the quarry without saying a word to Delport or the other warders. About fifty warders were lined up behind him, carrying batons in their hands, some holding dogs on leashes, the wind whistling past their large, tightly wrapped khaki overcoats. Those warders already in the quarry remained rooted to the spot and the five warders on the sentinel posts stood up and pointed their rifles at us. Cofimvaba was running around checking on his men, checking on the prisoners, shouting at the top of his voice where this warder should be and where that, arranging and rearranging them all the time.

We stopped talking and the only sound that could be heard from our section was the beat of the hammers on the stones, the squeaking of the laden wheelbarrow and, from time to time, the heavy crack of sledgehammers. Cofimvaba continued to dash around, howling at everybody, and finally, when all his preparations were complete, he screamed at us to assemble in front of the major.

Slowly we put down our tools and moved forward in a bunch to a spot in front of the major. There must have been four hundred of us, looking grave and mutinous in our scanty prison clothes, our jackets flapping wildly in the biting wind.

Quickly the warders closed in to form a circle round us, while the hundreds of other prisoners in the quarry dropped their sledgehammers, put down their wheelbarrows and stood watching. Cofimvaba rushed tensely at them and ordered them to resume work, which they began to do in a half-hearted way, positioning themselves so that they could continue to keep watch in our direction.

The warders surrounding us were edgy. Kellerman remained still for a while, then looked around.

'So you chaps don't want to work?' He paused. 'I am ordering you to take your stones, move up, and work.'

We tried to reply, our lips frozen in the wind, that we were willing to work, but that going up into the icy gale was a form of victimisation. He told us abruptly that he was not interested in anything we had to say, he was simply telling us we had to move, we had to obey, and afterwards we could say what we had to say.

We refused to move, we just stood there shivering. Then he too became agitated and started shouting. 'I'm giving you chaps only five minutes and if you don't move, you'll be responsible for the consequences.'

The warders were eager, they moved in closely, batons at the ready; the dogs were pulling at the leashes as if they, too, were conditioned to understand exactly what was going on.

'Give us the word,' the warders shouted. 'Let's get stuck in. Give us the word, Chief.'

We were completely quiet. The prisoners elsewhere in the quarry put down their tools again. Suddenly, some of the leading

PAC members broke away from the group, moved through the circle of warders, and began to pick up their stones, and before long all the PAC men had followed suit.

That caused considerable confusion and a few of our comrades started moving with the line, myself included. But we turned round and saw that the bulk of our comrades had remained still, refusing to move, and we turned back to rejoin them. By now, all the PAC prisoners were breaking stones in the wind on top of the dyke, while the ANC prisoners stood in a circle, trembling with cold, waiting to see what would happen.

Kellerman looked around at us, clearly pleased that we were divided.

'You have exactly five minutes to get back to the top of the dyke!'

As he looked at his watch the warders became even more urgent and aggressive, shouting: 'Let's get them, Chief, they're the leaders, they're the agitators. *Julle gaan vrek* – you're going to die.' They exchanged views loudly among themselves about how best to attack us, and Kellerman kept looking down at his watch; the time went very slowly, we were freezing.

When five minutes were over he looked up. 'I'm giving you one last chance, you can have one more minute to fetch your stones.'

We all stood very quietly, shivering and tense. Kellerman looked at his watch again. We did not move. 'Take them back to the jail!'

There were about two hundred of us and we formed up in fours, starting to talk to each other again, speculating about what was to happen. 'This is it,' we thought. We had made our stand, and now we were going to pay. The warders and dogs accompanied us, the dogs barking the whole way, the warders telling us we had been asking for it, now there was going to be real fun and games, we would see who ran the jail. It was a long walk back, and we looked at our thin comrades and joked: 'Man, I don't think you're going to survive this day, you're just skin and bones.'

'Man, it's you guys who are in trouble, the dogs will go for the fat, juicy ones, not us thin fellows.'

We entered the jail, waiting for further instructions, and the warders came inside with us, ready for the command. Cofimvaba appeared and ordered us all to be locked up in one cell, so we were squeezed into a cell, the door was locked, and we carried on waiting, talking excitedly. Any minute we expected a baton charge with dogs; we were cramped, sitting one against the other, laughing and nervous.

About an hour and a half passed, and then we heard the cell door being unlocked. We braced ourselves as a warder entered. 'Get your supper. Quick! Run!'

We trooped out to collect our plates, buzzing among ourselves, nothing had happened.

Next day, virtually all the prisoners in our section including those in the building *span*, the cleaners, the gardeners and so on, were ordered to the quarry, which was really full.

Delport again addressed us, repeating that we should take our stones to the top of the dyke and chop them there. Once more, all the PAC men, including the new ones, picked up their stones and began to work, while all the ANC comrades – now about four hundred – stayed put.

'I repeat, get to the top of the dyke.'

We did not move.

'All right, it's your look-out, if that's what you want, you can just stand there, it will be a long, cold day, but that's your look-out.'

We stood there, icy cold, hour after hour, the whole day, talking about news items to keep up our spirits, rubbing our hands together for warmth, moving from one leg to the other, frozen and tense.

At the end of the day we were ordered back to our cells. Our muscles were cramped up, and we were pleased to be moving again, getting some warmth into them.

On the third day Delport once again ordered all the prisoners to the top of the dyke, and once more we refused to go, but this time we noticed that, as the other prisoners moved off, about twenty or thirty of the more mature PAC men stayed behind with us. We did not say anything special to them, we simply treated them as though they had been with us from the start, talking to them, joking with them, making them feel part of our group.

On the fourth day the bulk of the PAC men trooped as usual to the top of the dyke, while we waited for instructions. Delport came along waving his arm: 'Ach! Go and work anywhere you like!'

We then marched off, all the ANC comrades and the few solid PAC prisoners with us, collecting our stones and preparing our place at the foot of the dyke.

The bulk of the PAC prisoners sat freezing in the wind at the top of the dyke while we, down below, were enjoying the lovely sunshine, feeling really good, and not long after, they picked up their hammers and stones, descended the dyke, and joined us in our warm shelter.

FORTY-NINE

'We Warders'

One day a common-law prisoner was brought in, dead, to the prison hospital. He had been working as a domestic servant for a warder's family, and he had a bullet-wound right through his chest. Word got around that he had been having an affair with the warder's wife, something he had been able to do quite safely because of the rigid working hours of the prison. But one day the warder had come home early and, finding the prisoner in bed with his wife, had pulled out a revolver and shot the prisoner dead.

A few days later, we read in a smuggled newspaper that a prisoner who had attempted to rape a warder's wife had been shot dead in a chase; immediately afterwards the warder was transferred from the Island.

Department policy for warders was the same as it was for us: no one talked in terms of 'we', only in terms of 'I'. The punishments meted out to the warders were severe: weekend duty, night duty, post duty, cancellation of leave, and even heavy fines. The food for the bachelors was bad: badly cooked and badly served, and never enough. Compared with what we were getting, it was fit for kings. But by civilian standards it was very poor and, what is more, they had to pay for it.

For a long time they did nothing about the situation and then, when they saw us taking part in hunger strikes, the entire complement of fifteen hundred prisoners standing together and keeping it up for days, they started to think.

A couple of months later, the warders informed the Island administration that, as a protest against the bad food, they would boycott the canteen until their demands for improvements were met; and one of their leaders was Meintjies, who had been the most vociferous in jeering at us.

After two days they were met by senior officers and, subsequently, we noticed that they were getting much better meals, served in a much better way.

We noticed that Head Warder Delport was beginning to spend his spare time studying and we learned that he was preparing for his matriculation exam. We also learned that in two successive years he had failed. He called on Saddick Isaacs, a former schoolteacher serving twelve years for attempted sabotage, to coach him in English, history and geography. English, even though it was only treated as a second language in his course, was just too much for him; it was his real Moses, and he failed it for a third time.

Delport eventually passed his matric and was promoted from head warder to chief warder. We heard that even his attitude to his family, almost all of whom worked for the Prison Department, had begun to change, that he was much less rough with them and had begun to smile at them.

Delport no longer used terms like '*kaffir*', '*koelie*' and '*boesman*', and even started referring to us as '*kêrels* – chaps'. He was impressed by us, by our determination and willingness to struggle to the limit of our abilities to achieve something we felt to be right. He had also seen the unity which we maintained, despite every effort of the Department to break us up. One little example: every warder and officer told us that prison regulations forbade us to use the word 'we', that we were in prison as individuals and not as a group, but we persisted in saying 'we' and 'us' when speaking to those in charge, however high their rank.

The various campaigns we had launched, including many against Delport and his behaviour, had also had their impact, and that, too, seemed to change him over the years so that when he began to look upon further study as the only way out of his job difficulties, he started openly to show his respect for us.

He even became something of a friend to political prisoners at that stage, listening to our grievances and taking them up. When we had problems we would take them to him and he would attend to them. He knew each one of us by name, and he was so changed that we would even see him smiling on occasion; smiling, even at us, and quite often. He would come and joke with us at work, which by this time had become much less unpleasant.

Jordaan, who spoke English and Xhosa fluently, which was most unusual for a warder, was a strange person. He was well into his fifties, having spent most of his life in the prison service, and was referred to by all his colleagues, high and low, as *Oom* (uncle). He was drunk more often than sober and told us that he wasn't interested in promotion. He was a bright person who had never got beyond head warder all those years because of his drinking.

He was a real Jekyll and Hyde towards us. Sometimes he was quite pleasant and then, without warning, he became very brutal and was responsible for some of the worst atrocities. For example, he would stand and watch other warders torture prisoners and would not hesitate to hit out himself, yet, on other occasions, he would greet us properly and for days on end would treat us like ordinary prisoners, talking and laughing with us – sometimes even taking up some of our problems.

After many years in the quarry he was transferred to the

censorship section in the office and was the one who checked and censored our mail. He also accompanied us to the visiting quarters on visiting days; sometimes he gave us a lot of freedom with our families, but on other days he would stand right on top of us and listen to every word. We never knew beforehand what his mood would be, whether he would let us go on or cut us off before our short period was up. He was just waiting for his pension day . . . and so were we.

The whole jail was talking about the love affair between the common-law prisoner and the warder's wife. He was a Malawian chap very close to us, who called us 'comrade' and smuggled in newspapers. He had been in prison about twelve years and we had great confidence in him, even though we were not sure if we could believe all his stories, especially those about this woman: how she used to wait for him, how she had started it all long ago; he even gave us explicit details of their love-life. With him it was just a question of enjoying himself as much as he could; it seemed that he had no special feeling for her and did not find her particularly attractive, or at least so he said.

We did not know how to take those tales. He told them very vividly, full of convincing detail, but there were lots of wonderful story-tellers among the common-law prisoners, and they were always boasting about things that they could never have done. One had even told me that he had composed the tune 'Have you been across the sea to Robben Island' – 'Galway Bay'!

One day this chap was brought back from work, handcuffed and beaten to pulp, and locked up in the isolation cells. The warders told us that he had been caught trying to rape the chief warder's wife and that about six warders had come to her rescue and beaten him up.

He appeared in court and received one year's extra imprisonment for attempted rape, and was then removed from the Island.

At last Dr van den Bergen was replaced and two new doctors

arrived: Dr Samuels and Dr Rom. They were both much better; they actually examined us and spoke to us like patients, not prisoners. Dr Rom in particular was different from almost anyone else we had met on the Island, relating to us as human beings, a real doctor.

FIFTY

Stars and Stripes

Great preparations were being made on the Island: the place was being cleaned out. Old prisoners' clothing was replaced by new; the very old blankets were changed for newer ones; the quality of food suddenly improved, and the warders became civil. 'Good morning, chaps.' We knew that somebody was due to arrive. We always prepared in advance, whether the visitor be a prison official, the biggest fascist possible, a Red Cross official, or anybody else. We appointed about five or six prisoners to represent us, and on this occasion I was in the group. We heard early in the morning that two gentlemen had arrived on the Island and were busy having a discussion with Nelson Mandela.

We got ourselves into a position working in the yard that would allow us to intercept the visitors when they arrived, and just before lunch we saw the commanding officer, a couple of senior warders and two strangers approaching. The group went to the prison library and spent some time talking to the prisoner librarian, then they went to the study section.

I dashed to the librarian and was told that the main visitor was McNichol, an Australian journalist, and as the group reappeared from the study section, our group of five placed ourselves right in front of him. I greeted him and said we would like to raise a few things about the Island with him. He looked straight through us, as though we were not there, and a warder roughly pushed us aside.

They moved off to the kitchen, and when the lunch bell rang we saw the visitor walking around the kitchen, tasting the food and, later, examining the dustbins. When they re-emerged into the yard, our little group once more placed itself in front of them, and this time we said, more boldly, that we had some complaints that we wanted to raise with him. Once again we were rudely pushed away, and once again he just walked off as if we did not exist.

Later we heard on the grapevine that Comrade Nelson Mandela had a very punchy interview with him, starting with a request that he congratulate the new Australian (Labour) government on their victory and send greetings on behalf of the prisoners and the South African people to the government and the people of Australia. When the journalist had expressed surprise that he had known about the elections, the Commissioner of Prisons had said, 'Yes, these prisoners smuggle in newspapers.' Mandela had replied that that was correct, and that they would continue to do so for as long as they were criminally deprived of news.

When asked how he felt about the radical policies that had led to his imprisonment and that of hundreds of others a decade earlier, Mandela had replied that he was more convinced than ever of the correctness of the ANC policy.

There was one visitor to the Island whom we never saw, but we heard from the normally reliable grapevine that he had definitely come, spending a day together with some Minister or other hunting pheasant and buck in the bush not far from us, and that he was the Ambassador of the United States of America.

FIFTY-ONE

The feast

The people who had been boasting over the years about how fast they had run the mile or how high they had jumped, were challenged to prove their ability. There were at least three prisoners who had been telling us that they had been Victor Ludorum at their schools, and now we were organising the first athletics meeting on the Island, called the mini-Olympic Games, which would put them to the proof.

We started laying out the field and working out a programme. The Games would be a two-day affair, we decided, ending on Monday, 16 December, which was a public holiday, the so-called Day of the Covenant. Preparations were well advanced. We had divided the prison population into four teams to sharpen the competition, and were ready to put our proposals to the authorities when fifteen of us, the key organisers, were arrested. We did not know why, but learned afterwards that it was because we had chosen 16 December, which was not only the Day of the Covenant but also the day of the launching of our armed struggle. So we spent six months in the isolation section, hearing distant cries and shouts from the spectators when the Games were eventually held on a 'neutral' date.

On our release from isolation, we immediately got stuck into organising the second Robben Island mini-Olympics, and I must say it was a tremendous success.

We marked out the field as accurately as possible, made hurdles of any old scraps of wood we had been able to find, and put sea sand in a pit for the long jump. We managed to get a large piece of scrap iron for the shot-put, more or less round, but had greater difficulty with the discus, our blacksmiths never managing to get the weighting right, so that it was always wobbly in flight. We attended to everything: armbands for the judges, a winners' stand, records, a scoreboard, stop-watches borrowed from the warders, even announcements on a loudhailer. The only thing that we could not get was a gun to start the races.

Before, our main enemy had been physical cruelty, now it was boredom, isolation, the psychological decay of an endlessly unproductive and confined existence; so the Games were an important way of getting ourselves mobilised, using our inner resources to smash the routine and monotonous futility of prison life.

We started with a parade of the teams, dressed in different football jerseys, making quite a display of colour.

'On your marks . . . Get set . . . Peep!' The whistle blew, and the athletes streaked towards the finishing line, cheer leaders raising a tremendous hullabaloo in favour of comrade X or Y or their team. Even some of the younger warders began to shout and scream, quite carried away by the occasion.

At the end of the day, all the results were carefully noted in a special book, and we had a prize-giving ceremony. There was some conflict with the authorities over that, since we had wanted to distribute chocolates, biscuits, cakes and sweets to the winners in bulk so that they could be redistributed amongst us all, to have a little feast to round off the proceedings; the warders refused, insisting that we hand out the prizes individually.

'Winner of the 100 yards . . .' The prisoner walked up to receive his bar of chocolate, waited while we all applauded, and then walked over with his prize to our Catering Committee, who put it in a collective pile. Soon, we were tucking into our first feast on the Island; the food tasting even better because of the struggle to get it.

It was a specially memorable day for me because it was just four months before my release and I made what was, in effect, my farewell speech to the prisoners, handing over the reins of the many offices I held. 'Gentlemen, gentlemen, please . . .' There was silence, 'First, on behalf of the organising committee, may I thank all those who made this occasion such a success.' Applause. 'Second, I wish to announce my resignation from a number of bodies, for reasons which you will understand.' Mild booing. 'Seriously, comrades, it is with very mixed feelings that I shall be leaving. I look forward to the joy of being released and being back in society after these ten long years, but feel extremely sad at leaving behind comrades and friends with whom I have lived more closely than anyone I have ever known; closer even than with the members of my family.'

I got a good brush, and felt very emotional.

FIFTY-TWO

He-wena, wena, wena

We are all sitting in the hall having our supper, amidst the usual hustle and bustle of voices and spoons and laughter. 'Listen, comrade, when you get out, look up my wife for me. Tell her that I'm still going strong and to have courage,' someone is saying in my ear, but I find it difficult to concentrate on him at the moment.

A prisoner comes in with a list, at last, and we all stare intently at it, as if to read the names even from this distance.

'Man, I haven't had a cent in ten years, just organise five rand for me, that's all I ask . . .' another voice.

It takes some time for the hubbub to die down, with here and there a 'Sh . . . sh . . .', and someone shouting, 'Give him a break, give him a break, man!'

The prisoner jumps on to a bench, looks around, and waits. He lifts up the paper, pauses, looks around again, and a big grin lights up his face; he is taking his time, keeping us on tenterhooks.

Then suddenly he becomes tense, stern, we all sit in an agony of suspense.

'*He-wena, wena, wena, wena . . . !*' he calls out in a loud baritone voice, '*he-wena, wena, wena, wena.*'

Someone in our clique whispers, 'It's coming, it's coming . . .'
'Sh . . . sh.'
He-wena, wena, wena, wena, wena . . .
Indres Naidoo!

Up go the cheers, everybody starts clapping hands, I feel hard slaps on my back and shoulders, I'm being pushed this way and that, I do not know whether to laugh or to cry; I am feeling intensely emotional, the cheering and clapping continue. I am about to be moved, in exactly twelve days' time I'll be out of prison, back in twilight freedom (as we call it) with my family and friends, but also separated and torn away from the comrades crowding around me now.

Other names are being called, but I cannot hear anything. I see people surrounding Reggie and Shirish, and they too have stunned looks on their faces.

'Don't forget . . . records for us . . . try and get Pete Seeger . . . and Dollar Brand . . . Miriam Makeba . . . and "Z", you know, Theodorakis . . .'

'Give them a break, give them a break.'

Everybody is talking at the same time, and someone comes up to me and takes me gently by the arm. 'Didn't you hear, Comrade Indres, you must go and collect your things and move to B One [the departure cell]?'

'And, comrade, don't forget, the struggle continues,' someone is whispering in my ear.

One by one the prisoners come to us, giving us a last hug as we move off towards our cell, kissing us on the cheeks, many crying. George Naicker takes out a soft khaki handkerchief and wipes the tears pouring down my face, then those pouring down his face, then those on my face again. For the first time since my torture, ten years ago, I am crying, and the tears come flooding down.

In our cell, Sonny Singh is darting around, with his head forward, neck out, laughing, folding up our blankets; somebody

241

else is packing our toilet things.

'Goodbye, Mr Assoc, goodbye Mr Assoc.' An escort of prisoners accompanies us, carrying our things, all of us with tears rolling down our cheeks.

PART THREE

FROM THE ISLAND

FIFTY-THREE

The chains unbound

The Island starts slowly moving back; the reverberations in the boat increase; the engine noise gets louder, and we feel the prison dock being torn from us. We are standing, silent, each at his own porthole, having our last look at what has been our home for ten years.

There is a strange optical effect: the Island seems to get bigger as we get further from it. First we see only the little dock, then the rocks and bushes at either side and, finally, the whole expanding coastline, a complete island; a green and picturesque stretch of land in the ocean, the harsh monotony of its internal life totally hidden by its outer physical beauty. Then, as the boat speeds further and further away, the Island starts to contract. It gets smaller and smaller and eventually all we see are the waves splashing against the portholes and seagulls screaming overhead.

Goodbye, Robben Island, may we never see you again, may all who live on you be liberated, may you go to hell, may you sink into the sea and become part of the bitter memories of the past, of our past, of the past of apartheid.

Aucamp's face leaps into my consciousness; the grim, sad-looking, crinkled, hostile face, threatening us to the very end. How many times had we heard that he was dying, and he always came back; how many times that he was retiring, and he was always there, hard and bitter, a sure bearer of misery every time.

'Behave yourself' – his last words – 'or you'll be back, our government is very strong.'

We turn our attention to Table Mountain, getting bigger and bigger, the giant granite cliffs revealing little cracks and fissures; no longer just a blob in the distance, but a mountain with its own personality and features. Three tall towers look incongruous at its base; and they, too, go through the strange alterations of perspective, growing bigger up to a point and then diminishing and sinking down while the skyscrapers on the foreshore – formerly so small – suddenly emerge, enormous, blotting out all behind them, even the mountain.

The engine noise cuts out, the boat floats along serenely, and we see people moving around on the docks in front of us, some dressed in workers' overalls, others in business suits: the different clothing of a different world in which everything is different, every detail.

It not only looks different, it has different sounds, sounds familiar and yet strange at the same time: an engine shunting – how many years since we heard a train? – cars hooting, a radio playing loud pop music, not stolen music, just sound at large for anyone to hear.

Our boat is tied up, and we dash upstairs carrying little plastic bags with all the belongings accumulated in ten years: toothbrush, toothpaste, soap, facecloth and razor – eager to set foot on land.

'Oh, so you chaps are in a hurry, hey?'

It is Magalies standing there grinning, ready to take us back to Leeuwkop, ten years older, but unmistakable. 'Where do you think you're going?' We do not reply to his question, but he waits cordially next to us, getting us to queue before we clamber off.

'Well, that's goodbye to Robben Island, see you don't come

back.'

We jump off one by one, still saying nothing to him, taking in as much as possible of all the things and movement on the docks, talking freely amongst ourselves and to whoever comes by.

In front of us is a black van, shiny new, and as we climb in we see it has benches and windows that let in the light, and a little pipe and bowl for peeing in.

Grey blankets keep us warm in the chill air, the early morning sun flickers on the smoke filling the van, and we lean back on the benches against the metal walls, each dreaming our own dreams, having our own memories, three common-law prisoners sitting silently in front.

Through the windows we see endless barren land flashing by, here and there clumps of dry bush, stones and more stones. The landscape is open and deserted for miles and miles. What life there is, is on the road and as cars and trucks pass we break out of our reveries and speak excitedly to each other. Only the three common-law prisoners with us remain silent, repressed, cautious.

'It's a man, I tell you.' The big, shiny car comes closer and closer; opulent, polished and glistening in the sun; soft leather upholstery with a smooth cashmere blanket on the back seat; elegant sun-tanned arms on the steering wheel. We are fascinated by the driver.

'Rubbish, it's a woman.' We could almost smell the scent and luxury of that car, and sense the long, blonde, wavy hair; lots and lots of hair travelling at speed, looking so free and easy.

'Ten years, and you've forgotten what a woman looks like.' The car whizzes out of sight and we carry on arguing and laughing, eventually settling back on our benches and drifting once more into our dreams.

I see the gardens of the Island in my mind: patches of lawn, rockeries, flower beds; everything produced by our patient labour. What arguments we used to have about those gardens: some saying it was wrong for us to beautify the Island, making it a show piece; others replying that we were doing it for ourselves, our own dignity, we had a right to see beautiful things, it was up to us to transform the Island in terms of what we wanted, not what the warders said.

We stole plants and grass and made quite a presentable series of gardens. When we tried to relax there during time off, the warders would order us off, saying it was prison property. So the opponents of the gardens would say they had warned us, and the rest of us would say, 'Well, one more battle to fight, that's all.'

The three young common-law prisoners sitting in the partitioned section in front of the van look dejected and harassed. But we are relaxed in the unproclaimed silence, wondering who these prisoners are, what their crime was, where they are going, what will happen to them and whether they will survive this jungle.

The road goes straight for ever. Our van speeds past flat dry land until suddenly we see an old black couple in tattered clothing, with bundles on their heads, walking by the roadside – the first sign of an approaching town. Later we pass ragged children playing barefoot in the sand; a collection of mud-and-zinc houses crowded on top of one another with smoke emerging here and there and a few thin dogs with long tails snapping and barking at the wheels of our van. 'Look at those miserable sick-looking dogs.'

For a few moments it is the arid bush again and then we see, rising up on the horizon, a big, imposing, modern church, all triangles, a bright new structure with a lovely green lawn and a few trees between it and the road and, as we get close, a large black car shining in the yard behind.

'Hey, what model is that? It's a beautiful Mercedes, they haven't changed the shape much, have they?'

We pass beautiful houses of all shapes and sizes, and then a modern police station, shops, a hotel with shiny cars parked diagonally outside, and see groups of elegantly dressed people walking about with all the arrogance of the rulers of our land, one holding a plump, smooth-coated dog on a lead in front of him.

'Where are the bloody mini-skirts?' We look this way and that, having read for years in smuggled newspapers about the new craze, but the skirts we see are long, near the ground; they had gone up and up and up . . . and now they had gone all the way down again.

The journey is long and monotonous, and we find ourselves sitting staring in front of us, each thinking his own thoughts. I recall the Koeloekoetz comrades standing in the lime quarry, dust everywhere, their eyes blinking from the white glare, specks of white in their hair and on their clothes, Nelson Mandela, tall, athletic, his shoulders a little hunched now, his eyebrows white, his cheeks caked with gleaming powder, the blueness of his jersey almost blotted out by layers of white powder, digging with his spade into the chalk, surrounded – I imagine – by a group of others. 'Kathy' with his glasses covered with chalk, Govan Mbeki no longer looking grey-haired because everyone was white-haired, dreamy Billy Nair appearing more ghostlike and spiritual than ever. I can see them all, earnestly discussing some world event, or possibly some aspect of the South African struggle.

Comrade Mandela – with him you had no choice, you had to respect him. There was something about his large calm physical presence and assured thoughtful manner that carried people along; his manner of always approaching problems in a correct way and guiding us in solving our day-to-day difficulties. We sensed his leadership even when he was not with us. And Comrade Sisulu, also impressive, always with us, but different in style: a strong leader, but more fatherly in his manner.

We sit staring at our legs, the blankets on the floor, the van lit up by the bright Karoo sun, and I think of what the other comrades would be doing now, of how they would love to be in the van with us, speeding home; those making bricks in a small yard, others collecting seaweed or crushing it for fertiliser. Where would Delport be, now that the quarry was closed, and he was in an office? Who were the new warders coming to the Island to keep our comrades isolated, fresh forces in the war of spiritual attrition, new warders to be broken in by the prisoners?

The common-law prisoners ask us in a whisper through the partition mesh if we could pass them a cigarette, and as we hand over three lit smokes we see, for the first time since they have joined us, a slightly happy expression touching their faces, a subdued flicker of warmth.

The sun is beginning to go down and we place the blankets on our shoulders once more, staring at the open veld speeding by, trying to keep warm, nourishing precious new thoughts about a future which we can now allow into our consciousness.

A side door is opened and we are in a small, icy-cold Karoo town; a warder is shouting, '*Kom uit, julle bliksems* – come out, you!'

The three common-law prisoners tumble out of the van, falling over each other, ducking the blows and the kicking feet of the warders standing outside.

'*Hardloop!* – Run!' They streak for the jail gates and disappear into the prison, and as the doors at the back of the van are opened wide we hear the same voice. '*Kom uit julle bliksems!*'

We get up slowly, fold our blankets neatly and place them in a pile

'*Kom uit, kom uit!*' The voice is shrill with impatience, but we take our time getting to the back, and descend one by one. The warder raises his hand to hurry the first of us along, and we suddenly move quickly, gathering round him. 'What are you doing? Leave us alone. What do you think you are doing?'

He is absolutely taken aback and pulls away, shocked. The other warders are equally astonished. '*Met wie praat jy* – who are you talking to?'

We all smile. It is the old story of '*baas*' of ten years ago, and

250

we notice Magalies approaching us, pretending to be aware of what has been going on. Calmly, in a straightforward way he tells us to enter the jail, so Reggie, walks up to him and says in an equally calm tone: 'Just tell that warder who we are and that he shouldn't mess us around.'

'Ach, come on, get inside.'

We walk slowly into the jail and find ourselves lodged in a cell with no mats, but plenty of dirty old blankets. Slowly and methodically we clean out the cell, shake out the blankets, make up our beds, and start to discuss our journey and the things we have seen.

The door opens and there behind the grille we see the same warder standing looking intently at us, a cigarette in his mouth, pretending to count us, as if there was some doubt about our number. After repeating the process in an exaggerated way a couple of times, he takes the cigarette out of his mouth, puts it between finger and thumb, and flicks it through the bars of the grille into our cell. For a moment it lies burning there, the smoke curling upward, and we look down at it and up at him. He looks back at us, down at the cigarette, waiting for us to dive for it. One of our group gets up, walks slowly across, lifts his foot and crushes the cigarette firmly with his heel, kicking it out of the cell. 'Don't dirty our cell, it's not an ashtray.'

The warder, once again stunned, stands there for a few moments, shakes his head in amazement, then storms out, slamming the door behind him. We smile at each other. Obviously Magalies had spoken to him about us and he was trying, in the only way he knew, to be friendly.

＊

As we cross the long, narrow bridge over the Vaal river our anxiety begins to mount. We are only a few hours' drive from our home. This is our territory: the world of factories, mine dumps and

locations. We see huge new road-signs: Vanderbijlpark ...
Sharpeville ... Johannesburg.

'Good God! Look at those beautiful pylons right next to the
road.'

Our memories go back to the days when we were always
looking for targets; the Struggle will have new tasks for us now,
and we wonder what they will be.

'Hey, chaps, look how Lens has grown.' We stare in dismay at
Lenasia, the vast racial Group Area set aside to accommodate the
people of Indian origin who had been kicked out of the centre of
Johannesburg. It was just beginning when we were arrested, and
though we know that our people have not been able to hold out
after all the years, especially when the school was moved, to see
the reality of the new ghetto still comes as a surprise and a shock.
There are so many houses there. It is so big and so bare, so far
from town, so much a monument to the continuing vigour of
apartheid.

In front of us we see another vast township, rows and rows of
identical houses, some completed and others still being built;
people all around; the traffic very heavy. Another completely new
Group Area, this one for Coloured people. What is it called? Where
have the people been moved from to go there?

Not far away, another huge conglomeration of matchbox-type
houses extends to the horizon, filling an enormous area; thousands
upon thousands upon thousands of them occupying the flatland,
going over the hills, little pockets of smoke hanging over some
sections: SOWETO. It is bigger than we remember it, enormous,
endless, and our anger increases as we drive past. That was what
we were fighting against ten years ago: to see an end to this, but
it grows bigger and bigger, and more and more soulless. There is
still a hard struggle ahead, there is no easy journey to freedom.

We are amazed at the relatively clear air over Soweto, always
there used to be a heavy blanket of smoke in the late afternoon,
and as we enter the zone of mine dumps, huge man-made

mountains of sand on both sides of us, we get another surprise: there is grass growing on some of them, even trees and flowers. The world of apartheid is being cleaned up, the environment is being made more beautiful, pollution is being controlled, only apartheid remains as cruel and inhuman as ever, more cruel. Let the explosion come, let the people be free, comrades, here we come!

We speed past Uncle Charlie's roadhouse, glad to see at least one familiar landmark still there, and shoot up a totally new roadway built high on stilts, a beautiful piece of engineering that plunges us right into the heart of Jo'burg.

'Look, there's my school.' I am excited, and point towards the building in which I spent so many years, now rapidly getting nearer and nearer.

'My God! Look at it.' It is more like a jail than a school. A feeling of disgust hits me. It has fencing around it, windows are broken, the paint is peeling off, it is dead, it has been converted into a storeroom.

The Johannesburg skyline is dramatic. Giant new skyscrapers of glass and stone rise on all sides, picking up the rays of the setting sun; black, green and blue buildings are outlined against the darkening sky, a wonderland of shapes and colour.

The high-rise motorway forks out in many different directions and we fly even higher now, surrounded by other motorways with traffic speeding under us, motorways to the side of us, trucks and cars flowing along in every direction, and buses, hundreds and hundreds of green buses jampacked with tired black workers, crushed against one another, on their way home after servicing the city during the day.

We look for Electricity House, once the tallest building in the southern hemisphere, and it is nowhere in sight; totally blotted out by the vast conglomeration of new skyscrapers that we have not seen before. The top deck of the motorway gives us a fine view of the city, but I know that I will never see my little house in this vast jungle of new buildings.

Suddenly, looming up right next to us is a massive green building, a huge façade of glass and concrete whizzing past only metres away. What place is this? Could it be the new John Vorster Square police headquarters, through which so many of our comrades have passed? Was this beautiful structure the building from which Comrade Babla was thrown to his death, only months after bringing us those packets of food?

We see our first hippies, almost as though they were invented in our absence: groups of strange-looking people standing around under the lamps on the pavements, men with big unkempt beards and hair hanging down their backs; some with bands across their foreheads, wearing colourful loose-hanging shirts, long trousers with patches and splotches of paint, and old worn sandals; women in clumsy long dresses, hair long and unruly, lots of bangles and necklaces, and big round earrings; a few with red or yellow dots on their forehead; one or two even barefoot, in spite of the cold. They move slowly, seemingly without a care in the world; untidy, unwashed and unworried. They do not even look up at our prison van going by as the other pedestrians do, and we wonder how they survive without working, what their attitude to apartheid is, and what the regime thinks of them.

The motorway curves right through the centre of the city, neon signs flash on and off in all colours, and we speed over railway lines running into tunnels beneath the vast building complex that contains the station. The city is full of people and traffic on the move, and signs flashing Coca-Cola, the bold white letters of IBM, B-O-S-C-H flicking on and off; lights everywhere, all colour and movement.

The pavements are filled with thousands of workers rushing to form queues at the bus station, some with big overcoats, some in jackets, others in overalls, carrying parcels of supermarket food, many with newspapers in their hands, thronging forward; a mass of people, the working class of Johannesburg on the move.

'Look chaps, look!' We wonder why the comrade's voice is so urgent. 'Quick, chaps, quick, there on the wall!'

Flashing past in big bold chalk letters is the word AMANDLA! We start cheering in the van and shout '*Amandla!* Power to the people! The struggle continues!' There is great excitement.

The motorway plunges into a deep cutting with heavily cemented walls rising steeply at the sides. In the centre islands rushing past are long narrow flowerbeds on which groups of black gardeners are collecting their forks and hoes, and sweeping up grass trimmings.

We hurtle along and suddenly the walls give way to the beautiful open scenes of the luxurious northern suburbs of Johannesburg: huge parks, lovely green golf courses, a hillside with its own waterfall; and mile upon mile of elegant accommodation: houses in the Spanish style, houses with fake black timbers imitating English Elizabethan architecture, round houses, square houses, houses of plate glass with gardens running right in, all the houses with walls and hedges and large driveways containing one, two or three cars; many with tennis courts and swimming pools and lawns and neatly kept gardens, orchards at the back with apple trees, peach trees, mulberry trees, kennels and servants' quarters. It just goes on and on, vast expanses of good living, beautiful landscaped nature and elegant houses; here a maid keeping two little white kids on the pavement, there a gardener putting a petrol-driven lawnmower back in the shed, delivery men returning in vans and on bicycles to their employers, a barefoot kid running from house to house stuffing *The Star* into mailboxes, chased all the way by well-fed dogs; lights on everywhere, street lamps, floodlit lawns, and windows aglow.

Hundreds of cars shoot on and off the motorway, beautiful cars with beautiful couples in them, men and women looking alike in coloured trousers and elegant tailored shirts, with fluffy shampooed hair; women without noticeable make-up, men neatly groomed, in cars of all shapes and all colours.

'Look, copper . . .'

'My God! Burnt orange . . .'

Bright red, pastel blue, canary yellow, silver-grey, gold; hardly a black or grey car in sight. Only the Volkswagen looks like a Volkswagen used to. We are amazed.

The van speeds along in the heavy traffic, past the lovely houses and parks and cars and beautiful people. We are attracted and repelled at the same time, the amazing luxury is endless, and each of us wonders how long it will be, how long, before the people whose sweat and humiliation were the price of all this beauty will be able to enjoy some of the simple decencies of life for themselves.

'Hey, chaps, look! There's another one.'

We glance at the motorway embankment rushing past and see, painted in black letters, FREE MANDELA!

The traffic is thinning out. There are a few red tail-lights of vehicles in front of us, and the van slows down. We turn off into open farmland and the first thing we see is two large stone lions staring at us. Leeuwkop. We are back again.

The cell door is open and the senior officer standing behind the grille looks down and reads from the Complaints and Requests Book in his hand. 'Indres Naidoo!'

I walk over to the grille and wait.

'You requested to grow a beard and a moustache?'

'Yes.'

'Well, the commanding officer has denied your request to grow a beard. Your moustache – you can wear a moustache!' He snaps the book closed and walks off, and as I turn round the comrades start laughing.

'What kind of moustache are you going to grow in six days, Indres?'

'I haven't shaved for a few days, so I've something of a start.'

'A droopy one? A big fat one? A thin pencil one? Or a Charlie

Chaplin one?'

There are two serious young prisoners with us whom we found in the transit cell when we arrived and they are puzzled by the way we joke about everything. They are from the Black Consciousness Movement, this is their first time in prison and they are on their way to Robben Island to serve five-year sentences for incitement and for being in possession of banned literature. We do not know them very well, they do not know us, or of us, and there is caution on both sides. They want to find out if the rumours they have heard about the Island are true and how they should conduct themselves when they get there. So we tell them that some of the hard times and terrible suffering have passed because of our struggles, and we stress that there is only one way to get through, and that is to remember, each and every day, that they are political prisoners fighting for a just cause, that they must always stand together and never lose sight of their goal. We remind them that the people of South Africa, and of the world, will always be standing by them, that they will never be forgotten, however isolated they might feel, and that we are confident that the ANC will continue the fight and bring victory to the people of our country.

*

A young white warder in his late teens is standing in the yard talking to an elderly black warder who is frowning very severely in our direction. 'Induna, you watch them, I'll be back soon.'

We see who the warder is speaking to: Kumalo, our tormentor from before, who looks fiercely at us and walks aggressively in our direction.

'*Ja, nkosi* – yes, *baas*,' he says to his departing 'superior'.

As the warder leaves the yard and Kumalo reaches us he suddenly starts smiling and greets us as if we were old friends. 'Well, you've done very well,' as though he was giving us a decoration.

'Oh, so you remember us, the dynamite coolies you used to mess around.'

He just smiles at us and continues talking in a friendly way until the young white warder returns, and then he starts to frown and shout at us once more.

My hair is neatly brushed into place, my face is shaved except for the top lip. All of us have straightened our clothing and are trying desperately to look presentable as we walk towards the Visitors' Room. We enter and wait; there are footsteps and voices outside and we wonder who it is who has come to see us on this, the last visit of all.

The footsteps get closer and the first person to enter is a young girl in her teens, with shoulder-length hair neatly combed, slim and elegantly dressed, very lovely; she smiles and waves as she moves towards me, looking carefully at my face as though waiting for a response. I am puzzled. There is something familiar about her, but I just cannot place her. She stops and waits in front of me, staring expectantly.

Then she walks on to the next person – Reggie – stops again and gives the same smile and the same tentative half-wave, once more expecting some response. I look at Reggie and see that he is stunned, trembling; a long time passes and he remains dumb while she stands there, still uncertain, puzzled, unsure.

My mother and two brothers come sweeping in, triumphant, full of joy. Members of Shirish's family, a little more restrained, move past me and Reggie and go to greet their son.

'Indres,' my mother calls out, 'just one more week exactly and we'll be coming for you.'

You can hardly notice the wrinkles on her face and her grey hair, she is so radiant, and I reply joyfully to her, trying to respond fully, but find myself looking all the time over my shoulder at the young girl standing half-smiling in front of Reggie, who is still trembling and pale.

'Excuse me, Ma . . .'

'You recognise her?'

I look again, still uncertain.

'It's Reggie's daughter.'

'What?' I jump up and rush over to where Reggie is standing and, without addressing him, say enthusiastically: 'Hey, do you remember me?'

She stands for a minute, smiling shyly. 'Yes, you must be Uncle Indres.'

'What? I'm not Uncle Indres. Just Indres!'

I ask her jovially to move back so that I can have a full view of her. Then I tell her to turn around. She just stands there. So I say, 'Come on. Turn around,' and she slowly turns giving Reggie and me a complete picture of her.

'My God! You've really grown up beautiful. The last time I saw you, you were a little nipper with snot running down your nose, I used to bully and tease you.'

I remember how I always used to chase her out of the room and tell her to go to the shop to buy me biscuits, always the same kind, Romany Creams. She just smiles at me, and I leave her to her father who has come out of his shock and starts talking to her. The arguments we used to have about whether or not his daughter should visit him. She was only six years old at the time of our arrest and not allowed, by prison regulations, to see him until she turned sixteen. So when her sixteenth birthday came we said, 'Good. Now she can come.' But Reggie was opposed to the idea, saying that he would soon be out and he did not want her to see him for the first time, after all those years, in prison. 'Nonsense,' we told him, 'she will be proud to see her father inside for fighting for the cause of peace and justice.'

In fact, one of the strong feelings we always had was that if we died and South Africa was still not free, our children would always be able to turn around and say that their dads had contributed towards the struggle of the people of South Africa, that they would

259

never feel ashamed of us or accuse us of having failed to fight.

My mother is calling me. 'Indres, what do you want for your first meal outside?'

All of a sudden I cannot think of anything, too many dishes flash through my mind, I cannot choose. I look at my mom and tell her to decide, she knows my favourite dishes.

'Do you want a meat dish, or a vegetable dish?'

She is being tactful. Visions of steak, chicken, huge plates of biriyani, tomato chutney, curried rhubarb – or, even better – cooked mango, a slice of buttered bread with cheese, and a cup of good coffee, fill my head.

'No, Ma, you decide everything.'

'Even meat?' She is being very tactful.

'Yes. Even meat.'

My brother butts in to say that they will be leaving some clothing for us; what type would I want to have?

'No, man, we want to leave in prison garb.'

This is the best visit we have ever had, full of joy and expectation. My brother tells me that they have painted my room and bought a beautiful hi-fi set, and my other brother chips in to say that if I'm not put under house arrest – which is quite possible, since the Special Branch has been visiting them and making enquiries – they will throw the biggest party Johannesburg has ever seen.

Before we know what has happened the warder shouts, 'Time up!'

We cannot believe it, and protest. But my brothers look at their watches and say it is true, the time has really passed by. All the excited mothers and fathers and brothers and sisters and daughters say last minute goodbyes, and begin to troop out.

'Oh, Uncle Indres. Do you still like Romany Creams?' She is smiling; more settled; her eyes wet with tears, yet filled with joy.

Coffee, green soup and bread. Not even real coffee; a tin mug of

260

what they call coffee and what, I must admit, we have come to regard as coffee over the years, even to enjoy as coffee. I push the food aside and say, 'No, not this time. I'd rather have my next meal outside.'

My comrades remind me that there is still a full night to go, that I'll be hungry, and who knows what will be waiting for us on our release, I mustn't be stupid. But I am adamant and ask the young Black Consciousness guys if they would like my portion. They are hungry, but reluctant to deprive me of my food, but I insist, and they quickly dispose of it all. Food is food.

'Tell us what Nelson Mandela is really like. Who is he?'

We explain, each one chipping in and interrupting the other, adding detail on detail: how Mandela came from a chief's clan in the Transkei, went to Fort Hare University, was chucked out as a rebel, studied law and qualified as an attorney together with his comrade Oliver Tambo, the two of them setting up legal practice together in Johannesburg, going in and out of prison all the time for their ANC activities; Oliver Tambo being sent out of the country by the ANC at the time of Sharpeville to get international support for our struggle; Nelson Mandela going full time underground and becoming Commander-in-Chief of Umkhonto we Sizwe.

This is all news to them, and we are amazed that people so dedicated to the struggle against oppression could have been so effectively cut off for so long from what, for us, had been common knowledge, part of our lives.

'What is Umkhonto? Is it the same as MK?'

We explain how Mandela went out of the country and received military instruction in Algeria, how hundreds of young people were smuggled out of the country to receive military training or to take up scholarships abroad, while some of us stayed behind to sabotage apartheid institutions and undermine the economy.

We are all talking at once. These guys do not stand a chance as we pile one piece of information after the other on them: about the Defiance of Unjust Laws Campaign when thousands voluntarily went to jail, about the Freedom Charter,* our basic document, which declares that South Africa belongs to all who live in it – they are doubtful, but listen. Of the army being built up outside the country, of the ANC guerrillas who fought alongside our Zimbabwe comrades trying to get down to South Africa, of the guerrillas who, we were sure, were getting back into the country all the time.

The army. They keep asking us to tell them more about the army. We pass on what we know about Mandela's famous 'I am prepared to die' speech, explaining the need for armed struggle; about the great successes achieved by our acting president, Tambo, in getting international backing from independent Africa, from the Socialist countries, the Scandinavian states, international workers' and church organisations, and from the United Nations itself, creating conditions for our people's army to grow. We tell them about the good relations established with Swapo, with MPLA and with Frelimo.

'But why do you always say "Acting President Oliver Tambo"?'

We tell them of the great loss suffered when our President, Chief Luthuli, was killed and how Oliver Tambo was elected acting president to fill the gap. 'We are an organisation of the people,' we tell them, 'not just of the leaders. But we are proud of our leaders, always in the thick of the struggle, intelligent, courageous, disciplined, with a clear strategy uniting all our forces, carrying out their historic responsibilities. Tambo is one of the great leaders of Africa.' We are enthusiastic.

'And Mandela?' They keep coming back to him. 'What is he like as a person? What does he look like?'

And we tell them about our struggles on the Island, the hunger strikes, McNichol's visit, the tall, slightly hunched figure of

---

*The Freedom Charter was adopted at the Congress of the People held at Kliptown in June 1955.

We are walking down a passage in our khaki prison clothes, excited and intensely nervous, wondering what sort of reception we will get outside.

It is 12 May 1973. How we jumped out of our blankets when the morning bell rang. A gate is unlocked and we walk through it and up some stairs, Kumalo escorting us from behind, telling us all the time how the world has changed, that black men are getting on now, that he is a chief warder while Head Warder Rodney, who used to be in charge of us before, is now a lieutenant in charge of all Transkei prisoners. We should try to adjust to the new world we are going to.

A second gate is unlocked and we go down another passage, getting more and more tense as we move along. What is this new world like? Will we be a decade out of date? Are we Rip van Winkles, waking up after ten years' sleep?

A third gate is unlocked, and we find ourselves in the reception area where we see three brown parcels waiting for us with our names on them.

We are told to change – we cannot keep our khaki uniforms, they belong to the prison – so we open the parcels: for Reggie a fine suit, for Shirish a smart jacket and trouser set, and for me a floral shirt and a pair of bell-bottomed pants. Bell-bottomed pants! Everybody laughs, imagining me wearing such an outlandish piece of clothing, but there is no alternative and I try them on, seeing my feet disappear underneath the cloth, all of us roaring with laughter, wondering how I will be able to walk in trousers that flap from side to side.

I am feeling as smart as possible, but uncomfortable. My hair combed back, straight cut at the back, ears visible at the sides, thin pencil moustache on my top lip, the pants and shirt out of keeping with the style I remember.

Kumalo is laughing louder than anybody. 'God, you're already a *tsotsi* [street tough].'

We are feeling different, and free. We are anxious to be out of the building as soon as possible, but first we are ordered to call in at the officer's section.

'Reggie Vandeyar!'

Reggie is the first to go into the office and Shirish and I talk to each other while we wait for him to return. He emerges with a couple of documents in his hand.

'House arrest, chaps. After you get yours I won't be able to talk to you.'

I go in next and see two plain-clothes Special Branch men holding typed documents in a folder in front of them. I notice behind them a large plate-glass window, and behind it a garden, and behind that a big crowd of colourfully dressed people all gesticulating, waving their arms frantically in my direction, huge smiles on their faces.

'Are you Indres Naidoo?'

'Yes.'

'Mr Naidoo, I am instructed by the Minister of Justice, in terms of Section 9(1) of Act 44 of 1950 . . .'

I am not listening, my eyes are searching out faces in the crowd in the distance. There's my mother, waving like mad. I cannot wave back. Who is that little girl standing next to her? Is that my brother's son sitting on my brother's shoulder?

'. . . absenting yourself from the residential premises situate at . . . except between the hours of . . .'

Three people are holding garlands, lovely flowers tied with glittering thread. There are more and more people waving frantically, they all seem to know me, yet I can only recognise a face here and there. It will be a great honour. I have never been garlanded before.

'Mr Naidoo, this is important, please pay attention . . . hereby prohibited from communicating with any other person whose name appears . . .'

My mother is bending down next to a little kid, pointing in my direction.

'. . . under the hand of the Minister of Justice . . . Is that all clear to you, Mr Naidoo?'

'Yes.'

'Sign here, please, and remember, you are prohibited from communicating with Vandeyar. You may go.'

We walk out of the open front door, shaking a little, a beautiful blue sky overhead, our muscles tense in the unfamiliar clothes; past the flower beds, hearing a buzz getting louder and louder, people waving furiously with both arms, jumping up and down; the men as colourfully dressed as the women: thick droopy moustaches, full beards and long hair lifting and falling over hidden ears. I feel very spare with my short-back-and-sides haircut and pencil moustache.

We have agreed on what to do . . .

Whose are all those faces in front of us, these strange people, each one trying to draw our attention as if we should know who he or she is?

We move toward the open gate . . .

The roar of the crowd is very loud, we hear our names and at the exact moment when we reach the gateway, we three raise our fists in the air:

'*Amandla!*' we shout. 'Power!'

'*Ngawethu!*' the crowd responds. 'To the people!'

We salute the world.

Epilogue to 2003 edition

We were released from prison after serving our ten years, every day of the ten long years, 3652 days of our lives, into twilight freedom. From prison bars and prison walls, into house arrest, prisoners in our own homes, and guards over ourselves. We were given five-year house arrest orders. The order read:

'WHEREAS I, PETRUS CORNELIUS PELSER, Minister of Justice, am satisfied that you engage in activities which are furthering or are calculated to further the achievement of any of the objects of communism, I hereby in terms of section 9 (1) of the Suppression of Communism Act, 1950 (Act No.44 of 1950), prohibit you for a period commencing on the date on which this notice is delivered or tendered to you and expiring on the 31ˢᵗ day of May, 1978, from attending within the Republic of South Africa or the territory of South West Africa . . .'

- We had to be indoors from 7 p.m. to 7 a.m. from Monday to Friday, on Saturday from 2 p.m. to Monday 7 a.m. and all public holidays.
- We had to report to the police station every Saturday between 7 a.m. and 2 p.m.

- We were not to communicate with any person or persons who were banned, house arrested or listed under the anti-communism act.
- We were not allowed to have any visitor whatsoever at home except a medical doctor for medical attention.
- We were not allowed to leave the Johannesburg magisterial district.
- We were not allowed to enter any factory building.
- We were not allowed to enter any building used for printing, publishing or distributing newspapers or other periodicals.
- We were not allowed to enter any education centre, school, university or kindergarten.
- We were not allowed to attend any gathering of more than two people (oneself included).
- We were not allowed to address any meeting/s.
- We were not allowed to write to or be interviewed or quoted by any press whatsoever . . .

All this was *'Given under my hand at Cape Town on this 12th day of April 1973'. (Signed) P C PELSER, Minister of Justice.*

The house arrest order meant I could not talk to my sister Shantie, who was in exile in London, and was a banned person in South Africa. Nor could I speak to my brother Murthie, who lived in the same house as I did and was a listed person. But I ignored it and spoke to both of them. My sister phoned me on the day of my release, to welcome me and to wish me good luck.

We were released into a totally new world. The world had left us far behind in many respects and it was very scary. For the first time we saw the fashions of the seventies: mini-skirts and bell-bottomed pants, men with long hair and some with long beards. New highways had been built in and around Johannesburg. Men had landed on the moon. It was mind-boggling. These were frightening times for my two comrades and myself – it was like waking up after a hundred years of sleep. Even people's social lives had changed, in some cases for the better but in most cases for the worse. The apartheid system was firmly in place. The oppression of the black people was at its height. Politics both in the country and around the world had changed. In Chile a new government under the leadership of Salvador Allende had come into power, to last only a few months. In South Africa the Black Consciousness Movement had become firmly rooted. On the surface the ANC and MK were not to be seen, but people whispered in corners about the underground movement.

In spite of being under such very strict restrictions, with the police keeping an around-the-clock watch on me and on our house, and even knowing that some of our neighbours were paid informers, the ANC underground made contact with me. I worked very closely with comrades like Joe Gqabi, Henry Makgothi, Robert Manci, Martin Ramogadi and others. I conducted political classes once a week with young activists from Soweto, many of them leaders in the Soweto uprising, with students from Wits University and with workers' groups.

I helped set up the Ahmed Timol Memorial Committee. Ahmed was an ANC underground activist who was killed in detention by the security police in 1971. The police harassed the committee and its meetings were banned. We changed the name of the committee something more 'kosher', the Human Rights Committee. To all intents and purposes the HRC was an internal ANC grouping. The idea was to keep ANC philosophy and the teachings of the Congress Movements alive in the minds of the people. The committee helped with the funeral arrangements for Bram Fischer, a leading member of the South African Communist Party and a loved and respected freedom fighter. Bram had been sentenced to life imprisonment for his role in the Struggle. He died in May 1975, shortly after being released into the custody of his brother in the terminal stages of cancer.

The HRC organised meetings and rallies on important national liberation days such as May Day, 26 June and South African Women's day (9 August). On 26 June 1975 the HRC quarterly bulletin carried the story of 'Two Important Days': the independence of Mozambique and the twentieth anniversary of the Freedom Charter. For the first time since the banning of the ANC and the Freedom Charter, the latter was published and distributed all over the country. The publication was popular and there were demands for more copies both in South Africa and abroad. The Freedom Charter caused great excitement throughout the country. Many people had never heard of it before. The government banned the publication immediately as well as all subsequent copies of the bulletin.

On 18 March 1976 Joseph Mdluli, the ANC leader in Natal, was detained and in less than twenty-four hours he died in detention. The South African security police alleged that Comrade Mdluli had fallen over a chair and died. Comrade Phyllis Naidoo, who lived in Durban and whose banning order had just elapsed, sent me photographs taken by the undertaker of Comrade Joseph's body. There were torture and bruise marks and severe swelling and cuts all over his body. They were the most horrifying colour photographs imaginable. With the assistance of a Dutch national, a former Roman Catholic priest named Toine Eggenhuisen, I smuggled the photos out of the country to my sister in London. They were exhibited by the ANC in the Houses of Parliament and also at the United Nations in New York. They were shown worldwide as testimony to the horrors of the apartheid regime. I was arrested and taken to the notorious John Vorster Square police station in the centre of Johannesburg where I was questioned about the photographs. It was alleged that I had sent them to the ANC in London. I admitted sending the photos to my sister but not to the ANC, and that I had mailed them from the Johannesburg central post office. The security police looked shocked but I was released after being told that I would hear from them again.

Toine was 'removed' from the country in November 1976. He became active in the Anti-Apartheid Movement in Holland and thereafter worked full time at the ANC London office. Today he works at the ANC head office in Luthuli House in Johannesburg.

By 1976 tension was running high in the country. Hundreds of people were detained, many died in detention and hundreds of young people disappeared overnight. The government was becoming more and more ruthless in the methods used to crack down on our people. The student uprising of 1976 was completely predictable. Students throughout the country were up in arms, and hundreds of young people were killed. The economy of the country, which had been booming only a few months earlier, began to crumble. ANC underground and MK units were active throughout the country and students and young people left in droves for military training in the ANC camps outside the borders. The ANC underground was overstretched and under great pressure. Soweto hit the world headlines on 16 June 1976 when thousands of schoolchildren marched in protest against the government instruction that Afrikaans had to be used as one of the media of tuition in secondary schools. They were fired on by the police and fifteen people died that day, while scores were injured.

Some time after the Soweto uprising a priest came to see me. He told me that he had met Thabo Mbeki in London, and had had a long discussion with him on the progress the ANC was making. I listened to him without comment. He then suddenly opened his briefcase which was filled with thousands of US dollars. I had never in my life seen so much money at one time. He claimed it was from Thabo, to finance underground operations. I felt uneasy. Was this a trap by the Special Branch or was he genuine? I refused to touch the money and sent the priest packing. It was only much later when I was in exile in Lusaka that Thabo confirmed that the priest was genuine. I have never seen him again.

Amongst the many people who helped in the underground

operations were the Reverends Reinhard Brückner and Horst Kleinschmidt, both of whom worked for the South African Council of Churches. From time to time they provided money for transport for ANC cadres to leave the country, helped to hide underground cadres and even gave us their cars to transport cadres to Swaziland. The Reverend Brückner was detained just after the June 16th uprising. On his release from detention he was given twenty-four hours to leave the country.

On 31 December 1976 Comrade Joe Gqabi was detained but he managed to smuggle out a message that Henry Makgothi, Martin Ramogadi and I should leave the country immediately. On 2 January 1977 the ANC underground structures took me out of the country into Swaziland. It was the first time in my life that I had been in a free country and the feeling was overwhelming. I felt on top of the world. The ANC structure in Swaziland kept me in hiding for a week and then transferred me to Mozambique. In Maputo I felt free, with no house arrest order hanging over my head. I could come and go as I pleased. The Mozambican people were very helpful, not only to me but to all my comrades.

In Mozambique I was put in charge of Internal Political Reconstruction in the Maputo region, under the leadership of Comrades John Motsabe and Mac Maharaj who were based at the ANC head office in Lusaka.

Life in exile had its ups and downs. The government and the people of Mozambique gave the ANC all the support and assistance possible. They gave us shelter and protection and, as far as possible, logistical support. The radio, the newspapers and television gave the ANC and the Struggle in South Africa a lot of coverage. The Solidarity Movement 'AMASP' organised rallies and fundraising events and mobilised mass support amongst the Mozambicans for the freedom struggle in South Africa. Their slogan was *We are forty million people* (South Africa, thirty million, and Mozambique, ten million).

In September 1977 I was invited by the United Nation Special

Committee on Apartheid to address their session in New York. My presentation was on the conditions of political prisoners in South Africa, the torture and deaths of detainees in South African police stations, the brutality of warders in the prisons. Scores of detainees had died mysteriously in South African prisons and police stations throughout the country from the early 1960s right up to the 1990s. Comrade 'Looksmart' S Ngudle, an ANC militant and workers' leader, was killed in detention in 1963. Suliman 'Babla' Salojee, a close friend and comrade, was killed in 1964. I also spoke on the executions carried out by the apartheid regime. Comrades like Vuyisile Mini, Wilton Khayingo and Zinakila Mkhaba, all three trade union leaders, were hanged in 1964 after being found guilty of sabotage. John Harris, an active Liberal and organiser of the campaign against racial discrimination in sport in South Africa, was hanged in Pretoria after being found guilty of murder. He had planted a bomb at the Johannesburg station and a woman and child were killed.

I travelled extensively in America, Europe and Africa on speaking tours and addressed demonstrations and mass rallies against the apartheid regime.

In December 1979 one of my underground contacts from South Africa, Linda Bernhardt, came to see me in Swaziland. She told me that Stephen Lee was in hiding in Johannesburg at Esther Leviton's house. Comrades Stephen Lee, Alex Moumbaris and Tim Jenkin had escaped from Pretoria Central Prison a few days earlier. She said that my brother Prema and Shirish Nanabhai were the only other persons who knew about Steve's presence in Johannesburg. After planning and plotting, the MK underground unit went into action and brought Steve safely out of the country into Mozambique. Later, Steve described the action as very professional. Years later, in April 1982, my brother Prema, Shirish and Michael Jenkin were sentenced to three years' imprisonment, two years of which were suspended for five years. They were found guilty of harbouring and assisting a dangerous terrorist on the run.

Many South Africans, mostly women, were married to Mozambicans. A number of them joined the ANC and MK and played an active role in the armed struggle and in the political struggle. Some of them paid the ultimate price for it.

Foreigners, who came in their hundreds to help the development of Mozambique, supported our struggle. They came from Zambia, Tanzania and England through an organisation called MAGIC (Mozambique, Angola, Guinea-Bissau Information Committee), based in London. The 'Afrika Group' from Sweden, CUSO/SUCO of Canada, the Holland Africa Committee, and many other non-governmental Organisations, gave moral and financial support to the movement. Chileans and Brazilians living in exile in Mozambique also took an active part in our struggle.

Helene Pastoor and Klaas de Jong are amongst the many heroes and heroines of our struggle. In February 1981 we had to bury twelve of our comrades who had been murdered by the South African Defence Force on the outskirts of Maputo, in a place called Matola. They had been killed in the early hours of the morning while they were asleep. It was a blazing hot day. The temperature was about 40 degrees Celsius and I, as many other comrades, had spent the whole morning and better part of the afternoon at the funeral service. I arrived home hot and tired. Just then we heard a lot of noise in our neighbours' yard. The neighbours, Ann, a Tanzanian, and her Belgian husband Mark Wuyts were good friends of ours. I shouted, 'Hi, Ann, you are making a hell of a noise!' She replied: 'Jump over and meet some friends of ours from Holland.'

That was when I met Helene and Klaas for the first time, and it was the start of a good friendship. Later, I recruited both Helene and Klaas into the ANC and MK. They both agreed to smuggle

ANC propaganda material into South Africa. They did a wonderful job, knowingly risking their lives. At the end of 1981 Comrade Joe Slovo asked me if I could find someone to take arms into South Africa. I approached Helene and Klaas and they agreed. And that was the beginning of their long courier service as ANC/MK freedom fighters. They went into South Africa at least once a month, smuggling arms and ammunition like AK47s, Makarov pistols, limpet mines, grenades, Sam Six rocket missiles. Finally they were arrested in 1987 in South Africa. Helene was sentenced to ten years' imprisonment, while Klaas managed to escape from the South African Police and took refuge at the Dutch Embassy in Pretoria for over a year. Finally the Dutch government managed to get him out of the country. Klaas became active in the Anti-Apartheid Movement in Holland. Helene, after being released from prison, went to work in Brazil.

In August 1982 the ANC and AMASP brought over the great South African jazz pianist Abdullah Ibrahim, his wife, the jazz singer Bea Benjamin, and a group of musicians to perform at our Freedom Concert. Every performance was completely sold out. It was at this time that the Centre for African Studies of the Eduardo Mondlane University in Maputo, together with UNESCO, organised a seminar on Teaching Social Science in Southern African Universities. Comrade Ruth First was one of the organisers. On the last day of the seminar, 17 August 1982, she was murdered by a letter bomb sent by an apartheid hit squad. Others in her office who were injured were ANC National Executive Committee member Pallo Jordan, Ms Bridgett O'Loughlin (an American citizen), and the director of the Centre of African Studies, Professor Aquino Braganza, who was a political adviser to President Samora Machel. It was a traumatic time for all of us. Our first reaction was to call off the last concert. The Freedom Concert Committee met and decided to continue with the last show, and to dedicate it to the memory of Ruth First and all those murdered by the South African regime. We got the backing and support of Frelimo, the ANC and Comrade Joe Slovo, husband of Ruth First. The Vice-President of Mozambique, top members of the government, leaders of Frelimo, the diplomatic corps of Maputo, the top leadership of the ANC and the Slovo family attended this last farewell concert. It was a solemn, dignified event, but also a magnificent jazz concert.

One year later the South African Communist Party and the African National Congress held a Ruth First memorial lecture, 'Fifty years as a member of the Communist Party', delivered by Jack Simons. On the second anniversary Comrade Joe Slovo delivered the lecture: 'Why the armed struggle in South Africa?' The hall was packed with Mozambicans, foreigners, ANC members and the diplomatic community. Even the racist South African Trade Mission representative Collin Patterson was there. As chairperson I welcomed the guests, making special mention of his presence. After the lecture, people gathered to show support for Joe Slovo and the ANC. Collin Patterson shook hands with Joe Slovo and offered his sympathy. A few days later a Johannesburg-based newspaper carried a story of the first ever meeting between an official South African representative and the ANC.

In 1983 a South African Defence Force plane bombed three places in Maputo and Matola at six in the morning, hitting an ANC residence, killing one ANC cadre and a Mozambican citizen, and also hitting a jam factory where three Mozambican citizens were killed. Fortunately, the day care centre adjacent to the jam factory had not yet opened. The apartheid regime claimed that the jam factory was an ANC arms and bomb-making factory. Reacting to this, the Mozambican authorities took the diplomatic corps to see the bombed sites. The British Ambassador in Maputo at the time said: 'I might be old and senile, but what I see here is a jam factory and nothing but a jam factory'.

A few days later, while I was having an afternoon nap, I heard a loud bang over our house. I ran outside to find out what was going on, only to see a big black cloud of smoke in the sky. Everybody was talking about a South African plane being shot down over Maputo. People were singing and dancing in the streets with joy. Later we discovered it was a drone sent over Maputo by the South African regime, on a reconnaissance mission. It was a great victory for the Mozambicans.

On 16 March 1984, the racist South African President P W Botha and the Mozambican President Samora Machel signed the Nkomati Accord, a non-aggression pact between South Africa and Mozambique. It caught us by total surprise. We could not believe that the Mozambican government would do this to us. Not only were the ANC members angry, but a large number of the Mozambicans and almost all the *cooperantes* were angered by what was regarded as a sell-out of the South African revolution.

On 22 March I was preparing a party for my son Bram's ninth birthday when he came and told me that a number of Mozambican soldiers were outside our gate. I approached the soldiers to find out what they wanted. They informed me that they had been ordered to search our neighbours' house. I told them that the neighbours were on holiday and would only return at the end of the month. Irritated and angry, they asked to use my phone to call their headquarters. They were given orders to wait outside the house for further instructions. In the mean time I discovered that the army had raided all ANC houses and the ANC office. We had a problem on our hands that had to be solved fast. The fact was that we always took advantage of the absence of our neighbours to hide arms and ammunition in their house. Although the soldiers were swarming around us, my Comrade Sonny Singh (also known as Bobby) and I managed to move the weapons to safety. Only after the house was 'cleaned', did I give the soldiers the keys to enter it. They searched the premises from top to bottom and left about two hours later empty-handed, little realising that they had been searching the wrong house.

In terms of the Nkomati Accord, the South African regime had to stop its support for Renamo, the Mozambique terrorist movement that was causing total destruction in the countryside, murdering hundreds of people. The Mozambicans were to discontinue their support for Umkhonto we Sizwe and to stop harbouring ANC/MK cadres in Mozambique. This meant that hundreds of MK cadres had to be transferred to Zambia, Tanzania, Angola and other places. Many of our comrades went into Swaziland, others infiltrated into South Africa and lot disappeared into hiding in Mozambique, while we sent out a lot of old people and children to make up the numbers that had to leave the country. Officially only ten of us and our families were to remain behind to staff our diplomatic office. This caused a problem with donor countries, because they had been looking after thousands of our cadres in the past. Now they were threatening to look after ten families only. We had to convince them that hundreds of new freedom fighters were still crossing from South Africa into Mozambique regularly. We also had to admit to them that hundreds of MK cadres were still in the country under cover, which meant we had to break security by revealing their presence. This was a violation of the Nkomati Accord and a security risk to the MK combatants.

On 8 March 1986 Comrade Moses Mabhida, the General Secretary of the South African Communist Party, died in Maputo. Frelimo insisted that the funeral take place in Maputo. They stated that Comrade Mabhida was not only an ANC/SACP leader but also a leader of Mozambican people and for that matter of the whole of the African continent. Comrade Mabhida was given a state funeral. His body lay in state at the Maputo city hall for two days. Scores of comrades from South Africa came to the funeral. Among them were Comrades Dorothy Nyembe and Archie Gumede. The speakers at the funeral were Comrade Oliver Tambo and the President of Mozambique, Comrade Samora Machel. Comrade Machel once again repeated in his speech: 'We are forty million, the racist regime will never defeat us.'

The Mozambican government offered a plane to transport our leaders and members in Lusaka to the funeral. One of their conditions was that all comrades must have valid travel documents. We agreed, but to my surprise more than half of the approximately 250 comrades who arrived had no travel documents whatsoever and caused so much chaos and confusion, that they all got through the border without immigration or customs checking them. To make matters worse, they were all carrying big, heavy suitcases. I discovered much later in the day that most of them were well-trained cadres, smuggling in arms and ammunition and that they were preparing to move in to South Africa soon.

Just seven months later, on 19 October 1986, Comrade Samora Machel was killed in a plane crash in the hills of South Africa, near the Mozambique border. Even today the Mozambican people, most South Africans and many in other parts of the world believe that the plane was brought down by the apartheid regime. I contacted Comrades Albertina Sisulu and Winnie Mandela and asked them to attend the funeral on behalf of the South African people. Initially the apartheid regime agreed to provide them with travel documents, but at the last minute they were refused.

Many of our comrades were killed in Mozambique and in many other Southern African countries too. Some were poisoned, like Comrade Gibson Mondane, others were shot and some were killed by bombs. Our lives were in constant danger from South African hit squads. There were times when the Mozambican authorities would inform us of possible attacks on ANC houses, which meant we had to sleep at friends' houses.

On Christmas Eve 1986 the President of Mozambique, Comrade Joaquim Chissano, received a letter from President P W Botha, informing him that there were six South African terrorists who were responsible for 92 per cent of all terror activities in South

Africa. He named these six as: Jacob Zuma, who was then the chairperson of the Political-Military Committee; Suzanne Rabkin, then secretary to the PMC; Mohamed Timol, then in charge of security; Keith Mokoape, and Sonny Singh and myself who were then in charge of propaganda. In his letter he stated that if we were not removed from Mozambique soon, he would not be responsible for what might happen to us. He threatened to blockade the port of Maputo and disrupt the Beira corridor project, which was a US$100-million project. Comrade Chissano immediately called a meeting with Comrade Oliver Tambo, sending his plane to Lusaka to bring him to Maputo. After lengthy discussions it was agreed that the six of us should leave Mozambique. We insisted on leaving only after 8 January, the ANC's seventy-fifth birthday. We had worked so hard on the preparations to celebrate this event.

Shortly before the celebration, a South African Afrikaans newspaper carried an article alleging that I had made a statement to the effect that the Mozambican government was kicking us out of the country. The reality we experienced was quite the contrary. The Mozambican authorities were very concerned about our welfare and safety and ready to take whatever action we felt was necessary to protect us. Our President had agreed that it was best for us as well as for the Mozambicans that we were transferred from Maputo.

The ANC's birthday party was a great success. Over a thousand guests attended, including the entire diplomatic corps in Maputo. For the first time ever, the Federal Republic of Germany, British and American diplomats attended one of our functions. Comrade Jacob Zuma, on behalf of the ANC and on behalf of the six of us, thanked the Mozambican people for being such good hosts to all of us. I took the opportunity to attack the Afrikaans newspaper for carrying fabricated stories about us.

The following day, 9 January 1987, we left for the ANC head office in Lusaka, Zambia.

I spent over one year in Lusaka, working most of the time in the Secretary General's office. In between, the ANC sent me to Sweden on a six-month course in Civil Administration. At the end of March 1988 the ANC appointed me Deputy Representative of the ANC in the German Democratic Republic. I decided to fly to Berlin via Maputo. I arrived there on 1 April 1988. Albie Sachs picked me up at the airport, promising to take me back a week later for my departure to Berlin. While I was still living in Maputo Albie quite often asked me to look after his car, a maroon Honda Civic, while he was out of town. He was still driving the same left-hand-drive car which I knew so well from the past.

The Mozambicans gave me a warm welcome and a number of dinner parties were organised. On 7 April, which is Mozambican Women's Day and was to be my last day in Maputo, I was busy with last-minute chores and farewells. As I arrived home at about 10 a.m. I bumped into a Brazilian comrade, Pedro Chaves. I could see immediately that something was wrong. He was pale and shaking, clearly very distressed. He said: 'Albie Boom.' I looked at him, not comprehending. I asked, 'Pedro, what are you saying?' He repeated: 'Albie Boom', throwing both his hands into the air. Immediately I rushed to the flat in Avenue Julius Nyerere were Albie lived. The streets around Albie's flat were completely sealed off. I managed to get through the security using my ANC membership card. What I saw then was incredible. I couldn't believe my eyes. Albie's car was a complete wreck, pieces of it scattered far and wide. There was blood everywhere and, even worse, pieces of flesh. It was a horrendous mess. There was total pandemonium. People all around were crying. A number of other cars had been damaged and windows shattered. It was a scene of utter carnage – broken glass, ripped car parts and blood. I could not believe that anybody could have survived such an attack.

The police chief in charge told me that Albie had been taken to the general hospital. I dashed there, only to find the hospital sealed off. Once again, I managed to make my way through security using my ANC membership card. A number of our Mozambican comrades were attending to Albie. What I saw was shocking. Albie was unconscious. Almost every inch of his body was lacerated. His eyes seemed to be damaged, his right arm had been severed, and his left hand was badly damaged. There were about ten doctors around him – Dr Manuel Leite, Dr Ivo Garrido, Dr Tino and others. Dr Manuel Leite, who used to play bridge with Albie and me, told me that Albie's condition was stable and that the doctors were working around the clock on him. I thanked him and the entire team. Manuel responded: 'Don't thank me. After all, you and Albie are our comrades. It is our duty.' I left the hospital feeling shaken and miserable. That night the Mozambican television news was delayed half an hour. When it finally came on, they showed the most horrific, graphic pictures of the explosion. It was like watching a James Bond movie, only it was real. I was told that this news item was flashed throughout the world.

On the following morning, the day of my departure for the GDR, I went to see Albie. The first thing he said as I entered his hospital room was: 'Why are you looking so serious? Come, hold my hand.' Imagine how I felt, with Albie lying there, one arm amputated and the other badly damaged. But he seemed in good spirits. We talked about everything but the explosion. As I was about to leave Albie said: 'Sorry, Indres, I will not be able to take you to the airport.' I was amazed that Albie, with the most horrible injuries imaginable, could find the courage to be humorous. It was all I could do to manage a smile. That evening I boarded my flight to Berlin.

A year or so later, I got a call from the Johannesburg-based newspaper, *The Weekly Mail*. The journalist informed me that they had finally traced me via London. I was asked to confirm or comment on a story that the car bomb was meant for me and not for Albie. This caught me by surprise. The journalist told me that, according to information they had received from a member of the South African Military Intelligence and Civil Cooperation

Bureau (CCB), the CCB knew I was in Maputo and on my way to Berlin. They knew that I used Albie's car quite often and that was why they had planted the bomb in his car. My only comment was: 'Albie was the victim and not me. I know no more.'

This story was confirmed on my return to South Africa many years later by a CCB/MI hit man. This man had applied for amnesty to the Truth and Reconciliation Commission (TRC) for the car bomb attack which nearly killed Albie and for the killing of a number of our comrades whom he named when we met in Johannesburg in July 1998. Present at the meeting were some of the comrades who were on his hit list: Sue Rabkin, Mohamed Timol, Sonny Singh and myself. According to him, I was one of the main targets to be eliminated and many attempts had been made on my life. They just never managed to get me. He said to me: 'You are very lucky to be alive today.'

We also learned at this meeting that the apartheid regime under then President P W Botha had made many attempts on our lives. We were told that in 1988 a group of CCB/MI hit men were to make a two-pronged attack on ANC targets in Swaziland and Maputo. They arrived in international waters close to the Maputo harbour in a submarine and waited for instructions to land in speedboats. They had orders to eliminate all six of us: Jacob Zuma, Sue Rabkin, Mohamed Timol, Sonny Singh, Keith Mokoape and myself. The CCB/MI hit man was in charge of that operation. He told us that they were fully equipped with heavy war equipment which they were ready to use.

The attack in Swaziland went badly wrong. They accidentally kidnapped a Swiss couple, which immediately created an inter-national outcry, and they had to call off the attack in Maputo. Because of that failure, they planted the car bomb which nearly killed Albie, a soft and defenceless target.

On 9 October 2000, some eight months after publication of the first South African edition of *Island in Chains*, the TRC granted amnesty to former South African Defence Force member Henri van der Westhuizen for the attempted murder of Albie Sachs. At the hearing, which took place in Johannesburg, Van der Westhuizen stated:

'The car bomb in which Professor Albie Sachs was injured was meant for Mr Indres Naidoo and not Professor Sachs ... What's important is the fact that Albie Sachs was not the target, because Indres Naidoo was the target ... The entire aspect with regard to who was a target and who was not a target was a process that was followed within the working group, within the so-called Trevits working group who sat in Middelburg, where the entire intelligence community, in other words the security branch, military intelligence, national intelligence, they all came in and said "Who are the members who had to be taken out that would have an impact on the ANC's day to day circumstances within a certain target area?" And within the Intelligence Community it was valued that Mr Naidoo played a very important and prominent role in terms of the infiltration of MK members to Natal and Eastern Transvaal, who on their part found their way open to the PWV area [Pretoria, Witwatersrand, Vereeniging] and then that he would also be involved or had knowledge of where ANC members housed themselves in Mozambique, as well as where the arms came from and where these arms were channelled.'*

My flight from Maputo to Berlin was uneventful. I arrived early in the morning, dressed for the European winter. From what I had been told, the European winter was supposed to be very cold. But, to my surprise, it was a hot April day. I felt on top of the world, coming to Berlin to represent my organisation. I went through immigration with no trouble. At customs, my baggage

*Minutes of the TRC Amnesty hearing, 9 October 2000, Mayfair, Johannesburg, pages 62-65.

was put through the X-ray machine. Two of the officers looked into the bag, and then one of them looked at me and asked, '*Was ist das?*' I didn't understand German. They pointed at the X-ray machine and said, '*Sehen Sie sich das mal an!*' Very confused, I looked at the X-ray machine and saw that there was a bayonet in my suitcase. I remembered putting the bayonet into my suitcase some time before in Maputo and had then completely forgotten about it. There was a lot of confusion. Me speaking in English, they speaking in German, neither understanding the other. Eventually, a senior official who spoke a little English came along. I explained to him that I was a member of the African National Congress and the bayonet was meant for my protection in Maputo. After some anxious moments, he finally gave orders. The bayonet was confiscated and I was on my way out of the airport. My comrades picked me up and we drove to the ANC office in Berlin-Pankow, a diplomatic suburb in East Berlin. As we approached the many embassies, I saw the ANC flag flying high and felt great pride at seeing our flag flying side by side with those of the other nations of the world. Tears of joy filled my eyes.

The ANC enjoyed full diplomatic status in the GDR. We had an office-cum-residence for our chief representative and three flats for the other ANC staff members. We had three cars with CD registration and wherever we went we enjoyed diplomatic recognition. For the first time in all my years in exile, I earned a salary from the GDR Solidarity Committee and did not have to live on handouts. And for the first time in my life I was in charge of my own financial arrangements. I travelled the length and breadth of the GDR, speaking at public meetings, at schools, factories, church groups and solidarity groups, and also at diplomatic gatherings. Wherever we went, we were given a warm welcome; people wanted to know more about South Africa and about the liberation struggle. I found the people, both young and old, to be well informed about events in Africa, and Southern Africa in particular.

In a town called Ilmenau, there is a school called Nelson Mandela Schule. Every year on 26 June the town and the school had a South Africa Solidarity Day of festivities, including sports and cultural events. The ANC was always invited to speak and the ANC students' musical group in the GDR, which was called *Amandla*, was always invited to perform.

In addition to other forms of support for the ANC, the GDR also gave us at least one hundred scholarships a year for trade schools, technical schools, secondary schools and university education. From the early sixties, many of our people had gone to the GDR for military training. A number of the ANC leaders who are in government today studied there. I was put in charge of all our students in the GDR and the surrounding Eastern European countries.

Another of the GDR contributions to our struggle was to publish and distribute books, pamphlets, and other material for the ANC and the SACP, from the early sixties right up to the collapse of the Berlin Wall in 1990. Among the publications were the ANC monthly journal *Sechaba* and the Communist Party quarterly journal *The African Communist*. More importantly, they also provided medical treatment for our sick and wounded comrades. There was a 'Solidarity Ward' at Buch Hospital where ANC, Swapo, PLO and other freedom fighters were treated. In some cases our comrades from South Africa were secretly brought into the country for medical treatment, and returned to South Africa through underground channels. They entered and left without their passports being stamped, evidence of the trust the GDR government had in our organisation. The Solidarity Committee covered all travel expenses. The Committee also paid for my trip to the UK for the seventieth birthday bash, organised in London, to demand the release of Comrade Nelson Mandela.

On 9 June 1988, I went to London to take part in celebrating the seventieth birthday of Comrade Nelson Mandela. On 11 June, the

Anti-Apartheid Movement (UK), with the collaboration of Anti-Apartheid Movements worldwide, organised one of the biggest birthday bashes ever seen, the Wembley Concert in London. It was a beautiful warm day. A hundred thousand people crammed into the stadium. ANC flags were flying and hundreds of pictures of Comrade Nelson Mandela were on display. T-shirts carrying the words 'Free Mandela' – 'Happy Birthday, Mandela' were on sale. Banners were hung across the stadium reading 'Happy 70th birthday Mandela'. The atmosphere was electric. There was a spirit of celebration in the air, but there was also anger that Mandela was still in prison after twenty-five years. The twelve-hour concert was broadcast live on television and radio all over the world but not, of course, to racist South Africa. Many of the world's top artists performed, including Hugh Masekela, Yousou N'Dour, Stevie Wonder, Amampondo, Joan Armatrading, Harry Belafonte, Jackson Brown, Tracy Chapman, Peter Gabriel, Jonas Gwangwa, Miriam Makeba, Simple Minds and Little Steven. It was estimated that more than a billion people worldwide watched the concert on TV. There was no doubt that Nelson Mandela had become a hero to the people, an icon of international standing.

From Wembley Stadium a group of twenty-five people, myself among them, boarded the train to Glasgow to start our 'Free Nelson Mandela Now' march. On Sunday 12 June, twenty-five thousand people attended a mass rally at the Glasgow Green. I was handed a symbolic key to Mandela's cell by ANC President Comrade Oliver Tambo to carry with us on our march to London. The speakers at the rally included Comrade Oliver Tambo, Archbishop Trevor Huddleston, and the General Secretary of Swapo, Andimba Toivo Ja Toivo. Jim Kerr, of the band Simple Minds, sang the song 'Mandela Day'.

Finally we were on our way, the historical march to London, one thousand kilometres away. We passed through something like forty towns and were given a roaring welcome everywhere and a warm send-off the following day. We arrived in Coventry on Sunday 10 July to be welcomed by a huge crowd of people. Still sweating and exhausted from the day's walk, we attended a service at the Cathedral. Coventry Cathedral was destroyed by the Nazis during the Second World War, and the rebuilt cathedral is now a symbol of peace and reconciliation. At the service the clergy washed the feet of six of the marchers in a symbolic gesture.

On 16 July we arrived in Finchley, North London. We were welcomed by thousands of people, including Adelaide Tambo and Richard Attenborough.

On the 17th we set off on the last leg of our journey to Hyde Park, after a gruelling one thousand kilometres and thirty-six days of marching. Over thirty thousand people joined us in the march, among them Dr Nkosazana Dlamini-Zuma, Ja Toivo and other well-known international figures. By the time we reached Hyde Park the march had grown to over one hundred thousand people. At Hyde Park another hundred thousand people waited to welcome us. Across the huge stage were emblazoned the words 'Free Nelson Mandela'. We were welcomed on stage by Bob Hughes (now Lord Hughes) to a tremendous roar from the people and the singing of 'Free Nelson Mandela'. I handed the symbolic key to Archbishop Desmond Tutu.

The march had been exhausting. Most of us had sore feet, tired legs and aching bodies, but it was a wonderful experience, an experience of a lifetime. None of the twenty-five marchers had ever taken part in such a long walk before. Amongst the marchers was a man who was the same age as Comrade Nelson Mandela. But it had all gone well, thanks to the GDR Solidarity Committee which provided all the medical requirements for the marchers – bandages, ointments, knee and ankle guards.

I arrived back in Berlin filled with a wonderful sense of achievement. The people of Europe had unequivocally shown their solidarity with Nelson Mandela and the African National Congress. I was certainly not expecting what awaited me on my arrival home.

My key would not open the door. Eventually I learned the reason.

Two nights before I left for London, Gabriele and I had invited a number of people, including some diplomats, for supper. We prepared everything ourselves. It was a good party and our guests stayed late. The next morning we went to work as usual. When we returned home in the evening we decided to have a simple supper of leftovers from the night before. We started off with the salad. We had just begun eating when I felt something hard in my mouth. I immediately spat it out – it appeared to be a piece of glass. Apart from wondering how the glass could have ended up in the salad, we didn't give it too much thought. The salad went into the bin and I commented that it was fortunate that none of our guests had found the piece of glass the previous evening.

The next morning I left for London on an early flight. Gabriele went off to work and when she returned home that evening she found that the front door was not double-locked, as it always was, and that the passage lights were burning. She is a security conscious person and clearly recalled double-locking the door. She was also conscious of the need to conserve energy and would not have left any lights on. However, she was tired after the day's work and began to doubt herself. She poured herself a long drink from the bottle of rum we had opened the previous evening and settled down to watch the news on television. When she took the first sip of her drink she found her mouth full of granules which cut her mouth slightly. She spat out the drink and poured the rest of the contents of the bottle down the kitchen sink. When she tried to pick up the glassy granules she had spat on to the carpet, she could not find them. All that remained was a dark wet spot on the light-coloured carpet. She decided she would clean up after the news.

But while watching the news it suddenly occurred to her that if there had been pieces of glass in the bottle they would not have been floating on the surface. The laws of physics would dictate that glass would sink to the bottom of a bottle containing liquid.

Glass in the salad the day before, and in the rum today? The events of the past few days began to worry her. Someone had been in our flat. She immediately called some comrades and they met her outside the flat. After hearing her story, they became convinced that this had been an attempted poisoning and the police were called. After they left, and after a new and additional lock had been installed on the front door, Gabriele began checking and cleaning the entire flat. All the food went into the bin.

The following evening Gabriele was approached by Mike, a Zimbabwean friend and diplomat, outside our block of flats. He asked if we were OK and if everybody who had been present at our dinner was all right. It transpired that a Zimbabwean diplomat had been hospitalised that very morning with what appeared to be a heart attack. However, the doctors were suspicious about his symptoms as he was a young man with no history of heart disease. They eventually identified poisoning as the cause of his illness and were able to save his life. To us, it was clear that this was the same kind of poison that had killed people in Mozambique.

The question remained: who had tried to poison us, and what type of poison was it?

We found out in 2002. During the trial in South Africa that year of Dr Wouter Basson, also known as 'Doctor Death', confessions were made which shed some light on our question. It emerged that this apartheid era chemical warfare scientist had invented a crystal-like poison that was supposed to dissolve on coming into contact with liquid. This substance had been used on many opponents of the apartheid regime, and many had died as a result.

Basson explained to the Truth and Reconciliation Commission that they had experienced some failures in the use of this poison – sometimes it did *not* dissolve when it came into contact with liquid. He had never established why this happened.

After the Berlin Wall came down in 1989 our safety and security could no longer be guaranteed. The apartheid regime had no respect for the sovereignty of other countries and continued to carry out acts of brutality, murder and even bombings. There was the bombing of the ANC offices in London, the killing of Dulcie September in Paris, the air raid over Maputo, the killing of innocent men, women and children in Angola, the massacre of innocent civilians in Lesotho, and many other atrocities.

At this time there was a great deal of social and political unrest in the German Democratic Republic, particularly in Leipzig. When the Berlin Wall came down there was a call for the unification of Germany. During this period of transition, we in the ANC office were not sure what our status would be in the future. The GDR Solidarity Committee was beginning to collapse. Within weeks after the unrest began we noticed strangers keeping surveillance on us. It was an uneasy time for us.

I was still in Berlin when Comrades Walter Sisulu, Govan Mbeki, Ahmed Kathrada, Raymond Mhlaba, Elias Matsoaledi, Andrew Mlangeni and Wilton Mkwayi were released from prison.

For the first time I managed to book a call from East Germany to South Africa. At first the operator refused to make my call, but after long arguments and explanations, I was connected about an hour later and was able to speak to Comrades Kathy and Walter. There was no link between East Germany and racist South Africa, so the operator had to get special permission to put me through.

In February 1990, while I was visiting Comrade Sisulu and others in Stockholm, the news came of the unbanning of the ANC and the SACP and the imminent release of Nelson Mandela.

I was in Berlin when the Wall came down and the German Democratic Republic collapsed. In March 1991 I received a fax from Comrade Thabo Mbeki from the Johannesburg ANC head office, instructing me to return home. I was told to apply for a visa to enter South Africa and for indemnity from crimes committed against the state. I filled in the indemnity form as best as I could.

Then I faxed both forms to the ANC head office in Johannesburg and was soon assured that all was well.

In April 1991 my sister Shantie and I arrived at Jan Smuts Airport in Johannesburg. I was very nervous, not knowing what to expect. Shantie, carrying a British passport, had no problems clearing immigration. During all my years in exile I had travelled on an Indian passport which stated plainly that it was valid for all countries other than the Republic of South Africa and Israel. To make matters worse there was no visa or indemnity waiting for me. The immigration officer was quite pleasant and friendly. He checked a book marked 'ANC Returnees', but my name was not there. I felt I was in big trouble, but he had a good laugh, pointing out the clause in the passport 'not valid for the Republic of South Africa'. After much delay and discussion, the immigration officer gave me a one-week visitor's visa for South Africa.

We entered the arrivals hall to a huge welcome from family and friends. It was my second homecoming. There were garlands and flowers and banners and placards reading 'Welcome home'. Once again I was confronted with the same problem I had had on my release from prison, eighteen years before. Who were all these people? These strange people, each one trying to attract my attention, as if I should know them. Of course I recognised my mother and my brothers. That was not a problem. But my nephews and nieces had been small children, some of them had not even been born, when I left and now they were grown men and women. I recognised Shirish and Reggie, my comrades in arms, in the crowd. It was a wonderful homecoming. We were driven through the heart of Johannesburg to my brother's home in Lenasia, the Indian township created next to Soweto by the apartheid regime for South African people of Indian origin. This creation was part of their grand plan for separate development. All day long friends, comrades and family arrived to welcome my sister and me home, all of them bearing presents and food. We partied till the early hours of the morning.

In November 1991, we gave my mother a big eighty-fourth birthday party, which was attended by family, friends and comrades. Amongst them were Comrades Walter and Albertina Sisulu, Ahmed Kathrada, Mac and Zarina Maharaj and Helen Joseph. It was the first time in almost thirty years that she had all five of her children with her. From 1963 onwards, at least one of her children had been behind bars or in exile. My mom, Manonmoney Naidoo, was better known to her generation and to the Mandelas and Sisulus as 'Mama'. To the generation of the sixties she was known as 'Amah' (which means mother in Tamil), not only by her own children but also by thousands of people in the Struggle. She died on Christmas Day 1993 at the age of eighty-six. One of her most fervent wishes was to see freedom in South Africa and to vote in the first democratic election. She saw freedom, but unfortunately died a few months before the election in April 1994. My mother always remembered that her comrade and friend Helen Joseph had died on Christmas Day, and felt it was a wonderful day on which to die. My mom died one year later to the day. We had had a family Christmas dinner at a friend's house. Mom was there, happy to be with her family, when her heart failed her. She died peacefully later that day.

April 27 1994, the day of the first democratic election in South Africa, was the greatest day in the history of our country. Although it was the beginning of winter, it was a warm day. I felt on top of the world, overjoyed with excitement and happiness. After so many years of struggle, imprisonment, torture and death, our country was moving towards democracy at last. Standing for hours in that very long queue in Yeoville, Johannesburg, I waited to enter the polling booth for the first time in the fifty-eight years of my life. When at long last the moment came, I was very nervous. I could not believe that the time had finally come, the time to put my X on the ballot papers.

The ANC won a resounding victory and celebrated at a party at the Carlton Hotel in Johannesburg. All the leaders were there – Nelson Mandela, Walter Sisulu, Thabo Mbeki – and we, the rank and file, as well. We celebrated long into the night.

I was appointed a Senator in the National Parliament for the province of Gauteng. My partner Gabi and I arrived at Cape Town International Airport on 19 May 1994 and were driven straight to parliament where all the formalities of filling in forms, taking of photographs and briefing on the parliamentary system were gone through. Later that evening we were taken to our hotel, only to find that our suitcases were missing. I had travelled comfortably in jeans. I was due to be sworn in the next morning and I could not believe that I might have to experience one of the proudest moments of my life in such casual garb. After a frantic and lengthy search our suitcases were finally found.

Friday, 20 May 1994 was the opening of the first democratically elected Senate in our country. We were up and on our way to the parliament buildings early that morning. I was walking on air. There were scores of journalists from television, radio and the press taking photos and eager for interviews. By 10 o'clock we were all seated in the Senate Chamber. The public gallery was packed. The sixty ANC Senators were on the right-hand side of the Chamber and the thirty of the opposition on the left. The Usher announced the Honourable Chief Justice, Mr Justice M M Corbett, who read prayers. Members were then called in alphabetical order in groups of five to take an oath or solemn affirmation. When my turn came, I heard the Chief Justice say: 'Do you swear to uphold the constitution of the Republic of South Africa?' I held up my fist and declared in a firm voice: 'Amandla'.

Indres Naidoo
Cape Town, December 2002

And Robben Island?

Some people called it Devil's Island, some called it University of Makhanda, and others called it Mandela University. But the name Robben Island remains. For centuries thousands of people were banished or imprisoned on the Island. Hundreds died there. The Island was universally known as a place of cruelty and brutality. It saw the suffering of thousands of our people; their blood and sweat drenched its rocks and sand.

Today Robben Island is a prison no more. The United Nations Educational, Scientific and Cultural Organisation (UNESCO) has declared it a World Heritage Site and it is protected as a national monument. Thousands of people visit the Island every day. Ordinary tourists as well as world leaders come to pay their homage to everything the Island symbolises, particularly those who suffered and gave their lives for freedom, justice and peace.

Since 1994 I have taken hundreds of people on guided tours to this historic site, which today is one of the major tourist destinations in the country.

It is my hope that the collective response of all who make the pilgrimage to the Island will be a united voice saying: 'Never again'.

Postscript to the first edition

Nelson Mandela and the others serving life sentences with him are – at the time of handing over this manuscript to the publishers – still in their prison within a prison on Robben Island. They have been there nearly two decades now and have become the focal point of struggle inside and outside South Africa against apartheid. When the youth rebelled in Soweto and elsewhere in 1976, the name most frequently on their lips was that of Mandela. Petitions circulated recently with great courage inside South Africa have called for his release while the United Nations, the Organisation of African Unity, and presidents and prime ministers of many lands have publicly and privately insisted that no talk of dismantling apartheid will have any meaning unless Mandela and the other political prisoners on the Island are released and permitted to take a leading part in that process.

Robben Island was intended to be the place for the destruction of anti-apartheid militants, but instead has become a centre of resistance and the symbol of the indestructibility of the movement for the creation of a non-racial democratic South Africa.

This book was prepared with great difficulty as a contribution towards that movement. After his release from prison in 1973, Indres Naidoo, like virtually all other ex-prisoners from the Island, lived the life of a banned person, prohibited by ministerial order from writing or publishing anything, and subject to house arrest weekends and evenings. In spite of these restrictions, many ex-prisoners played an important role in linking the Soweto uprising to wider struggles, and the reports which Indres and the others spread by word of mouth, concerning the way in which prisoners identified with the ANC continued to struggle on the Island, did much to keep the flames of resistance burning in people's hearts throughout the country.

When eventually in 1977 Indres was instructed by the ANC to leave South Africa clandestinely, the possibilities of writing this book arose. He was called upon by the UN to testify on conditions on the Island, and invited to address audiences in the USA, Holland, Norway, Belgium, the United Kingdom and other countries, but always his account was necessarily abbreviated. Our objective was to convey the meaning of Robben Island through the experiences of one prisoner told extensively and concretely. We collaborated during our spare moments, working at nights and over weekends, anxious to finish the story as soon as possible, but also anxious to do justice to it by making it as accurate and readable as possible. This required submitting the manuscript to the scrutiny of others who had been on the Island, and this caused further necessary delay; we have no doubt, however, that the helpful comments we received greatly enriched the book. Getting the manuscript typed at its various stages also took time – here too we were helped by dedicated people. Our hope, now that the book is out, is that each reader will be stirred by the story it tells into thinking about the contribution he or she can make to the closing down of the Island prison, the release of all political prisoners in South Africa, and the ending of the system which results in the best sons and daughters of our country finding themselves behind bars.

Albie Sachs
Maputo – London, 1981